The Complete Guide to Buddhism:

How to Meditate & Mindfulness Meditation to Reduce Stress, Anxiety & Find Lasting Happiness, For Beginners to Advanced

© **Copyright 2019 by Harini Anand - All rights reserved.**

This document is geared towards providing exact and reliable information in regard to the topic and issue covered. The publication is sold with the idea that the publisher is not required to render accounting, officially permitted, or otherwise, qualified services. If advice is necessary, legal or professional, a practiced individual in the profession should be ordered.

- From a Declaration of Principles which was accepted and approved equally by a Committee of the American Bar Association and a Committee of Publishers and Associations.

In no way is it legal to reproduce, duplicate, or transmit any part of this document in either electronic means or in printed format. Recording of this publication is strictly prohibited and any storage of this document is not allowed unless with written permission from the publisher. All rights reserved.

The information provided herein is stated to be truthful and consistent, in that any liability, in terms of inattention or otherwise, by any usage or abuse of any policies, processes, or directions contained within is the solitary and utter responsibility of the recipient reader. Under no circumstances will any legal responsibility or blame be held against the publisher for any reparation, damages, or monetary loss due to the information herein, either directly or indirectly.

Respective authors own all copyrights not held by the publisher.

The information herein is offered for informational purposes solely and is universal as so. The presentation of the information is without contract or any type of guarantee assurance.

The trademarks that are used are without any consent, and the publication of the trademark is without permission or backing by the trademark owner. All trademarks and brands within this book are for clarifying purposes only and are the owned by the owners themselves, not affiliated with this document.

FIND OUT MORE

Buddhism for Beginners:

How The Practice of Buddhism, Mindfulness and Meditation Can Increase Your Happiness and Help You Deal With Stress and Anxiety

Contents:

Introduction

Chapter 1 – The Foundations of Buddhism

Chapter 2 - The 5 Precepts – Buddha's Guide to a Simple Life

Chapter 3 - The Three Marks of Existence of Buddha

Chapter 4 - Karma and Zen in Buddhism

Chapter 5 - Ethics and Other Vital Things in Buddhism

Chapter 6 - Start Your Spiritual Path

Chapter 7 – Training The Mind With Meditation

Chapter 8 - Different Kinds of Meditation

Chapter 9 - Cultivating Mindfulness

Chapter 10 – Yoga and Buddhism

Chapter 11 - The Mudras and Basic Poses in Yoga

Chapter 12- Mastering Yoga Poses

Chapter 13 – How to Relax and Meditate Through Yoga

Chapter 14 – Center Yourself With Sound Healing

Chapter 15 - Vibrational Healing

Chapter 16 - Healing Instruments

Conclusion

Introduction

Learning about Buddhism at this day and age will help you understand that there is more to life than what you see. You only have to go past the material things and luxuries to realize that you are more than your physical qualities, you are not your ego nor your mind.

The founder of Buddhism, Siddhartha Gautama Buddha, is the epitome of what this belief stands for. He grew up surrounded by luxuries, but he opted to turn his back on all the riches to contemplate and gain enlightenment.

This book outlines Buddha's teachings that will have a great impact on your life. It will help you gain a deeper understanding of life.

To help you towards your journey to enlightenment and self-realization, this book has detailed information about the different kinds of meditation practices you can learn to perform.

This book tells the story of Siddhartha and how he became the Buddha. You will learn a lot from his teachings and concepts he was able to spread to his disciples. It also has a useful guide about Zen meditation, yoga, sound healing, and the other forms of meditation you can do as a beginner in the practice.

Enjoy!

Chapter 1 – The Foundations of Buddhism

It is believed that Buddhism started more than 2,500 years ago in India. It was founded by Siddhartha Gautama, born to a clan of a tribal chief in Nepal. A soothsayer predicted when Siddhartha was born that he will be a renouncer. His father tried to prevent this by showering him with all the luxuries he can afford.

Siddhartha lived a sheltered life. But he came to a point that he started to question life. His curiosity of what lies beyond the palace walls prompted him to ask his father to let him go out and see the world. The young Siddhartha set out a series of chariot rides to go around. It was then that his eyes were opened to the "real" state of life – far from the pleasures, fortunes, and riches he has grown accustomed to.

During his travels, the young man was faced with extreme forms of human suffering like illness, old age, and death. He also met an ascetic renouncer.

The realizations opened the young Siddhartha's mind of life's simple truths he was deprived of knowing while growing up - people grow old, get sick, and die. At that point, he realized that all life's pleasures were fleeting and only hide human misery.

He decided to leave his wife and son and devoted his time to expanding his knowledge about his newfound truths.

He first tried following the monk's sample. He denied himself of the pleasures in life and started leading life of utmost asceticism. He also tried severe abandonment in the forest to the point of almost starving himself. It was not easy as it almost took his life. Until one day, he heard someone uttered something about the strings of a musical instrument - that you can't make beautiful music if the strings were too loose and if they were too tight, they will just snap.

After understanding that starvation only added to his suffering, he began eating and spent a lot of time sitting underneath a tree while meditating.

Reaching Nirvana

Several known versions exist today as to how the young Siddhartha reached his goal. There were accounts that said it happened the morning after, while there are others stating that Siddhartha found Nirvana (Enlightenment) 6 months after. He knew he had found the answers to why humans suffer and how to eliminate suffering.

Becoming the Buddha

Once Siddhartha achieved Enlightenment, he became known as the Buddha (also called the Awakened One or the Enlightened One).

The Buddha began his mission of ending all human suffering by teaching his truths. Not long after, he became popular and gained many followers.

His most important teachings were the Eight-Fold Path and the Four Noble Truths.

The Four Noble Truths

1. Life is dukkha (suffering).

2. Human suffering is brought about by craving – for pleasures and things to be, unfortunately they are not. It is a person's refusal to see life as it is that causes suffering.

3. There's an end to life's suffering.

4. The means to end life's sufferings – Middle Way and Eight-Fold Path.

The Middle Way

The Middle Way, a characterization of Buddha's life, suggests that people must not indulge their body's every whim but to not totally deny the physical body either. Upon following the combined path of the Middle Way and Eight-Fold Path should one attain Nirvana and experience utter joy and peace.

The Spread of Buddhism

When the Buddha died, his celibate and wandering followers settled down at monasteries provided by married laityas. To return the favor, these followers shared Buddha's important teachers to them. In return, the monks taught these laityas of the important teachings of Buddha. They visited the Buddha's birthplace, started to worship the tree where the Buddha received enlightenment, they put images of the Buddha in their temples, and placed his relics in different stupas (funeral mounds).

In the 3rd century BCE, Ashoka, a famous king, and his son spread and taught Buddhism throughout Ceylon (Sri Lanka) and South India.

From its original Indian foundation, Buddhism began to spread to various countries around the globe. Currently, the estimated Buddhist population around the world is about 500 million. Myanmar, Cambodia, and Thailand have the highest recorded percentages of this religion among all their residents while the largest Buddhist population is in China.

Buddhism is also gradually getting practitioners in the United Kingdom, Australia, and America.

Within Buddhism are many schools or division and two major branches, which vary in the areas of focus. Mahayana Buddhism concentrates on educating about the ways to enlightenment and joint freedom from suffering. Its two offshoots, Tibetan and Zen Buddhism are the kinds many people practice in western countries. Theravada Buddhism concentrates on monastic life and individual experience and enlightenment.

Nirvana

The term, which literally means quenching or blowing out, refers to the ultimate goal of the Buddhist path. It is included in the cessation of dukkha or the Third Truth in the Four Noble Truths. It is commonly interpreted as the extinguishing of the "three fires" that results in samsara or freedom from the cycle of rebirth. It is also associated with other Buddhism terms, such as the states of sunyata or emptiness and anatta or non-self.

Nirvana refers to the state when you become free from rebirth and suffering, although it was given different meanings in various Buddhist traditions.

Chapter 2 - The 5 Precepts – Buddha's Guide to a Simple Life

The five precepts cover the foundation of Buddhist training. Buddha knew it would be challenging to apply these precepts to all areas of your life every day but also understand their virtue towards reaching higher forms of wisdom and development. These precepts are also referred to as the noble eightfold path.

This is a guide to end human suffering found within the fourth noble truth. The path is categorized into three – wisdom, mental discipline, and moral conduct.

The Eight-Fold Path

1. Samma Samadhin – Right concentration

2. Samma Sati – Right mindfulness

3. Samma Vayama – Right effort

4. Samma Ajiva – Right livelihood

5. Samma Kammanta – Right action

6. Samma Vaca – Right speech

7. Samma Sankappa – Right thought

8. Samma Ditthi – Right understanding

The Eight-Fold Path in relation to the categories they belong to:

1. Wisdom

Right Understanding – This is said to be the highest form of wisdom that sees the Ultimate Reality or seeing things as they are. There are two kinds of understanding in Buddhism. Penetration or pativedha is deep understanding. It means that you see through things without any label or name. You see things beyond their impurities. You can only gain this kind of understanding through meditation. The other kind of understanding, which is not quite deep, is known as knowing accordingly or anubodha. This is how your mind perceives things based on the information given.

Right Thought – It encompasses the right thought of all beings, such as non-violence, love, and detachment or selfless renunciation. Lack of wisdom in any areas of life, such as political, social or individual, result in thoughts about violence, hatred, ill-will, and selfish desire.

2. Ethical conduct

Ethical conduct, also called sila, is based on the wide concept of compassion and universal love for all living things. This is said to be the basis of the teachings of Buddha. Buddhism believes that two qualities make a perfect man – wisdom or panna and compassion or karuna.

Compassion represents the noble qualities of the heart and emotion, such as tolerance, kindness, charity, and love. Wisdom represents the great qualities and intellectual side of the mind. A man has to have balanced wisdom and compassion. Too much intellect without compassion may lead to becoming a genius but hard-hearted individual and too much compassion without wisdom may result in becoming a good-hearted fool. Compassion and wisdom are linked and inseparable in Buddhism.

Here are the three factors of the noble eightfold path included in ethical conduct:

Right Speech – It means refraining from saying harmful and wrong speech, such as:

- Gossip, and foolish, useless, and idle babble

- Abusive, malicious, impolite, rude, and harsh language

- Slander and backbiting and talk that could cause disharmony, disunity, enmity, and hatred among groups of people or individuals

- Telling lies

It means that one has to be careful when speaking. It is better to keep noble silence than to say anything unpleasant or hurtful. One has to speak the truth all the time and has to use words, which are useful, meaningful, gentle, pleasant, and friendly.

Right Action – It teaches people to stay away from dishonorable conducts, such as illegitimate sexual encounters, dishonest dealings, stealing, and destroying other people's lives. It prompts individuals to lead an honorable and peaceful life by following a moral compass.

Right Livelihood – It reflects the strong opposition of Buddhism to the use and trading of lethal weapons and arms and any kind of war. It teaches people to stay away from sources of income that may cause harm to others, which include cheating, killing, selling poison and intoxicating drinks and trading lethal weapons. A person should earn a living through means that won't cause harm to others, blameless and honorable.

3. Mental Discipline

Right Effort – Teaches people to find balance in cultivating enthusiasm and positive attitude. It should produce an attitude of cheerful yet steady determination. Human beings should cultivate clear and honest thoughts and do away with negative and jealous feelings to produce right effort.

Right effort simply equates positive thinking.

Right Mindfulness – It teaches people to be attentive, mindful, and diligently aware of the following:

- Things (dhamma), conceptions, thoughts, ideas
- Mind activities (citta)
- Feelings or sensations (vedana)
- Body or physical activities (kaya)

There are many kinds of meditation techniques that aim to develop attentiveness. Anapanasati or concentration on breathing is also a popular practice for mental and body development. A person has to be aware how the mind works and how thoughts disappear and appear at all times – if the mind is concentrated or distracted, filled with kindness or hatred, full of truth or deluded, and lustful or not. A person has to learn about the nature of their thoughts – from conception, suppression to destruction and so on.

Right Concentration – This last factor of mental discipline leads to recueillement or trance or the four stages of Dhyana, as follows:

- First stage – A person keeps the feelings of happiness, joy and other mental activities and discards skeptical doubt, restlessness, worry, languor, ill-will, unwholesome thoughts, and passionate desires.

- Second stage – A person keeps the feelings of happiness and joy while suppressing intellectual activities until the mind develops one-pointedness and tranquility.

- Third stage – A person keeps the disposition of happiness, but joy is discarded to get to the point of mindful equanimity.

- Fourth stage – Awareness and pure equanimity remain but all sensations, including sorrow, joy, and happiness are discarded.

The noble eightfold path is not to be used for sequential learning, but rather as the eight aspects of life which have to be integrated in your daily life. It creates an environment that will lead you further into finding the Buddhist path.

The path isn't religious in nature but more on the realization of one's completeness in terms of peace through intellectual, spiritual, and moral perfection, happiness, freedom, and utmost reality.

In Buddhism, it is meant to be used as a guideline to be considered, learned, contemplated on, and to be taken on when each step has been fully accepted to be a part of the life one person seeks to lead.

Buddhism does not teach its followers for blind faith, rather it asks people to promote the joys of learning and the process of self-discovery.

The five precepts were among Buddha's first teachings. He knew it would be challenging to apply these five precepts in all areas of life but will help a lot to ease a person's emotional stress and struggles. These precepts make a vital part of the noble eightfold path. In reciting the precepts, the target usually involves the following:

1. Never take lives, including insects.

2. Never steal nor get anything not given freely.

3. Never get involved in illicit sexual acts.

4. Never speak harshly, gossip and lies.

5. Never consume intoxicants that cloud the mind.

Chapter 3 - The Three Marks of Existence of Buddha

Everything that the Buddha taught his followers contained the three marks of existence or the three characteristics common in all his teachings. These three marks are anicca or impermanence, dukkha or suffering/dissatisfaction, and anatta or not-self. They apply to all things except for nirvana. Buddha said that in order to realize enlightenment, one has to appreciate and fully understand the three marks of existence. This concept is more emphasized in the Theravada school but is also taught in Mahayana school.

Anicca

Buddha always believed that everything changes. We should never think of anybody or anything as permanent. Even people's lives are not permanent. The moment that you forget the notion is when you feel hurt and stressed out.

Dukkha

Nothing is permanent, including emotions. You may feel satisfied with something, such as having a new car, eating a wonderful dish or spending quality time with friends, but the feeling won't last. For Buddha, life is dukkha, but it doesn't mean that it is always filled with unhappiness. What he meant was that ultimately, the feeling will pass, and you will realize that it is not enough to feel the same way for the rest of your life.

Anatta

Nothing is permanent, including the existing self inside each individual. There is no absolute identity. There is no "I" or "self". Having an illusion of a permanent self bind you to dissatisfaction and suffering. You do everything to protect your notion of "self" but by doing so, you develop certain cravings that lead to suffering, like what was told in the four noble truths.

By learning more about the teachings of Buddha, including the application of the eightfold path, you will develop less attachment to material and other impermanent things. Upon discovering the truths behind the three marks of existence, it will be easier to learn the important factors towards enlightenment. These factors are serenity and equanimity or the point when you can no longer be controlled by your likes and dislikes.

Chapter 4 - Karma and Zen in Buddhism

The Law of Karma

The term and concept of karma have been used in different religions in India before the time of Buddha. He interpreted the term as the intention or the cause of action. He formulated the doctrine, which is now considered as fundamental in Buddhism. One of the insights that Buddha learned on the night he was enlightened was about karmic conditioning and how it dictates the intentions behind the actions. This means that the intention was brought about by the actions and consequences of what they have done. On that night, Buddha was able to see his past lives and the actions he took that brought him to his enlightenment.

Buddha believed that karma is mutable even though it comes from the result of the karma you have accumulated from your past to present lives. Each day gives you an opportunity to change the negative into positive and to follow his teachings towards a better tomorrow.

For Buddhists, nothing in this world happens by accident. In one way or another, a person deserves whatever happens to them. The reasons may be traced either in their present life or past life. A person is responsible for his own misery and happiness. You create your fate, as well as your own heaven and hell.

Zen in Buddhism

Zen, formerly known as the Chan School, started during the Tang dynasty in China. It is a school of Mahayana Buddhism that later on branched out into different schools. Its formation is traced to dhyāna, and Indian practice that means meditation.

Zen focuses on understanding the true nature of things, meditation practice, and strict self-control. It promotes interaction with a qualified teacher and spiritual practice to achieve direct understanding. It veers away from emphasizing mere lessons about doctrine and sutras.

Dhyana or jhana refers to the practice that leads to the state of perfect awareness or equanimity. It is commonly called meditation, which trains the mind to disassociate from instant responses to the impressions of the senses. It was included in the pre-sectarian Buddhism's core practice, along with other practices leading to utmost detachment and mindfulness.

In Chinese Buddhism, dhyana incorporates different meditation techniques and important practices applied in the preparatory stage. The five main meditation techniques practiced in the process include the following:

- Contemplation on the Buddha
- Contemplation on the 12 links of pratītyasamutpāda

- Loving-kindness or maitrī meditation
- Mindfulness of the body's impurity or paṭikūlamanasikāra meditation
- Mindfulness of breathing or ānāpānasmṛti

The goal of this technique is to understand the dhyana and purify the mind and improve its focus. The five techniques are also referred to as the ways for pacifying or stilling the mind.

In Zen teachings, students are taught to focus and count their breaths to control their minds. They either count both inhalations and exhalation or, only one of the two. The process is repeated until the mind is calm. Breathing for this purpose is often diaphragmatic. It means that the breath must come from hara or under the navel.

Chapter 5 - Ethics and Other Vital Things To Understand in Buddhism

Buddhism encourages people to examine their words and actions if they are causing harm to others or themselves. Anything that causes harm should be avoided or else, such words or actions will cause the suffering of oneself and of others. The eightfold path or the path of practice of Buddha encompasses ways to live ethically.

By living ethically, your mind becomes lighter and more free, which makes it easier to see things clearly and focus. You'll find it hard to concentrate during meditation when you know that you have done something wrong or you've said a lie. This will be harder for you to find your way towards spiritual enlightenment.

How to Deal with Fear

In Buddhism, it is believed that fear is a mistake in perception. It is something that is rooted in the made-up images that took over your mind. You have to deal with your perceptions in order to deal with fear. Feeling this way also means that you are lacking love and have attention problems. Those who stay at the moment and live with love and compassion are less likely to feel fear.

The seeds of conflict, according to Buddhism, come from selfishness, envy, and bitterness. When you have these emotions and you lack love, you become susceptible and an open breeding ground to fear. You have to feel stronger to conquer your fears.

One source of fear is attachment, with polar opposites include spiritual and mental peace. You develop an attachment when you become too focused on attaining things and emotions. After getting what you want, the next thing you will feel is the fear of losing them. The more attached you become to these things, feelings, or people, the stronger the fear you'll feel about losing them. As your fear heightens, the more attached you become to the sources of the feeling.

To avoid or overcome fear, Buddhism teaches people to accept that everything is temporary. You have to feel detached and accept that you don't own anything or anyone, not even your life. All that you have now, including your life, is only temporary. It is better to stop trying having things to lessen the chances of feeling fear.

Another factor that plays a great role in developing fear is the habit of dwelling on committed mistakes. This action feeds anxiety and fear. Mistakes are normal in life. The only way you can get past them is by learning from your mistakes. If you don't learn from them, you will only risk the chance of committing the same mistakes over and over again.

The fundamental essence of fear, according to Buddhism, is dwelling too much on rejection toward suffering. Pain equates to your understanding of fear and suffering is how you handle it. Suffering is said to be optional while pain is bound to happen.

Pain becomes too powerful and causes fear when you don't handle it well. To avoid fear out of pain, you must not suffer from the emotion by learning to accept pain. Only then will pain lose its power and instead of feeling fear, you will try to understand where it came from and try to learn from it.

When you deal with fear, you also deal with suffering. Buddhism suggests to always focus on the present to deal with fear. This kind of attitude will keep your mind from overthinking and feeding yourself with unfounded fears.

Learning how to effectively deal with fear takes persistence and patience. Meditating often will help in speeding up the process.

Rebirth

According to the teachings of Buddhism, a person is reborn after death. The cycle of death and rebirth will go on until one reaches the point of nirvana. The concept of a person in Buddhism is composed of perceptions, feelings, and thoughts that constantly interact. The mental energy doesn't stop after the death of a person. It will only reenter and establish again in another body.

There are different Buddhist beliefs about how long it takes before the rebirth process. There are some teachings that say it takes 49 days while others say that it happens immediately after death.

Other Vital Things to Understand about Buddhism

What does emptiness mean to Buddhist practitioners?

The term, emptiness, comes from the Pali word – sunnata or sunyata in Sanskrit. The term was met with confusion at first since it connotes a negative feeling. Later on, the concept of emptiness was expanded on Heart Sutra, a famous Mahayana scripture. It states that everything is relative or empty. Nothing exists with any substantial reality – from the mind itself to the tiniest of particles on earth.

Is it important to believe in rebirth to be called a Buddhist?

Most Buddhists look into their lives in the context of rebirth. This doesn't mean that they believe in it, but they see each individual as part of a bigger story and a bigger world. Many western Buddhists wouldn't find it offensive even if you don't believe in the concept of rebirth. You are your own boss. You can do and believe whatever pleases you, but it wouldn't hurt to prepare just in case you experience getting reborn. This will even make you a better person, you have nothing to lose.

How important is faith in Buddhism?

Faith isn't encouraged in Buddhism. It doesn't promote any particular belief. Even Buddha didn't want his disciples to rely solely on his teachings. Faith means a personal experience in Buddhism. It means to trust or be confident on your journey towards enlightenment. In many Buddhist schools, faith is defined as taking refuge in the dharma or teachings of Buddha. Most of them share the commitment to the path while being guided by the wisdom and example of sangha, dharma, and Buddha.

Chapter 6 - Start Your Spiritual Path

Going to retreats is a good way to start your spiritual path. This will allow you to explore not only Buddhism but more about yourself. In the West, you'll find a lot of Buddhist retreat centers that include monasteries and dharma centers.

For those who don't have time, reading books and learning the ways to meditate in a similar way like the Buddhists is a good start. Once you are ready to explore and experience what it is like outside the books, you can try finding the nearest centers in your place. If you can allot time and money, you can also join retreats in exotic places or into the wilderness.

The good thing about joining retreats is that you'll have a company and most of you are beginners. You will all learn together the protocols, nature of the exercises, meditation and other teachings involved in the process.

When joining a Buddhist retreat, it is important to manage your expectations. Do not expect anything luxurious. This is far from a vacation or a day at the spa. You will learn how to live like Buddha – simple and free from the riches. Certain facilities require the sharing of bathrooms. There are monasteries that expect the participants to help with the chores during their stay. Sleeping isn't a luxury either since monks will walk in before dawn with clanging bells to start a chanting program or an early meditation.

It is also likely that you'll be required to participate in Buddhist rituals. This is something that doesn't sit well on many postmodern westerners who don't approve of chanting unfamiliar words or paying homage to golden Buddha figures.

Despite certain setbacks, a Buddhist retreat for beginners is a once in a lifetime spiritual experience and a personal adventure. It will open your eyes to reality as you've never seen before. It will help you in finding greater spiritual intensity and depth.

It is not easy to find a good Buddhist retreat. You have to be on the lookout of the real ones that will not take advantage of you. You can try finding good retreat centers at directories online or known Buddhist publications.

If you want an authentic Buddhist experience, research about the centers you're interested in. There are certain centers, which advertise that they are Buddhist, but actually, they are not. Ask about the qualifications of the teacher who will conduct the retreat. An authentic one will be honest in telling you all about their Buddhism background and education.

A real Buddhist retreat place offers well-established practices. You can also opt to join centers that offer a fusion of practices and activities. They will be upfront about what they have to offer and explain the Buddhism aspects and the other practices involved in the retreat.

A beginner should always start in a beginner's retreat. You will need the experience before you can join the more intensive rituals offered at many dharma centers. Getting into an advanced retreat center without prior experience will make it difficult for you to understand the protocols and rituals. You might end up having a bad experience despite getting into an authentic retreat center.

How to Become a Buddhist Monk?

You can become a monk as long as you have a pure intent of becoming one. You have to be sincere in learning about the practice and all the Buddha's teachings.

Learning

1. You must first have the interest before committing yourself to the process. Understand the basic concept of Buddhism and familiarize yourself with the teachings of Buddha. You can begin by reading books and researching. You can then enroll yourself in classes headed by ordained Buddhist monks. The most basic concepts you need to learn at the start include the following:

    - The Eightfold Path
    - The Four Noble truths

2. Look for a sangha or temple that practices Buddhism. You'll find one anywhere in the world you are since the religion is practiced worldwide. Join and be part of the community. You have to commit your time to it. Do not give yourself a deadline when you enter the temple. This will serve as a test if this is the right path for you. You will learn a lot from the process but how long you would last will depend on your realizations. You can prematurely leave the temple if you can't see yourself following the same practices that Buddhists do for the rest of your life. You can also stay for weeks, months, or even years before deciding whether you want to adapt to the practice or not.

While in the temple, be an active participant as much as possible. The activities and teachings depend on the sangha you've enrolled yourself into. There are sanghas that focus on helping people grow in their faith, as well as ones that offer introductory courses about the religion. The Buddhist communities may vary. Others may have adapted to the changing times while some have stuck their teachings to traditional Buddhism. Your goal is to find the community that is most appealing and suited to your personality and beliefs.

You can try visiting various temples before choosing which one to join. This will give you a better idea of their similarities and differences.

3. You will need a mentor. In order to become a monk, you will need a spiritual guide or mentor. He will teach you and guide you throughout the process. You will learn a lot from your mentor – a deeper look into the religion, a step-by-step guide to fulfill your goal and understanding what to expect once you become a monk.

It will be easier to find a mentor once you have joined a temple. They will often invite Buddhist leaders to share their experiences and the teachings of Buddha. You can ask about them and choose which one you will approach to become your mentor.

Preparation

1. Commit your time in meditating as you prepare yourself for the monastic life. A Buddhist monk meditates every day. They are consciously doing it to change how their minds work. It is essential to commit most of your time meditating when you live in an abbey. It's not easy but it can be done through practice.

There are many kinds of meditation you can practice in Buddhism. It can include focusing on postures, a meditation on the Lamrim, transformation, and breathing. You can begin doing the practice twice a day for at least five minutes each session. You can gradually increase the time you spend in the process until you can last 15 minutes per session twice a day. You will learn from your mentor that monks spend hours in meditating.

2. You'll be required to follow the code of conduct called Vinaya to become a Buddhist monk. This means that you'll need to support yourself for up to three years. It is stipulated in the Vinaya that nuns and Buddhist monks can't work a normal day job to earn a living.. In certain cases, the abbey you're situated in will give your basic needs but in most cases, you need to have sufficient savings to support yourself.

3. You have to get used to a life without luxury. As a monk, you only need to possess what you need and nothing else. You will live as a mendicant without worldly possession. You'll get supplies of your basic needs – sundries, clothing, and other things you'll need from day to day. You cannot have anything that could evoke possessiveness, envy, or greed. You will lead a simple life.

4. It is important to discuss the decision with your family and let them understand the changes that will happen once you become a monk. You'll be devoted to your advocacy to help those in need and your Buddhist community will become your new family. You'll have very limited interaction with your family.

There are certain monasteries who only accept single people without strong relationship ties. There are others that don't allow married candidates to become monks. They prefer people who can devote themselves to the religion without any distractions, such as relationships and strong ties outside of the monastery.

5. Practice chastity before committing yourself to become a monk. Monks are required to take a vow of chastity. They can't get involved in any kind of sexual behavior. There are even instances when female and male monks are prohibited to talk to one another about topics not related to Buddhism. This is done to conserve energy and put it to matters considered more important than the self.

6. Talk to your mentor about the kinds of commitment you can choose from before deciding on the matter. There are certain traditions that will require ordination for several months or years. There are other traditions that require a lifelong commitment to the practice after getting ordained.

For example, many men in Tibet complete ordinations of two to three months to gain a clearer perspective about their spirituality before pursuing their careers or getting married. If you are unsure about yourself but still want to try the life of a monk, you can try the shorter span of ordination. If you liked it, then you can join the lifelong ordination or if not, you still have time to leave and pursue the other things your heart desires.

Ordination

1. When you have decided that you really want to pursue the life of a monk, you have to train at an abbey. You have to meet the requirements and rules set by the specific abbey you're in to be obtained. In some cases, you will need a referral from an elder to appoint you as a candidate to become a monk.

2. The ordination can only be done by an ordained monk. You have to attend the ceremony wherein the monk will hand to you the Five Precepts and three Jewels. You will also be given a Buddhist name.

3. The one who ordained you will teach you about what to do next. You'll be briefed about the rules and what to expect on the monastery you'll be part of.

4. You will take the Bodhisattva Vows, which focus on searching for enlightenment, working for the good of all human beings and doing compassionate action. You will become a Bodhisattva or a person whose life is devoted to Buddhist practice. You have to recite the vows regularly. They serve as a reminder of what you're

striving for and to your commitment to a selfless service throughout your life.

Chapter 7 – Training The Mind With Meditation

Many people's idea of meditation is that of a Tibetan monk peacefully sitting on a mountaintop or a yogic practitioner with eyes closed and chanting the sound of "Om" in a candlelit room.

There are many ways to meditate and it could mean different things to different people. The clear idea here is that it offers many health benefits and can be done by anyone.

Untrained minds are hard to satisfy. You will constantly feel the longing to attain more even when your ego tells you to stop. Meditation helps in making you realize that you are different from your ego, your personality or your mind.

Behind the physical qualities, you are composed of a limitless ocean of pure bliss. Once you realize this truth, it will be easier to reach your highest potential and experience true contentment and joy.

Dealing with Stress

You will find it hard to meditate if you are often stressed or get easily frustrated over petty reasons. Learn how to deal with stress first by doing the proven techniques to get rid of it.

1. Imagine yourself as a child without too many things to worry about. Let your mind go on a trip down the memory lane. Try to remember as many happy memories as you can when you were little. Observe how your feelings become lighter as you remember those fond memories.

2. Recall how your parents dealt with your naughtiness and how they were able to control their temper a lot of times when you were young. Go back to the times when you did something untoward. Imagine how your parents handled the situation with calmness. You can use these memories to soothe your temper and control your anger whenever needed.

3. Free yourself from all gadgets while at home, especially when you are not expecting calls or messages from work. Instead of watching TV or using the computer, play soothing music, sit back, relax, and enjoy the

sound. If you want, you can turn off the music and learn how to enjoy the silence for silence is good.

4. Sleep. Your physical body may already be too tired from everything you've done. It may be the cause of your grumpiness and the heaviness you are feeling inside. Rest but don't oversleep. Oversleeping will only worsen your feelings of fatigue.

    If you have difficulty sleeping and you badly needed to rest, go in your room, and set the temperature the way you like it. Play some soothing music, diffuse some relaxing essential oils, and wear your most comfortable clothes. Forget about your worries as you dive into your bed to give your mind and body enough time to rest and recharge.

5. Get comfortable and be your natural self when at home. Look and act silly if you must. Everybody needs this kind of feeling every once in a while, to be at a place where you don't have to prove yourself. Enjoy yourself when you're at home and leave all your worries in the office or school. You have to give this time to yourself to feel better and be prepared for the next busy days.

6. Many people find their kitchens the most relaxing spot at home. Cook or bake and indulge in the kinds of activities you enjoy. You will feel lighter in the process

and happier as well. You can choose not to do anything in the kitchen but to smell the scents of your favorite ingredients. No matter what you do, take your time, and enjoy the process. See things as if you're seeing them for the first time as you explore your most favorite spot at home.

7. Clean. Cleaning can help in relieving stress, especially for people who can't stand anything dirty and in disorder. You can set a date when you will do a complete makeover of your home. Do it at times when you are experiencing too much stress. The result of the activity – a cleaner and more organized home, will make you feel lighter and relieve your stress as well.

    You can also spend the first 10 to 15 minutes of your day in tidying up your home. This is considered as an exercise, which can help in boosting your mood and energy.

8. Turn your home into a sanctuary. Always remind yourself that this is your place and you can do anything you want as long as it pleases you. Turn your home into the kind of place you will look forward coming to after spending a stressful day at work. Paint the house with your favorite color or shades that help in calming the nerves, such as white or green. Display images, figurines or toys that make you feel happy. Put new

curtains and diffuse relaxing scents whenever you're at home. The scent will linger inside when you go out and welcome you with its invigorating effect when you go back.

Other Effective Ways to Get Rid of Stress

There are days when you get hit by too much stress that you find it hard to focus, concentrate, and meditate. You can't control the nagging voice inside your head. There are too many distractions and you're getting defeated by them. When you find yourself in the situation, here are some of the most effective ways to deal with too much stress:

1. Laugh more often

   When you are feeling weary due to stress, laugh at the situation and laugh at yourself. Laugh hard and give it your all. Try to remember a funny situation or a joke you heard that made you laugh so hard. You can also watch your favorite funny video clips. Even without reason, you can force yourself to laugh. It may seem unnatural at first but as you go on laughing, you will start to find something amusing about the process and the laughter will come out naturally. This is a good exercise in relieving stress. Laughing relaxes your muscles and helps in releasing endorphins in the brain.

2. Listen to nature

This is a good way to remind yourself that there is a bigger world you are a part of. The circumstances may not be working in your favor at the moment, but this phase will pass. For now, you have to calm your nerves to pacify the mind and think clearly. You can do this indoors or outdoors. If you are in the office, excuse yourself for a while, go out, sit on a bench and close your eyes. Listen intently to nature sounds, like the animals nearby and the whistling of air. Indoors, you can listen to a seashell and imagine that you are in a paradise for that brief moment.

You can also put a miniature fountain at your desk and listen to the sounds as you try to relax, sit back and allow yourself to feel comfortable and soothed.

If you are technologically savvy, you can download some apps you can use for this kind of activity. There are apps with nature sounds you can use to help relax your mind and body.

3. Smell your favorite essential oils.

There is a part of the brain responsible for governing your memory and emotions. Near this area is the part that processes scents. The latter can induce good emotions and help in calming your mind.

A study published in 2008 proved that the use of essential oils in nurses who work in intensive care units helped in alleviating and managing their tension and stress. You can dab a small amount of oil with your favorite scent in your clothes or skin. You can also use a diffuser to allow all the people in the room to benefit from its scent. The essential oils known to relieve stress include lavender, ylang-ylang, and peppermint.

4. Perform breathing exercises. A minute of this exercise is enough to ease the tension inside of you. Close your eyes, breathe deeply and let your mind focus on your breathing. Feel your body when you breathe. You will feel better when you go back to the current moment. You will also notice that your mood is lighter and your outlook in life clearer.

5. Give yourself a brief massage. The stress triangle in the body is found at the neck and shoulders. Stop what you're doing when you're stressed out. Try to relax as you massage your neck and shoulders. Focus on how your hands and fingers are moving and how the massage alleviates your tiredness and stress. Focus the massage on your stress triangle.

6. Dance. This is a good form of exercise as it helps in releasing and pumping up the endorphins in your system. Put on your earphones and play a tune. Let

your body dance to the beat as if no one's watching. Continue even when there are people around. This will make you feel better and happier.

Getting Started with Seated Meditation

If you want to learn how to meditate, you can start by following these steps:

1. Find the perfect spot where you can meditate undisturbed. It can be indoors or outdoors, as long as it is peaceful and quiet. Make sure that the space can give you a total solitude during the process. Clean the spot and keep it neat. It will be hard to focus in a cluttered space. Set the mood and ambiance by lighting a candle but you can skip this part if you are not fond of its smell. Place anything in your chosen spot that will make it easier for you to get "in the zone," such as music or incense.

2. It will take time to get used to the process. As much as possible, minimize the possible distractions when you begin. The biggest distraction will be your own mind. No matter what thoughts it comes up with, keep your focus and try to go back to meditating. Set a goal on what you want to achieve, including how long you intend the session to last. You can start the practice

with 20 minutes per session. You can gradually add time through the days and as you get more used to it.

3. Keep proper posture all the time while meditating and make sure that you are comfortable with it. Sitting properly will minimize the discomfort and pain while proper posture helps you breathe deeper and easier.

   You can choose to sit however you like - with a cushion or without, on a chair or on the floor. You can also opt to stand if you'll find it more comfortable. No matter how you position yourself, never lose your balance, never lean on anything and never slouch. Adjust your position if you feel any kind of pain. As to constantly meditate, you will find the best and appropriate position for you.

4. Focus on your breathing - how the air flows in and out of your system, your belly getting filled and empty and upward and downward motion of your chest. Breathe slow but not deliberately. Feel the ebb, flow, and rhythm of the process.

5. Be aware of yourself and all the areas of your body. Learn how to recognize where the discomfort or tension is coming from. There are certain parts of the body where stress usually gets "stored", such as the face, neck, back, shoulders, and legs.

You have to relax as you meditate and the best way to do this is by getting rid of the tension and stress. Imagine the tension coming out of your system as you breathe out until you have released all the tension and you finally feel at ease.

Refining Your Meditation Practice

After learning the basics, you can focus on training your mind. Concentrate on how to reach true happiness, compassion, inner peace, and patience.

Here are the steps to follow to improve your concentration while meditating:

1. Practice mindfulness. Concentration and mindfulness are referred to as the two wings of meditation in Buddhism. They are opposite but work together like wings. Mindfulness remains open and relaxed at times when concentration is one-pointed. Mindfulness becomes expansive while concentration is focused.

   At this point, you have to learn how to grow and expand your awareness. Feel your breath as air is distributed all over your system, senses, emotions, thoughts, and mind. Whenever something comes to mind, accept it and release so that you can go back in opening and freeing your awareness.

Observe everything present in the moment but do not grasp anything all at once Learn how to recognize things, emotions, and thoughts and let them go. As you practice meditation, it will be easier to rest, stay peaceful, and come to this state.

2. Improve your mental discipline through control and focus. You have to learn how to focus your attention. This aspect of meditation seems simple but it's actually one of the most difficult to control.

You can begin by choosing one thing as the object you'll focus on. It can be your breath, the flame of a lit candle or a mantra. Hold your attention to your focus. Take a mental note of whatever distracted you as you're doing the process.

Distractions come in many forms - a random thought or feeling, noise or an itch. As you set aside the distraction, bring back your attention to your focus.

It is normal to find this activity hard in the beginning. There will be times when you'll get distracted not only by things or your thoughts but also by certain emotions, such as boredom and frustration. Just hold on to the practice and keep on doing it. You will get better at it in time.

Through continued practice, your mind will find it easier to become more steady. You'll be able to allow distractions and thoughts fade from sight without affecting you. The object of your focus becomes a calm refuge, a sanctuary or an island that you can go back into whenever you need healing.

3. You don't silence your mind when you meditate, contrary to popular belief. It is not your enemy, but it can be a powerful tool and your friend with the right training and attitude.

When you pay attention, you will realize the same thought pattern repeating in your mind as you practice mindfulness or concentration. The recurring thoughts may be telling you something. They may be fantasies, dreams or memories that exist to teach you. They will serve as the keys to open any mental blockage, which includes subconscious thinking that refrains you from reaching your full potential, fears, and deeply held beliefs.

Just let the thought come in and do not fight them. Befriend your thoughts instead, including the unpleasant ones. Invite all the learnings you've gotten from the thoughts as you find out more about your inner workings - why are you like that and why do love doing the things you love to do. Your goal is to make the unconscious conscious. You can achieve this by bringing into the light the darkest and deepest parts of your mind.

4. As you cultivate pure awareness through meditation, you have to practice non-judgment. Learn not to judge your thoughts whether they are right or wrong and good or bad. Let all the feelings, memories, and thoughts flow through your awareness. Do not label them but merely observe what is happening. Having bad thoughts don't mean that you are a bad person, same as having good thoughts make you a good person.

   Observe your fantasies and memories as they unfold and listen to your thoughts. Your mind doesn't define who you are.

5. Do not identify yourself with the voice in your head – the voice that constantly plans, worry, remember, label, judge, and repeat thoughts over and over again. You are not your personality, mind, and ego. They are all lies that you can get yourself freed from through meditation. The process empowers the truth of what and who you really are. You can make that happen by first, stopping from identifying yourself from your fearful ego.

You are not required to silence your ego. That would be impossible. You simply have to shift your personality to become an observer and spectator. Whatever you are thinking are only thoughts. Thinking happens and you don't have anything to do with it.

When you reach the point of realization and successfully shifted your personality, you will feel what it's like to be free. You will feel lighter as if a heavy burden has been lifted off your life. The thoughts in your head must never limit who you are and your full potential. Always remember that you are a pure and vast ocean of awareness that becomes a witness to everything inside and outside of you. You can do whatever you want because you are free.

6. Meditation allows you to uncover recurring thought patterns, such as limiting beliefs, judgments, and fears. The process helps you understand what the rest of the world expects from you and most important of all, develop your basic concept of who you really are. Once you allow meditation to transform you, it will shape your character and how you relate to other people, your behavior and all aspects of your life.

The process leads to the point of understanding that most of your thoughts aren't true and they only form barriers and try to limit you. Let go of these limiting thoughts and beliefs.

7. The most difficult skill you have to develop as you meditate is the art of letting go or surrendering. You have to let go of your so-called self, get rid of who you thought you are and realize the limitless potentials and opportunities.

Every time you go to your sacred place to meditate, you have to be open and aware. Give yourself fully to the experience, the stillness, and silence.

It will be easier through time. Make sure that you never compare your progress to others. You are unique and this is a good way to realize what kind of unique you are.

Chapter 8 - Different Kinds of Meditation

Metta Meditation

This type of meditation helps its practitioners develop compassion, which is one of the main goals of Buddhism. This is popular, universal, and accessible to everybody.

The word, Meta, is a term with no literal English translation but it conveys fellowship, compassion, goodwill, benevolence, non-violence, friendliness, and warmth. The word comes from ancient Pali or a language from the most ancient scriptures of Buddhism. To give it an English translation, the term loving-kindness was made.

The practice and philosophy of this kind of meditation can be rooted in the Hymn of Universal Love - the Karaniya Metta Sutta of Buddha. Through this Hymn of Universal Love, Buddha taught his disciples proper contemplation and development of compassion and universal love to achieve spiritual perfection and liberation.

In order to perform this kind of meditation properly, you must first understand what compassion is all about. Compassion, while having a meaning close to empathy, differs from the latter. Empathy allows you to feel other's suffering as if you are the one going through it. While it can be said that compassion is an extension of empathy, it doesn't end to feeling the other person's suffering. Empathy makes you feel stuck. It is draining, stressful and not helpful to you or the person who is going through something.

When you take empathy to the next level, that's when you will feel compassion. At this point, you will identify with the sufferer and not merely relate to how they are feeling. You'd have a desire of taking off their baggage and you will feel love and warmth towards them.

According to studies, compassion and empathy stimulate different networks in the brain. The positive feelings, such as kindness, love, connection, and warmth are associated with networks with underlying compassion. Negative emotions, on the other hand, are associated with networks that underlying empathy.

Compassion puts the feeling of empathy to good use. It is proactive because you will realize that you are also helping yourself as you help others.

Compassion has numerous benefits according to research. They include the following:

- Alleviates chronic pain
- Alleviates migraine
- Alleviates signs of aging
- Alleviates stress
- Prompts positive changes in the brain

Compassion is also beneficial to emotional and mental wellbeing:

- Boosts positive emotions
- Heals self-criticism
- Improves mood and emotions
- Boosts emotional intelligence
- Helps in treating mental disorders, such as schizophrenia and PTSD
- Reduces the symptoms of depression

Some of its social benefits include the following:

- It helps you become more cooperative and helpful
- Boosts your social connection
- Helps in dealing with bias and prejudices

Here are the steps on how to practice Metta or Loving-Kindness Meditation

1. Find your sacred place and position yourself comfortably. Keep your back relaxed and straight without feeling any pain.

2. Practice a simple breathing meditation for the first few minutes. Inhale deeply as you scan your system for any tension, pain, and stress. Exhale slowly while you release the negative feelings with each exhalation. Keep focused on your breathing while adjusting your position whenever needed. As you go through the breathing exercises, allow yourself to go deeper until you reach the state of total relaxation.

3. Once the body is completely relaxed and your mind is at peace, chant words that will make you feel calmer. The chant has to revolve around yourself like these:

> *"May I be joyful, peaceful, and safe."*

> *"May I discover the real me."*

> *"May I be free from pain and suffering."*

You must first cultivate loving-kindness to yourself because you can only give love and compassion to others if you love and feel compassionate about yourself. Chant the words while feeling happy, at peace, free, and smiling. Imagine that you are in a perfect world where happiness is everywhere, without danger or fear.

As you recite the words, imagine a vision of complete serenity. Feel the love in your core and accept the feeling and the warmth it brings. Accept who you are, love that person, forgive and be kind to yourself. Stay in this state for 2 to 3 minutes.

4. You will now direct the loving-kindness to other people. Think about the closest or those in your inner circle. You will think of them one by one. The chant can be similar with the first one but this time, you'll address your chants to each of your loved one like:

> *"May you be joyful, peaceful, and safe."*

"May you discover the real you."

"May you be free from pain and suffering."

Imagine your loved one being free, happy, and well as you perform the chant. You will visualize them overcoming problems and challenges. Imagine them discovering the divine and infinite being.

5. You will chant the same thing as what you said in the previous step but this time, you'll think about other people who don't belong in your inner circle. They can be anyone you can think of – a person you met on the street or at the mall, your neighbor or co-worker. Relax the chant whole thinking of the person who first come to your mind. Think about them while wishing for their well-being. Be sincere with your desire for them to attain spiritual freedom, healthy body, and peaceful mind.

6. At this point, you will think of a person or people who have hurt or caused you pain. You will recite the same chant in steps 4 to 5 while thinking about each of them. Call them out and silently chant the phrases. You will then observe how you feel as you perform the chant. You have to be aware if you are feeling any resistance or if feels like you are still holding resentment, pain, anger, and frustration towards them. You can move forward to the next step if you feel like you have already forgiven what they have done. If not, you will need to

work on forgiving these people until can recite the chants like you mean them

7. You will now include all living things in your chant. Using the same chant in steps 4 to 6, you will recite them while thinking about all living things in the universe, including animals, plants, and humans. As you say the chant, imagine your mind and heart like a fully bloomed lotus flower. Visualize all living things on earth and all the universe as part of an infinite whole. Keep the vision until it feels real.

You can perform this kind of meditation twice a day at about 20 minutes each per session.

Moving Meditation

Everybody can meditate, even those who find it hard to sit still, such as people diagnosed with ADHD or ADD. You can try any of the following alternatives to the most common sitting meditation:

1. Mindful Walking

This walking meditation popularized by Buddhist monk Thich Nhat Hanh is done by simply walking while working on your focus and attention. This is best done outdoors. As you walk, focus on your breathing and on your every step. Keep your attention to your senses, breath, body, and whatever is happening at the moment. Relax as you walk. You can do this anytime and anywhere. You can practice this kind of meditation as you walk to or from home.

2. Painting or drawing

Bring out the artist in you and indulge on your talent. Art can heal. Most artists consider their art as sacred and more than a craft. The process of doing the art will get you in the zone, especially if it is your passion. In the zone means that you'll enter into the state of surrender and mindfulness. Painting and writing have long been considered as forms of meditation in the far East. They help them achieve peace, mindfulness and give them the feeling of freedom and spontaneity.

You don't need to be good to start with this form of meditation. Relax, loosen up, try something new and play with your imagination. Choose what you will use – crayons, paints or pen and choose space. This space has to be peaceful and where you can be left alone while seeking for a much-needed silence. This space must inspire you to work on your art while keeping your focus. Place all the materials you'll need within reach.

Decide on what you will draw or paint. It can be anything – an abstract, landscape, shapes, fruit or flower. Enjoy the process and let your medium go wherever it wants to go and create whatever they whatever it wants to create. Do not mind the end product. You don't have to show it to anyone, and it doesn't need to be perfect. Release your worries and focus on having fun.

3. Tai Chi

It comes from the term, *tai chi chuan*, which means supreme ultimate force. The exercise aims to balance and enhance the body's energy flow – the chi or qi or the cosmic life force. The practice involves a series of easy movements mostly inspired by nature. Many of the motions done in Tai Chi are similar to martial arts. You will focus on your breathing as you perform deliberate, gentle, and slow movements. You will continue with the practice until you become balanced, centered, and calm.

You will challenge yourself with more difficult movements as you get used to the practice. In time, you will also learn surrender to the flow of energy and still your mind. The practice will make you forget the difference between active and passive, motion and stillness, the rest of the universe and yourself. When you reach that point, you will realize that you are the ultimate supreme force. You are the Chi.

3. Martial Arts

This is preferred by those who aren't used to doing the gentle movements of Tai Chi and yoga. Martial arts have the elements of engaged and active meditation. You can train your mind as you train your body during practice. There are many forms of martial arts that you can practice, such as kickboxing, karate, taekwondo, aikido and many more.

Choose what you want to practice and prepare a space where you will do it. Make sure that when you decide to start on the practice, you will dedicate the time in achieving mastery not only of the skills and movements but also of your self, life, and mind. While at it, keep your attention to your body and breathing. Let yourself get lost and absorbed in the movements.

4. Dancing, chanting, or singing

You don't need props or instruments to start meditating. You can use your voice and body. You can allow yourself to get lost in the melody or rhythm. Sing and dance your heart out. Have fun and without realizing, you'll eventually get into a meditative state of surrender, mindfulness, and relaxation.

To perform this kind of meditation, listen to your heart and do whatever feels right at the moment. You can dance along with your favorite tune or sing along with relaxing music, such as Gregorian chants or the traditional Indian kirtans. Let go and lose yourself in the moment.

5. Running

Most runners will tell you that the activity can be more than an exercise. It helps you reach the state called the runner's high or the meditative state while in motion. At this state, you'll feel in the moment, intensely alive and free from inner turmoil and mental chatter.

First, you have to decide that you'll do it and commit that you'll run the same time every day. This time will be your sacred time. You can do this anywhere you want – in the backyard, park, beach or road. Like the other forms of meditation, focus on your breathing. Keep your attention to the rhythm created by your feet while in motion. Feel the air as it moves past or along your body.

Be aware of your surroundings – the sunrise or sunset, the trees, other people, the gushing wind, the smell of the grass. Imbibe the moment and experience the present. The experience will make you feel light and happy, emotions that you'll look forward to each time that you have to do the activity again.

6. Yoga (Asanas)

Yoga is more than the physical poses required during the practice. It is comprised of different meditative practices, such as breathing exercises, self-inquiry, meditation and many more, which aim to help you reach the point of being one with God.

Chapter 9 - Cultivating Mindfulness

Mindfulness is an important concept in meditation practices and Buddhism. It refers to the act of paying close attention to the "now" or whatever's happening at the moment without being biased, without labels and judgment. It is pure awareness that happens before your mind works by doing cognitive tasks and thinking.

To practice mindfulness, you have to observe everything around you without overthinking or over-analyzing what you see. It is normal for judgments and unrelated thoughts to come up during the process. When this happens, try to stay calm as you focus your observation on what you're thinking.

When you have gotten into the state of pure awareness, you will find it easier to see things as they are. Everything becomes interesting, music sound better, food tastes better, and you'll see goodness in people. You will see life in variety, full of richness and color. You will let go of the filter that used to blur your vision and understanding of the world around you. You will also develop sharper senses and a disposition free from destructive thought patterns that lead to illnesses, anxiety, and depression.

You don't need to spend your whole life meditating to get into this state. You also don't have to be a Buddhist to experience the state of pure awareness.

Here are some of the activities and exercises you can do each day to make it easier for you to attain mindfulness that will last from day till night.

1. Start each day by waking up mindfully.

This will set the mood for the rest of your day. The moment you open your eyes, focus your awareness of the present moment – where you are, what you are doing, how you are feeling. Observe how you fee and what you sense. Do this first thing in the morning before getting up and before reaching your alarm clock.

Be aware of everything – every sound, smell, feeling, and more. Listen to the sounds coming from outside of the window, the noise created by your fan or cooler, the ringing of your alarm. Focus on your body and feel if there is any tension or if your eyelids feel heavy. Gently stretch your muscles as you observe the subtle sensations you feel as you become more awake. Observe but do not make judgments or any mental notes.

2. Practice mindfulness when you're taking a shower. As much as possible, teach your mind to observe without making a judgment. In the shower, observe all the things around you. As you begin with the process, run your hands to the water and feel its temperature. Look closely and observe how the water touches and slips through your form. Be observant of the feel

and smell of your shampoo, conditioner, soap, lotion, body wash, and all other products you'll use in the shower.

Smell the towel or roe and feel its texture as it rubs against your skin and hair. Observe the differences in the feeling of being dry and wet. Observe the toothpaste as you put some to your toothbrush. Be mindful of its taste and how the bristles of the toothbrush feel once inside your mouth. Avoid talking if you can and make sure that you are aware of the moment throughout the process.

3. Practice mindful eating.

Practice mindfulness at the first meal you'll have in the day, your breakfast. When in the kitchen, observe your body and hear what it says. Listen to its cravings or what does it want to have for breakfast. Observe every step and every movement you do as you prepare your meal to the moment that you have placed it on the table. As you eat, focus on your food and your body. Once your food is inside your mouth, chew it slowly. Let the flavor linger in your mouth as you pause in between. Feel the texture of the food and how it moves to your throat and belly. You must also be aware when your body is telling you that you're full.

4. Observe your habits

At times when you are not in a rush, try to observe the most common things you do each day and how you do them.

Observe each step of the activities you do almost every day. Start upon waking up. Observe what you usually do when you get out of bed. Be aware of what your body prefers doing and how you feel in each task. Observe each step of the task. Focus on the things that you could have skipped so you can spend time doing other useful chores. This exercise will not only help in practicing mindfulness but will also prompt you to become aware and give you an opportunity to wake up.

5. Practice mindfulness whenever you find yourself waiting

When your mind is busy, you tend to get easily frustrated when things slow down. If you find yourself waiting due for different reasons – traffic, long lines, the bus failed to show up, your date is late, and so on, use the waiting time to practice mindfulness instead of getting angry. Instead of thinking negatively about your situation, observe and practice mindfulness. While waiting, try to close your eyes, inhale, and relax.

Focus your awareness to your system and how you are feeling. Feel the emotion, anxiety, stress or tension. Breathe deeply and let go of the negative emotions and thoughts. Let them all go. The situation won't get light by getting angry or feeling tensed. You won't get to your destination or your date won't show up the moment you get angry. Relax and focus at what's happening at the moment. Whenever you are left to wait, make sure that you don't get mad. Instead, focus on the present, be mindful, and be aware.

6. Practice mindful driving

Consider your time at the car as your "me" time. From the point where you came from to your destination, you have to be aware of everything that has transpired – your car's temperature, the music playing, the sounds you hear, people and vehicles on the street. You have to focus on how you are driving and on the road ahead.

The next day, turn off the music and drive in silence. Refrain from talking or having other distractions. Bring your focus on the road. What do you see on the road and how do you feel. As you look closely, bring the attention of your senses on your feet and hands and what they are doing while you are driving. Focus on the sounds you hear, like the hum of the engine or the wind outside. Do not get distracted by your own thoughts. Let them be. Breathe deeply and bring back your attention to the very moment in the present.

7. Give yourself time to unwind

Upon coming home after a day at work or school, do not go straight on the couch or look for something to eat. Sit somewhere peaceful and spend a few minutes doing nothing but unwinding and relaxing. Be at the moment. Focus on what happened to your day and how it made you feel. Process any frustration, anger or tiredness. Keep on resting until you feel calmer. Make sure that you leave all negative feelings at this state. When you go back to usual, you'll feel calmer, happier, and rested.

8. Practice active listening

Give your loved ones or friends your undivided attention. Instead of tuning them out, try to actively listen to what they are saying. Concentrate on listening to them and do not compose your response in your head. This will hone your mindfulness and nurture your relationships as well. It gives you a chance to connect and be intimate with someone you care for.

Chapter 10 – Yoga and Buddhism

Yoga is not a religious system but is sometimes performed as part of certain religious practices. This practice has certain similarities to Buddhism. For one, they both aim to achieve enlightenment through the development of insightful wisdom and intuitive skills.

Buddha was also a serious practitioner of yoga and yogic arts. He sought an experiential understanding of the practice and he was also knowledgeable about the Vedantic philosophy. Yoga and Buddhism have the same core teaching, which is compassion. Both practices also recognize that freedom from a dualistic mindset leads to enlightenment. One type of yoga, Krishna, focuses on teaching the essence of equanimity of mind.

Buddha has expressed many times during his lifetime that one will only achieve the real meaning of freedom when they are free from their preferences and wants. Wanting something and not getting it will only lead to sadness and disappointment.

According to the yoga sutras of Patanjali, yoga is achieved when you can no longer identify the wavering of your mind. Once the state is achieved, you will experience Samadhi or identity with self that equates to ecstasy, bliss, and happiness. It also states that good karma comes from the practice of non-harming of others, also called ahimsa.

The yogic text Astavakra Samhita believes that a person will become whatever he thinks. A person eventually becomes eternal when he identifies with something that is eternal. He will be bound if that's how he thinks himself to be and free if he thinks himself as free.

Buddhism and yoga encourage people to be compassionate and kind toward other beings because everything that you do – action, word or thought, will eventually come back to you. They are both geared in achieving enlightenment or the state when a person realizes the totality of Oneness of Being. In order to achieve Oneness, you have to completely remove otherness. Oneness, in Buddhism, is referred to as the emptiness of form. Since otherness is considered as an obstacle, you have to make it disappear through compassion or one's ability to deeply see themselves in other people.

Another similarity between yoga and Buddhism is the recognition that suffering exists, but it is possible to free yourself from it. Both teachings utilize the meditation technique for the mind to go beyond hindrances and fluctuations. Yogis refer to the state as absolute self while it is referred to as emptiness in Buddhism.

Despite the similarities, the two practices also have various differences. Buddhism doesn't believe that God or a fundamental self exist. For Buddhists, these ideas were only created by the mind. The illusion of the self and creation of life were explained through conditioning and karma. For them, one's self is not something enduring but only a fleeting feeling or thought.

Yoga practitioners, on the other hand, believe in the existence of God and Atman or an Inner Self. The latter refers to one's soul or authentic self and the true nature of a person's consciousness. For them, God is not only the creator of the universe but also its preserver and destroyer. In order to gain self-realization in a yoga practice, you have to surrender yourself to God and have total faith in the Atman. In yoga, Atman is different from Ahamkara or ego. Both Buddhism and yoga are meditative practices in the search for higher consciousness.

Beginners Guide to Yoga

In order to benefit from yoga and use the practice to meditate and achieve enlightenment, you have to do it properly. Yoga can be done alone. You can follow a guide and perform the sequences on your own but is recommended to get a trainer or join a yoga class, especially in the beginning. You will need help not only with the movements and breathing but also on how to stay focused all throughout the process.

Different Styles of Yoga

It is important to acquaint yourself with the different styles of yoga to make it easier for you to find an instructor or yoga class. If you have an existing medical condition, make sure to open it up first to your instructor so that they can adjust the movements and pace depending on the state of your health.

Here are some of the most popular styles of yoga that you can choose from:

1. Bikram Yoga

Yoga is done in a heated room with 45 minutes spent in doing standing poses and 45 minutes for floor poses. The movements help you keep in shape and at the same time, boost your mental concentration to help your physical state become one with your spiritual self.

2. Forrest Yoga

This yoga practice celebrates strength by releasing your emotional and physical tension. It is composed of tough physical movements and emotional exercises. The movements help in clearing your baggage to make enough room to welcome your spirit.

3. Ashtanga Yoga

This yoga, which is athletic in nature, teaches you the value of practicing and setting your mind that good things are coming. Your trainer will design exercises and movements depending on your strengths. You are only required to observe and follow without rejecting.

4. Baptiste Power Vinyasa Yoga

This yoga, which is physically demanding, is also done in a heated room. It requires 90 minutes comprised of vigorous sequences. It aims to help you in coping with the challenges that you may face in the future. The movements were designed to give you the freedom and attain a certain power to accept who you really are while having a peace of mind.

5. Iyengar Yoga

This yoga is perfect for beginners whose movements are still limited. It is comprised of subtle actions with the focus on proper alignment. It gives you a peek of the various movements that you can do in yoga. It also makes you aware of your physical capabilities, strengths, and weaknesses. After learning your body's limitations, this yoga will help in improving your flexibility.

6. Jivamukti Yoga

This is both physically exhilarating and intellectually stimulating. The focus is on the spiritual growth of the practitioner. It includes meditation, breathing techniques, and movements from different yoga practices.

7. Integral Yoga

This yoga helps you go back to your natural state with a clear mind, a heart full of love, and a happy and contented life. The movements are gentle, and it also includes meditation, chanting, and breathing exercises.

8. Sivananda Yoga

This yoga was inspired by the teachings of Swami Sivananda. It is known to be more spiritual than physical. Every session lasts for 90 minutes, wherein you'll be required to do 12 core poses, meditate, relax, and practice pranayama and Sanskrit chanting. It focuses on the five fundamental points of yoga – proper breathing, right exercise, corpse pose, positive thinking and meditation, and vegetarianism or proper diet. The yoga practice aims in helping the practitioner attain a higher level of consciousness.

9. Svaroopa Yoga

Svaroopa, a term that means the bliss of your own being, aims to help you in releasing tension to get rid of those factors that hinder you from having an inner transformation. Each session includes many floor and hand exercises. It starts and ends with the Corpse pose or Savasana.

10. TriYoga

The movements involved in this yoga practice aim to awaken your prana. Each session requires the performance of mudras, flowing asanas, Dharana, pranayama, and meditation. It teaches you spine movements and coordinated breathing.

11. Ishta Yoga

ISHTA or Integrated Science of Hatha, Tantra, and Ayurveda, is a yoga practice that balances the human organism to help you develop a stronger platform to attain spiritual growth. The movements give out varying energetic effects. It aligns your body, teaches you proper breathing techniques, hones your focus through meditation, and cleanses your inner being.

12. Kripalu Yoga

This yoga practice awakens the natural life force to help you in coping with all areas of your life. This can be extremely easy or tough. You'll be required to observe the sensations of your body and mind. This will give you time to understand the nature of the poses and how your body is benefitting from them. It also helps you realize how the decisions you make impact your life. The practice includes meditation, relaxation, asana, and pranayama.

13. Kundalini Yoga

Each session lasts for 90 minutes comprised of extensive movements aimed to push your body and mind to the limits. It typically begins with a chant and ends with the class singing. This yoga style, also referred to as the Yoga of Awareness, includes breathing exercises, mantras, mudras, and mini-meditations – all aimed in awakening your kundalini energy.

As you go about the process, you will experience spiritual evaluation that will lead to the transformation of your core.

14. Prana Flow Yoga

This yoga practice, which is both challenging and empowering, is a fluid form of Vinsaya yoga. It teaches you to connect with prana. Each session typically opens with Om and followed by creative near-continuous sequences with accompanying music.

15. Purna Yoga

Each session starts and ends with quick meditations intended to connect to your heart center. It aims to connect your body and mind to your spirit. The practice is composed of four limbs – pranayama, asana, nutrition, and lifestyle, and applied philosophy. This yoga practice is focused on the asanas combined with yogic philosophy and the alignment methods of Iyengar yoga.

16. OM Yoga

This yoga practice helps the practitioner achieve strength, clarity, and stability. It also helps you develop compassion with how you live your life. The movements, mostly composed of Vinsaya sequences, are done at a moderate pace aligned with compassion and mindfulness.

17. ParaYoga

This yoga practice boosts your self-awareness. It teaches you about how asana affects your energy and how you can develop a more refined prana. Each session is composed of the combination of a dynamic practice and tantric philosophy. You will be required to perform difficult asanas, mudras, bandhas, pranayama, and meditation.

18. Viniyoga

The purpose of this therapeutic yoga is to help you reach the point of discriminative awareness that is important in achieving self-transformation. The sequences were designed to coordinate the movements of the spine with your breathing. It teaches you to focus and cultivate the positive aspects of life and eliminate the negativities.

In deciding which style of yoga to pursue, you have to weigh the benefits of the process and choose the type that is best suited to your health, needs, and physical capabilities. If you don't want to join classes, you can still practice yoga on your own as long as you have the right guide, materials, equipment, and handy tools for first aid.

Benefits of Yoga

Yoga helps you become one with the universe through different techniques, poses, and practices involved.

1. It helps you develop stronger muscles that will reduce the risks of developing back pain and arthritis.

2. It boosts your bone health. As you progress with the practice, you will learn how to lift your own weight. Yoga reduces the levels of the stress hormone in your body and as a result, the calcium in the bones remains intact. The practice reduces your risk of osteoporosis and other bone diseases.

3. Yoga exercises help you in developing a better body posture. Poor posture can lead to health issues in the different areas of the body, including your neck, joint, back, and muscles.

4. The exercises will improve your body's flexibility through continued practice.

5. Aside from achieving enlightenment, yoga also helps you burn calories and stay fit.

6. It helps you stay focused.

7. The exercises boost blood flow and allow more oxygen to get into your system. Yoga reduces your risk of stroke and heart attack.

8. A well-balanced asana practice will result in a more flexible spinal disc since you will do lots of twists, forward and backbends.

9. Yoga helps in keeping your blood pressure normal and maintaining a regular heart rate. It protects you from heart ailments and depression.

10. It decreases the cortisol levels in your system. The opposite will cause health problems, such as insulin resistance, osteoporosis, high blood pressure, and depression.

11. It increases your system's good cholesterol (HDL) and decreases the levels of your bad cholesterol (LDL).

12. Yoga is calming and relaxing. It is a good form of meditation when you are faced with problems and stressors.

13. Your proprioception or your ability to feel where in space is your physical body and what is it doing improves as you do yoga more often. Through time and practice, you will develop a better balance and you will find it easier to perform the difficult yoga sequences.

14. The exercises in yoga require the joints to move in a full range motion. It helps the bones to become strong and less prone to injuries even as you age.

15. The yoga sequences, breathing, and meditation boost the body's immune system.

Chapter 11 - The Mudras and Basic Poses in Yoga

In the ancient Yoga Sutras of Patanjali, physical postures constitute one of eight limbs of yoga. The other limbs include breathing, conduct, and the power of the mind. All these limbs aim to bring out your divine inner qualities.

As you make yoga part of your lifestyle, you will understand how important is the practice to understand your inner self or who you are from within. All human beings have a physical and non-physical existence composed of different layers. Yoga aims to open and activate the principles that will hone each of these layers. To deal with the physical practices of yoga, you have to learn more about the asanas, mudras, and bandhas.

- Asanas – the physical poses, postures, and seats you need to learn to attain spiritual growth and a healthier nervous system.

- Bandhas – physical poses, which are static most of the time. They are geared in improving the areas of the body that block the flow of neurobiological energies from deep within. Yoga will teach you how to direct the energy to flow in the right direction and where it is needed.

- Mudras – composed of physical and dynamic poses geared to the areas of your body that channel the flow of the neurobiological energies to your core.

Among the three, asanas are more known worldwide and are being integrated into various exercises and physical fitness activities. In a way, they help in keeping the interest of many people in yoga.

Mudras and bandhas are separate practices with similarities and overlaps. They are both inward in terms of appearance and performance. They both train the natural physical processes in your core to awaken the Kundalini, where you will experience spiritual ecstasy.

Asanas, mudras, and bandhas are the three major ways in yoga in which you can connect your physical state and spirit.

More about the Mudras

Mudra is a Sanskrit word that means gesture or attitude. In yoga, mudras are performed in combination with breathing exercises to boost the flow of prana and stimulate all parts of the body involved in breathing. These mudras are often taught in the lesser-known and independent branch of yoga known as the Yoga Tatva Mudra Vigyan. The goal is to create a subtle connection with the instincts that affect your unconscious reflexes as you do the movements.

The mudras direct your focus to the gesture being done by your hands as you perform yoga poses. Mudras are also called seals and their goal is to create prana or pathways for energy by unblocking the chakras.

They also have healing effects since the hands have reflexology points and acupressure. Certain mudras are also symbolic in nature.

In yoga, the fingers and toes are believed to be charged with divine power. A mudra is a gesture that looks like a hand pantomime based on the rituals and carries a visual message similar to a hieroglyph. There are many types of mudras ranging from simple to complex.

Here are the most common mudras typically used in Hatha yoga:

1. Gyan Mudra. Relax your fingers. Move your thumb and forefinger closer and press them firmly while keeping the rest of the fingers straight. When doing this mudra in a cross-legged pose, lay the backs of your hands on your thighs. This is also called Jnana mudra or knowledge mudra, which symbolizes connection and oneness.

This mudra affects wisdom. It is done to meditate and disassociate oneself from the material world. It boosts the air element of the body and prompts creative thinking, enthusiasm, and eagerness. When done properly, this mudra can help in boosting your memory and the cognitive process of thinking. It can also relieve depression, drowsiness, and mental retardation.

2. Anjali Mudra. This is the most common mudra, which is also known as the prayer or Namaste position. Press your left palm with your right palm. The pose is said to bring harmony to the right and left sides of your brain. The pose gives instant calmness as long as it is done right.

3. Garuda Mudra. The pose, which resembles a bird, has the same origin as the eagle pose or Garudasana. It has an invigorating effect and it promotes balance. Cross your wrists with your palms to the direction of your chest. Hook the thumbs of your two hands together.

4. Vishnu Mudra. The pose is usually done when performing Nadi Sodhana or alternate nostril breathing. Put your index and middle fingers towards the direction of your palm. With the two fingers bent, keep the rest of the fingers extended.

5. Lotus Mudra. Put your hands together until your palms meet similar to the Anjali mudra. Gradually separate the middle parts of the palms as you spread your fingers without disconnecting your thumbs, pinkies, and the bases of your palms. The pose, reminiscent of the shape of a lotus flower, symbolizes openness and blossoming.

6. Dhyana Mudra. This classic Buddhist meditation pose is done by sitting down as you relax your whole body. Place your left hand on your lap with the palm facing up. Put your right hand on top of the left as you let your thumbs touch the top part of your palms.

7. Kundalini Mudra. This pose, assimilated with one's sexuality and unity, is done by forming a fist in your left hand as you keep the index finger extended. Grip that index finger with your right hand as you form a fist with this hand. Keep the thumb of your right hand lying on top of the index finger of your left hand.

Chapter 12- Mastering Yoga Poses

The first thing you need to do is to familiarize yourself with the proper ways of performing right mudra for each yoga pose suitable for beginners. You can start with the following three poses:

1. Toe Stand (Pandangustasana)

This pose, which is typically performed in Bikram yoga, helps in opening the hips and in strengthening the core of the feet. Perform hip stretches before doing the pose. Be careful with your movements, especially if you have knee problems. If the pain doesn't go away no matter how careful you are, stop doing the pose and perform other poses more suitable for your condition.

Stand in a half lotus tree pose. Stand on your right leg. Move the top of your left foot towards your right hip. Maintain your balance by taking several breaths. Slowly bend your right knee while keeping the left foot on top of the left thigh.

Start lifting your right heel until you are up on the ball of your right foot. Go on a squatting position while keeping your right heel in the center of your body. Make sure that you don't move the right heel under the right buttock.

While in that position, extend your fingertips to the floor ahead of you to attain more balance. Make your belly firm as you lift one hand or both, if you can, off the floor. As you do this, keep your balance on the ball of your right foot. Once you have achieved the perfect balance, move your hands and perform Anjali mudra.

Hold the pose as you inhale and exhale deeply for five counts. Gradually rise back to the half lotus tree pose. Rest for a while as you focus on your breathing. Shake both legs and perform the same sequence to the other side.

If you are having difficulty doing the half lotus pose, you can squat with your heels lifted and your knees together while keeping your balance. This may be difficult in the beginning, but you will eventually get used to it. Once you can do the pose effortlessly, try making it more challenging by coming in and out of the pose without allowing your hands touch the floor.

2. Deep Side Lunge (Skandasana)

You can do this pose in different ways depending on your capability. You can do this with one foot hooked at the back of your head while on a seated forward bend. You can also do the pose with the foot hooked behind your head while standing. The exercise works on your hips and hamstrings and improves your balance and core strength.

Start in a wide-legged forward bend or Prasarita Padottanasana. Gently bend your knee to a half squat. Keep your right leg straight as you extend your foot and lift your toes from the floor. Let your weight rest on your right heel. You can keep your hands on the floor if you are finding it hard to attain balance.

Once you are used with the pose, do it while bending your elbows as you bring your hands together to perform an Anjali mudra pose. Place your left elbow at the inner part of the left knee. Drop your hands to the floor for support as you gradually remove yourself from the pose. Rest for a while and focus on your breathing. Repeat the sequence on the other side.

Most beginners find it hard to get into a full squat. You will eventually get used to it through continued practice. While you still can't, keep standing on the ball of the left foot.

3. Revolved Lunge (Parivrtta Anjaneyasana)

This detoxifying pose requires flexibility, balance, and strength. By twisting your body, you will wring out your internal organs and give your chest enough room to breathe by the end of the pose.

Start in a regular lunge pose. Put your hands down and gradually twist to the right by stepping your left foot backward. You will end up in a high lunge pose with your knee directly facing your ankle and your toes facing forward. Reach through the back heel to make your weight stable and attain balance. Bring your hands to Anjali mudra in front of your chest and twist your body to the right.

Place your elbow and press it outside of the knee. Put your hands together and place them in the middle part of your chest. It is only usual to find it difficult to put your elbow down to your knee in the beginning, but you will eventually get used to it. For beginners, you can retain one hand in prayer position while the other arm is extended.

In case you're finding it difficult to sustain your balance, keep the back of your knee down with your toes tucked underneath. As a beginner, it is more important to keep your lower back safe than to perform fluid movements.

You can perform the twist in a low lunge pose to make it more comfortable or by twisting your rib cage while keeping the belly button up. Keep your chin a little bit tucked as you reach the crown of your head. Come out of the pose by doing the lunge position with your hands down. Step forward and roll up as gently as you can.

A Deeper Look into the Mudras

Aside from simplest forms of mudras already mentioned, there are many more types that range from rare to contemporary and done in various yoga practices.

There are also other mudras that people naturally do without realizing it. The most common example is touching your fingers to your hands, a gesture that brings a subtle change in your attitude and perception. It has a certain power that can affect and heal your body.

The yoga mudras have a direct relationship with the five elements of the human body. This concept is further explained in Ayurveda. According to Ayurveda, a disease is caused by an imbalance in the body that can either be due to the lack or excess of the five elements of the body. These five elements are found in the fingers, which make your fingers important electrical circuits. The role of the mudras is to adjust the flow of energy in the five elements of the body to imbibe healing.

It is important to learn about the five elements of the body because they are used not only in yoga but in a variety of healing techniques, including sound healing and meditation. Here are five elements important in attaining balance and healing:

1. Earth

This element represents the foundation of life and is strongly linked to the root chakra. It deals with emotions of insecurity and failure and basic structures of life, such as money, housing, body contact, work, and partnership. Its basic qualities include solidity, permanence, stability, and heaviness on one's environmental, physical, and mental state.

Too much of this element will make you feel heavy and sleepy. If you are experiencing sleeping problems, here's an exercise that can help you in dealing with it: Lie down in bed while keeping your mind's focus on your feet. Do it for 10 minutes or until you are fully aware of your feet. Use your imagination and think that you are no longer in the room but rather on a beach and your feet are covered by warm and soft sand.

The root chakra is also associated with a human's sense of smell. Newborn babies, for example, know the familiar smell of their mothers' breasts and milk. The baby feels secured upon recognizing the smell of their mother. This familiarity started when the baby was still inside the womb where the first two senses develop, sense of smell and sense of taste.

The way to strengthen the earth element is to imagine or envision. You have to take some time to focus on the image you want to envision and feel the connection.

2. Water

The water element of the body encompasses the sacrum to the point below the navel, an area comprised of a large percentage of water. Getting connected with the water element will boost your creativity, vitality, and sexuality. It will make you feel like you want to get reunited with the mother ocean, an emotion that started whole you were growing in the water inside of your mother's womb.

The basic emotion of the water element is anger. The tendency is to get frustrated and mad when the element is blocked. The energy of fire will help in releasing the negative emotions in the water element. If you are angry, for example, you will feel better after letting your steam off.

3. Fire

This element is found between the navel and beneath the sternum. Its basic emotions are love and understanding. You need to use the other elements to control fire in a productive manner. Use the container the earth element provides to give you fuel and strength. Use the water element to slow it down or extinguish the fire and the air element to stimulate it.

4. Air

The element is found at the bottom to the top of your ribcage, including the heart, lungs, and the thymus gland. A person gets depressed when the energy of the heart chakra is held close to the chest and cannot expand. Depression, the opposite of joy, is a sign of longing for something higher. To feel lighter and inspired, you have to do something for the heart chakra to expand freely. This element knows your passion and what makes you happy.

5. Space

This element, also called the ether, does not have a shape or color and fills the gap between objects and people. Nothing will exist without space and its absence will make you appreciate its importance. Its main characteristic is silence.

This element offers ultimate security because unlike Earth, it won't disintegrate nor carried away by wind or water. This is found from the collar bones to the bridge of the nose, the area of the body called the point of silence. It encompasses the mouth, eyes, ears, nose, and vocal cords.

The characteristics of these five elements are found in your fingers. Performing the mudras will adjust the flow of energy in your body to balance the five elements and promote healing.

There are basically two kinds of mudras in yoga. The first one involves the touching of the tips of different fingers with the thumb. The second one is pressing the first phalangeal joint with the thumb. The effects of the mudras depend on which fingers are touching or being pressed.

Additional Mudras to Know About

Here are the other mudras that you can do after you are done with the basic ones. You can do the following while doing yoga poses, such as cross-legged or lotus, or while seated on a chair:

1. Adi Mudra

Place your thumb at the base of your small finger while keeping the rest of the fingers curled over the thumb forming a light fist. Place your hands on your thighs with the palms facing up. Breathe deeply and be attentive how the mudra affects you.

2. Brahma Mudra

Position your hands similar to Adi Mudra. Place the knuckles of your hands together and place them in the navel area. Breathe deeply up to 12 counts. Be mindful of the flow of your breathing and how it affects your mind and body.

3. Chin mudra

Lightly touch each of your thumbs with your forefingers. Keep the rest of the fingers extended and straight. You can place your hands on top of your thighs with the palms facing up. Breathe deeply and focus on its flow. Relax and don't exert pressure on your fingers and hands.

4. Chinmaya Mudra

Form a ring with your thumb and forefinger and curl the three remaining fingers in your palm. Place your hands on your thighs with palms facing up. Take deep ujjayi breaths as you relax your whole body. Focus on your breathing and its effects.

5. Vaayu Mudra

This mudra is also called Vaayu Shaamak Mudra – Vaayu meaning air and Shaamak means to suppress. It helps in soothing your emotions. Put the tip of your index finger at the base of your thumb. Press the two fingers lightly as you breathe deeply.

This mudra decreases the air element in your body. It soothes your spirit and calms your mind. It also pacifies the nervous system and heals hormonal imbalance. This is recommended for people who are hyperactive, aggressive and have difficulty in keeping their focus.

6. Aakash Mudra

This mudra, meaning or space and Vardhak or to enhance, gives you a feeling of lightness. Gently touch the tips of your middle finger with the thumb to boost the space element in your body. For best results, perform this mudra from 2 to 6 in the morning or afternoon. Do not do this for more than 30 minutes each session if you have an active body.

It eases away your negative thoughts and worries and helps in dealing with anger, sadness, and fear. It has a detoxifying effect and is ideal for those who have problems with congestion, tummy, ear, sinus, and chest.

7. Shunya Mudra

This mudra also called Aakash Shaamak Mudra – Aakash meaning space and Shaamak meaning to suppress, has a healing effect for pains. It also decreases the space element in your body. Gently touch the tip of your middle finger at the base of your thumb and give it a slight press.

It prevents the feeling of numbness in your chest and head. It also helps in relieving ear-related pains, such as minor aches, tinnitus, impaired hearing, travel sickness, and nausea. You can perform this mudra any time you want. If you are doing this to get rid of earaches, numbness, and vertigo, make sure that you stop when the pain has subsided.

8. Prithvi Mudra

This mudra is also called Prithvi Vardhak Mudra – Prithvi means earth and Vardhak means to enhance, and Agni Shaamak Mudra – Agni means fire and Shaamak means to suppress. This is said to affect a person's strength and vitality.

Touch the tips of your ring finger to your thumb. This simple action decreases the fire element in your body while boosting the earth element. It allows you to heal, build muscles and encourage the growth of new tissue. It helps in boosting your energy and is effective for those who are suffering from dry skin and brittle nails, hair, and bones. It can also regulate the body temperature and metabolic process. This is recommended to skinny people and those who often experience ulcers, fever, and inflammation.

9. Surya Mudra

This mudra is also called Prithvi Shaamak Mudra – Prithvi means earth and Shaamak means to suppress and Agni Vardhak Mudra – Agni means fire and Vardhak means to enhance. It works by decreasing the earth element while increasing the fire element in your system. This is recommended when you are shivering due to low temperature and colds. Place the tip of your ring finger at the base of your thumb and gently press.

This is a good mudra for those who want to lose weight. It aids in digestion and deals with health concerns, such as constipation, lack of appetite, and suppressed thyroid activity. This can be done at any time during the day for 30 minutes or less for each session. Doing this mudra longer than 30 minutes will cause your body to overheat.

10. Varun Mudra

This is also called Jal Vardhak Mudra – Jal means war and Vardhak means to enhance. Gently touch the tips of your little finger with your thumb. The simple movement has a moisturizing effect and is recommended for those who are suffering from general dehydration, cramps, and hormonal deficiency.

It works by increasing the water element in your body. It also helps in relieving joint pains, arthritis, and improves the condition of those who have lost the sensation of taste and experience limited body secretions. It also deals with dry hair, eyes and skin, digestive health problems, and eczema. This is safe for everybody except for people who have problems with water retention.

11. Jal Shaamak Mudra

This mudra, which is intended for stability, means Jal for water and Shaamak or to suppress. Place the tip of your little finger to the base of the thumb and gently press.

It works by decreasing the water element in the body. This is recommended for people who have problems with water retention or edema, hyperacidity, too much glandular secretion, watery eyes, sweaty palms, runny nose, and too much salivation.

Chapter 13 – How to Relax and Meditate Through Yoga

A big part of learning in Buddhism is meditation and exercises aimed to give you calmness and enlightenment. After knowing about the mudras and the basic yoga poses, you can expand your knowledge and test your strength by doing the more complicated poses.

Asanas, which is one of the eight limbs of yoga, are now being practiced worldwide and have been adapted in the physical fitness industry. Asanas or physical postures are important in executing other styles of yoga. They are defined by types, benefits, anatomy, and many more.

There are many kinds of asanas and they depend on your initial pose upon doing the exercise and your purpose for the poses. These poses include standing, arm balance, balancing poses, binding, chest opening, core yoga poses, forward bend, hip opening, inversion, pranayama, restorative, seated, strengthening, twist, backbends, and bandha.

Before giving an example of a good yoga sequence for relaxation and meditation, you must first learn how to perform the warm-up exercises. Warming up is an essential part not only of yoga but all other kinds of exercises.

The warm-up yoga exercises depend upon the parts of the body you'll use during the exercise. Always make sure that the movements are gentle, and fluid and you always focus on your deep breathing.

Warm-up exercises for the whole body:

1. Start in Easy Pose or Sukhasana. Sit on the floor with your legs crossed. Make sure that your buttocks are comfortable. Put your feet below your knees. Place your hands on your lap with the palms facing downwards or upwards. Move your hip bones to the mat as you reach your hands on top of your head. Slowly drop your shoulders as you push your chest in front. Relax your face and stomach as you breathe through the nose. Hold the pose as long as you can.

2. Breathe in as you extend your fingertips in the direction of the ceiling.

3. Breathe out and let your palms rest on the mat.

4. Repeat steps 2 and 3. Twist your body to the left upon breathing out. Repeat and twist your body to the right. Repeat and upon breathing out, arch your body to the left. Repeat and arch your body to the right. Inhale and put your arms behind you. Breathe out as you lay your hands on the mat.

5. Bring your spine to a neutral pose with the shoulders down, the spine extended and your chest open.

Repeat the warm-up before you begin doing other yoga poses.

For the neck:

1. Begin the sequence by doing any seated pose. Keep your shoulders laid back, your spine extended and chest open. Breathe out as you lay your chin to your chest. Breathe in as you put your neck back to the center.

2. Breathe out and lay your head backward. Keep your shoulders down as you lift your chin and relax your mouth. Breathe in as you put your neck back to the center.

3. Breathe out as you move the lower part of your left ear to your left shoulder. Breathe in as you put your neck back to the center. Repeat the step on the other side.

4. Breathe out as you extend your chin to your left shoulder. With your body faced in front, gently twist your neck and look at any point behind you. Breathe in as you put your neck back to the center. Repeat the step on the other side.

For the shoulders:

1. Start by doing the Easy Pose.

2. Breathe in as you extend your arms in the direction of the ceiling. Intertwine your fingers and move your palms upward. Breathe out and arch your body to the left.

3. Breathe in as you extend your palms to the ceiling while keeping your hips grounded to the mat. Breathe out and arch your body to the right.

4. Breathe in as you reach your palms upward. Breathe out as you round your spine by pressing your hands to the front.

5. Breathe in as you extend your palms upward. Breathe out as you bend your right elbow on the back of your head. Repeat the step on your left elbow.

6. Breathe in as you extend your palms to the ceiling. Breath out as you slowly put your hands down.

7. Breathe in and make slow and large circles as you roll your shoulders up and down to the front and then to the back. Breathe out as you lay your knees to the mat.

A Sample Yoga Sequence to Help You Relax

Here is an example of a yoga sequence you can perform every day. This is aimed to calm your mind and train your brain to relax and was based on the teachings of the Mindful Yoga Therapy. The sequence is commonly used to help returning military service members suffering from the post-traumatic stress disorder.

The focus of the exercise is on the present and you will do this through proper movements and breathing. Your mind should focus on the moment and avoid thinking about the past or future. Through continued practice, you will notice the change in your attitude and the way you think.

To accomplish the goal and help you relax, perform the following poses:

1. Constructive Rest

Lie with your back on the mat while keeping your knees bent and your feet apart. Put your knees together to allow them to rest. Close your eyes and breathe. Focus on your breathing as you allow the breath to move through your body. Use your imagination to guide the breath as it travels to the body to nourish your organs, cells, and tissues.

If you are feeling any kind of pain, draw your mind to the spot. Breathe in and imagine the fresh oxygen washing away the pain. Exhale all the causes of the pain away from you.

Imagine a thing or person you are fond of. Focus on the image as your reason for doing the sequence. Do this part for as long as you like. You can also cut it short if you are certain that you have already achieved your set goal.

2. Supine Twist

This pose helps ease the tension on your lower back. Place your knees closer to your chest as you rest your right hand on your left knee. Extend your left arm straight out to the left. Breathe in and focus on your breathing. Breathe out and carefully roll your knees to the right. Take five breaths. Breathe in and put your knees back to the middle. Breathe out and squeeze your knees back to your chest. Breathe in and extend your left hand on your right knee. Stretch out your right arm. Breathe out and move your knees to the left. Take five breaths.

Breathe in and move your knees to the middle and squeeze them for the last time. Breathe out and release your feet to the floor. Twist deeper by reaching to your extended arm. This will push more air to your lungs.

3. Hands and Knees Balance

Listen to your body as you let it rest. When it is ready for this step, roll your body to one side and sit. Go down to the floor on your hands and knees. Place your hands a little bit in front of your shoulders and your knees under your hips. Focus your attention to your hands. Press your hands down to the earth. This pose intends to keep you grounded and remain at the moment.

Gently bend your elbows. Keep pressing to continue connecting with the earth. Get support from the floor or earth to remain grounded. Develop an instinct that you will get support whenever you need it.

Imagine there is an extra hand holding your navel and giving support on the underside of your body. Lift your core slowly and move it inward. The movement intends to support, protect, and strengthen the lower portions of your back. Be mindful in keeping this support throughout the exercise.

Breathe in and extend the right arm and left leg into the hands and knees pose. Grasp both of your limbs in contrasting routes to keep your body steady and even. Hold the pose as you take five breaths. Breathe out and move your extended arm and leg to the floor. Repeat the movements on the other side.

4. Plank Pose

Move your feet until you are in a Plank Pose with your hands directly under your shoulders. Straighten your body until it is similar to a long and even line. Press your hands through the earth and feel its rebound through your tailbone. Allow your senses to feel the connection from your head to your heels while you gather strength from the navel. Keep your collarbones and chest wide and do not allow your hips to hang. Take five easy Ujjayi breaths.

5. Downward-Facing Dog Pose (Adho Mukha Svanasana)

Knees and hands on the floor with your hands aligned under your shoulders. Push the earth with force using your hands. Curl your toes under and gently bend your knees. Push your body back until you are in an Adho Mukha Svanasana pose.

Focus on your hands firmly pressed to the ground and then to your sitting bones. Keep the navel support for strength as you stretch both sides of your waist. If you have tight hamstrings, bend your knees. Take up to 10 breaths. Move your hands to your feet. Breathe in and stand up.

6. Warrior Pose II (Virabhadrasana II)

Step your feet sideways until they are about 4 feet apart. Establish your footwork to give you support while making sure that you maintain the navel support. Twist your right leg and foot to the right. Move your back leg and foot slightly backward. Your right heel has to be in line with the arch of your left foot. Focus your attention on the ground through your legs and feet.

Breathe in as you extend your arms to your sides. Breathe out as you bend your right knee. Move your right sitting bone in the direction of your right foot. Do not allow your knee to go beyond your ankle. You will find stability through your back leg. Focus on your back leg and take 5 breaths. Keep yourself grounded. Breathe in and push to the floor. Extend your right leg and release the posture. Breathe out as you go back to the middle. Repeat the movements on your left side.

7. Extended Triangle Pose (Utthita Trikonasana)

Twist your right leg and foot out. Take your time as you align your feet similar to the previous pose. Breathe in, push your feet to the floor and extend your arms to your sides. From your feet, shift your focus through the crown of your head. Breathe out and use the navel support to keep your spine extended and healthy. Stretch out the right side of your body over your right leg. Reach your shin with your right hand.

Allow your left arm to extend to the sky. Take 5 breaths. Maintain the Ujjayi breath. As you breathe out, go back to the middle. Repeat the actions on your left side.

8. Tree Pose (Vrksasana)

Keep your gaze (Drishti) on one point to keep your body steady. Push your feet to the floor as you draw awareness from your heels to the crown of your head while maintaining navel support. Lift your right foot and press it against the left leg. Keep your foot above or below the knee. Push your leg back into your foot to create a contrasting feeling.

Put your palms together and bring it in front of your heart. Extend your arms to the sky while imagining that they were growing limbs of a tree. Find peace and make yourself calm. Keep your focus on your breathing and Drishti even when you feel like the tree is swaying. Take up to 10 breaths and repeat on the other side.

9. Supported Shoulder-stand (Salamba Sarvangasana)

Lie with your back on the floor and keep your feet and knees hip-distance apart. Breathe in and push your feet down as you begin lifting your hips. Turn on your shoulder tops and use a block to support your sacrum or the triangular bone found at the base of your spine. Place the block under the sacrum at the point where you are comfortable with its height.

Put your hands to your sides and push them to the floor. Move your chin in the direction of your chest. Refrain from moving your head from side to side. As you breathe out, pull your right knee to your chest. Breathe in and stretch your right leg. Take 5 breaths. Breathe out and pull your right knee back in. Breathe in and move your right foot back to the floor. Breathe out and pull your left knee to your chest. Breathe in and stretch your left leg upward. Take 5 breaths.

Breathe out and pull your left knee back in. Leave it there as you pull your right knee to meet with the other knee. When your feet are on the floor, focus on the support from your hands and the block under your sacrum. Breathe in as you extend your legs upward. Hold the pose for 5 breaths.

Pull both knees to your chest and allow them to come down as you breathe out. Breathe in and put your feet on the ground and pressed firmly on the floor. Lift your hips and remove the block. Gently allow your body to go back to the earth and take your moment until your spine has adjusted.

10. Corpse Pose (Savasana)

Lie with your back on the floor. Extend your legs and arms with your palms facing up. As an option, you can place a bolster under your knees if it gives you comfort. You can also perform the exercise without the prop by finding a posture you are comfortable with. Soften your gaze or close your eyes. Hold for at least 5 minutes. Draw your focus to your every movement.

The Asanas or Yoga Poses

Yoga asanas are important in executing other yoga styles. The kinds of asanas depend on your initial pose when doing the exercise and what you aim to achieve.

Samples of Standing Yoga Poses

1. Big Toe Pose (Padangusthasana)

Stand straight with the inner part of your feet parallel and about 6 inches apart from each other. Contract the front muscles of your thigh as you move your kneecaps upwards. Make sure that your legs remain straight as you breathe out. Do a forward bend from the hip joints to your torso and head.

Slide the index and middle fingers of your two hands in between the big toes and the second toes. Curl your fingers under, firmly gripping your big toes. Wrap the thumbs around the other two fingers to make the grip more secure and press the toes against the fingers.

Breathe in, lift your torso and extend your elbows as if you are going to stand up. Stretch the front part of your torso, exhale and lift your sitting bones. Carefully release your hamstrings and the hollow the part below your navel and lift it slightly towards the back part of your pelvis.

Keep your forehead relaxed as you lift your sternum as high as you can. Make sure that you don't overdo the action to avoid compressing the back of your neck.

Inhale as lift your torso strongly while contracting your front thighs. On the next exhalations, forcefully lift your sitting bones, let your hamstrings relax and make the hollow in your lower back deeper.

Exhale and bend your elbows to the sides. Pull up on your toes and stretch the front and sides of your torso. Lower the torso in a gentle manner by doing a forward bend.

Hold the position for one minute. Lose the grip on your toes. Place your hands to your hips and stretch your front torso. Inhale and swing your torso and head as if you are dealing with a single unit and go back to an upright pose.

2. Mountain Pose (Tadasana)

Stand straight with the bases of your big toes touching and the second toes in line with each other. Lift and spread your toes. Move the balls of your feet before putting them back again to the floor. Move your feet to the front and back and then from side to side to rock your weight. Gradually reduce the frequency of the swaying of your body until you are standing still. Carry your weight on your feet to give you balance.

Lift your kneecaps with your thigh muscles remaining firm and your lower belly relaxed. Lift the inner parts of your ankles. Imagine your inner thighs with a line of energy that runs through the groin to the torso, neck, up to the crown of your head. Move the upper parts of your thighs inward. Extend your tailbone to the floor and lift your pubis to the direction of the navel.

Keep the shoulder blades at the back before gradually spreading them across and releasing them to your back. Lift the top part of the sternum in the direction of the ceiling without pushing your ribs forward. Spread your collarbones and let your arms hang at each side of your torso.

Make sure that the top of your head is balanced. Keep your chin resting on the floor. Keep the pose for a minute as you breathe easily.

3. Dolphin Pose (Ardha Pincha Mayurasana)

This position opens your shoulders by working on your core, arms, and legs. Come down on the floor on your hands and knees, forearms on the floor and shoulders above your wrists. Press your palms together in a firm manner.

Curl your toes. Exhale and slowly raise your knees in a slightly bent manner and the heels away. Extend your tailbone and slightly press it in the direction of your pubis. Lift the sitting bones upward and draw your inner legs up to your groins.

Keep your forearms pressed to the floor while your shoulder blades are firm against the back. Extend the blades and draw them in the direction of your tailbone. Continue to extend your tailbone away from the pelvis as you lift the upper part of the sternum away from the floor. Hold position for up to a minute. Release your knees as you exhale.

4. Chair Pose (Utkatasana)

This position utilizes the muscles in your legs and arms and provides health benefits to your heart and diaphragm.

Begin by standing in Tadasana. Breathe in as you move your arms upwards until they are perpendicular to the floor. Keep your arms parallel with the palms facing inward. Slowly bend your knees as you exhale. Try to position your thighs parallel to the floor to push your torso slightly forward until it forms a right angle with the top parts of the thighs. Make sure that the inner thighs remain parallel to one another as you press the heads of the bones of your thighs in the direction of your heels.

Relax your shoulder blades until they are firm against your back. Move your tailbone to your pubis while keeping the lower part of the back long. Hold the position for up to a minute. Inhale and straighten your knees as you lift through your arms. Release your arms and put them on each of your sides as you exhale. Go back to Tadasana.

5. Eagle Pose (Garudasana)

This pose works by boosting your endurance, concentration, flexibility, and strength. Begin in the Tadasana pose. Slightly curve your knees and move your left foot in the direction of the ceiling. Keep the right foot balanced as the left thigh crosses over the other thigh. Position the left toes parallel to the floor. Press your foot and hook its upper part at the back of the lower right calf. Maintain your balance using your right foot.

Extend your arms spreading the scapulas across the back part of the torso. Put the right arm at the top of the left arm. Move the right arm in front of your torso and slowly bend your elbows. Put the right elbow into the corner of the left elbow and extend the forearms until they are positioned vertically to the mat. Make sure that the back parts of your hands are facing one another.

Move the palms until they are facing each other. Move the thumb of the right hand beyond the little finger of your left hand. Press your palms together with force. Lift your elbows and spread your fingers upwards. Keep the position for up to 30 seconds. Unwind your arms and legs and go back to the Tadasana pose. Repeat the sequence using the other side of your legs and arms.

Arm Balance Yoga Poses

The following yoga poses are intended to make you stronger, with an improved balance, by challenging yourself and conquering your fear of doing more difficult movements.

1. Eight-Angle Pose (Astavakrasana)

Begin by standing in a Tadasana pose with your feet spread wider than usual. Exhale and change into the Uttanasana pose. Push your hands to the floor outside of your feet. Slightly bend your knees and slide your right arm inside your right leg. Push your hand to the floor outside of your right foot. Place your right arm across the back of your right knee and bring the knee as high as the back of your right shoulder.

Keep your shoulders against the knees as you slide your left foot to the right foot. Cross your left ankle in front of the right and hook them up. Move slightly towards the left as you put more weight on your left arm. Lift your feet several inches away off the floor.

Exhale as you support the right leg with your shoulder and slowly bend your elbows. Lean forward, your torso should be parallel to the floor. Keep the pose as you extend your knees to stretch your legs out to the right while keeping them parallel to the floor. Keep the upper right arm in between your thighs squeezed and tight. Use the pressure to twist your torso to the left. Keep the elbows in proximity with your torso and your gaze to the floor. Hold the pose for up to a minute.

Slowly extend your arms while moving your torso upright. Bend your knees and unhook your ankles. Put your feet back to the floor. As you stand, rest in Uttanasana. Breathe in and breathe out for a few counts. Repeat the sequence to the left.

2. Crane/Crow Pose (Bakasana)

The pose can help in making your arms and abs stronger. Begin in Tadasana. Bend your knees while keeping your feet a few inches away from each other. You can use a prop if you are finding it hard to maintain the balance of your heels. You can place a thick blanket for support. Widen the gap between your two knees as you lean your torso forward. Extend your arms in front. Slowly bend your elbows as you lay your hands on the mat while the back parts of your upper arms are positioned against your shins.

Nestle the inner parts of your thighs against the outer areas of your torso and keep your shins in the armpits. Slide the upper part of your arms until they are close to your shins. Use the balls of your feet as you lift your weight and lean forward to transfer the weight to back parts of your upper arms. Keep your tailbone close to your heels as you perform the movements.

As you exhale, lean forward until the legs and your torso are balanced with the back parts of the upper arms. You can hold this pose if you are a beginner. The more experienced practitioners can continue with the rest of the steps.

Cuddle your legs against your arms and strongly push the inner parts of your hands to the mat. Inhale and stretch your elbows. With your arms slightly angled forward, keep the inner parts of the knees stuck to your arms up to the areas near the sides of your chest. Keep your head comfortable and balanced and your gaze on the floor. Keep the pose for up to a minute. Exhale as you release the pose. Lower your feet to the mat and go back to your original squat position.

3. Four-Limbed Staff Pose (Chaturanga Dandasana)

This position is part of the traditional Sun Salutation sequence. Begin in the Adho Mukha Svanasana and change into the Plank Pose. Keep the shoulder blades firm against your back ribs and push the tailbone to your pubis. As you exhale, lower your torso and legs until they are inches above the floor. Keep your tailbone firm and your legs active and turned in a slight inward manner. Pull your pubis to your navel.

Hold your elbows by the sides of your torso while keeping a broad space between your shoulder blades. Push your elbows back toward your heels. Push the bottom of your index fingers to the floor. Move the top of your sternum and head up as you keep your gaze upfront. Count up to 30 before you exhale as you release and go back up to the Adho Mukha Svanasana pose.

4. Firefly Pose (Tittibhasana)

Stand with your feet a little far apart and then go on a squat. Lift the pelvis a little to the front bringing the trunk in between your legs. Lower the trunk as you extend your legs until your pelvis is of knee height.

Move your left upper arm and shoulder under the back of your left thigh and reach as far as you can. Put your left hand to the floor at the outside corners of your foot while keeping your fingers pointing forward. Repeat the sequence on the other side.

Carefully lift your weight away from the floor. Push your hands to the floor and rock your weight from your feet to your hands keeping your inner thighs as high as you can on your arms.

Inhale as you extend your legs to the sides while keeping the pelvis high. Push through the bottom of your big toes while pulling your toes to your torso and spreading your toes apart.

Stretch your arms and widen your shoulder blades to lift the torso higher. Keep your neck relaxed with your head and gaze looking ahead. Breathe in a slow manner for about 15 minutes as you hold the pose. Release by putting your feet to the floor upon exhale.

5. Peacock Pose (Mayurasana)

This pose symbolizes immortality and love. Kneel on a mat with your knees wide. Lean your body as you push your palms to the floor and your fingers directed to your torso. Slightly bend your elbows as they touch your hands. Bend your elbows as you move your knees away from your arms. Move the front torso on the back of the upper arms. Cradle your elbows at your tummy.

Press your tummy against your elbows as you lower your head to the floor. Extend your knees and straighten your legs at the back of your torso. Keep the tips of your toes on the floor, your buttocks firm and your shoulders round and slightly downward. Slowly lift your head and keep your gaze forward. Transfer your weight a little to the front and lift your feet. Your torso and legs have to be aligned to the floor. Hold the pose for 10 seconds or longer if you can.

Lower down your head and feet to the floor as you bend your knees and lift your torso away from the arms.

Chapter 14 – Center Yourself With Sound Healing

To benefit from sound healing, it is important to learn how to center yourself. Trust the process, develop compassion and keep yourself grounded. These practices are similar to yoga, meditation, and other healing and meditative processes taught in Buddhism.

Sound healing involves all the levels of a person's energy. There are no rules but to follow your instinct on how to deal with your energy fields. The concept came from the notion that a human being is a center of energy subjected to the influences of other energies – color, light, and sound.

Sound is the most powerful energy among the three. Sound therapy focuses on soothing and healing sounds. It gives you a choice which sounds you want to reach your ear and brain. The therapy teaches you how to stay unaffected by noise and other unwanted sounds.

Noise is damaging to the ears and is the main cause of hearing loss. The ear is the first to react to its surroundings. It is also said to be the most sensitive organ both in humans and animals.

Noise gives off an unpleasant sensation and poses harm to the ear structure. A mouse exposed to the sound of a siren for a few seconds will likely suffer from a convulsive audiogenic attack. This serves as proof that noise can be fatal. Noise can cause disequilibrium that harms the nerve centers at the base of the brain.

Sound healing is a conscious and educated use of the energy gathered from sounds. Based on the concept that everything that surrounds you vibrates at specific frequencies; it helps in boosting one's health and wellness to reach identified goals. When an external source of sound plays, it will cause a significant change in the vibrational characteristics of the other objects that vibrate.

Sound healing, aside from being a good meditative technique, also offers the following health benefits:

- Raise one's consciousness
- Personal transformation
- Reduce stress
- Improve sleep disorders
- Enhance the immune system
- Help the patients relax
- Alleviates pain

- Enhance clarity and alertness
- Connect with one's spirit

Learning How to Center Yourself

Here's a brief guide to get this done. This will help you adapt the techniques and other factors important to sound healing.

1. Look for a square area or anything similar. Position yourself in any way you're comfortable with. Breathe deeply as you focus your mind to your navel, spleen, and solar plexus.

2. Feel your surroundings. Keep on breathing deeply as you turn your attention to the area above your head.

3. Turn your attention and look at your legs and feet. Move your toes and feel each movement. Be attentive of each foot until you feel something concrete and you've reached the point when you feel like you are well-grounded.

4. Turn your attention to your heart chakra. Keep on focusing until you are fully aware of it. Allow the feeling of softness spread in the vast space ahead of you.

You can easily apply the other techniques used in the process once you have mastered the art of centering yourself. For sound healing to work, you have to let go of your emotions and ego and allow your intuition and emotion to take charge.

Sound healing works by using silence and different sources of sound, including humming, your own voice, and musical instruments. You will use musical instruments according to their characteristics and the elements they attract. The first thing to do is to set your goal. Ask yourself what you want to achieve in the process. It is typically used for relaxation, to understand the seemingly vague areas of life, learning more about yourself, overcoming pains, and many more.

You also have to be patient whether you are the one undergoing the process, or you are the healer. Healing takes time. Do not expect a miracle to happen in a few hours. Its effects can be felt in different ways and different places and levels.

Another powerful and effective element in sound healing is the use of voice. With a wide range of sounds and letters found in human languages, you will find some sounds linked to the five elements.

Sound healing improves your health and life in general. It allows you to witness your own transformation as you experience the effects of the process. With the right goal and proper implementation of the process, you will experience positive changes and benefits, which include the following:

- Become more focused
- Understand that you are part of a big universe

- Develop a positive outlook in life
- Develop a healthy lifestyle
- Become happier

Sound therapy teaches you to choose what you hear and how to imbibe their effects. Instead of stopping the noise, you can diffuse it by playing a gentle sound. There are many therapies and techniques used in sound healing depending on the training and beliefs of the practitioner and the purpose of healing.

Sound healing is among the oldest forms of healing known to humans. It uses sound frequencies to bring the body and mind in a state of health and harmony. It gets transmitted in different ways, such as:

- Listening to music through earphones or headphones or a loudspeaker
- Listening to one or more instruments
- Use of voice with other voices
- Use of own voice
- Another individual's voice
- Use of own voice while listening to music

The Concepts of Sound Healing

1. Every person has a unique soul or root frequency. You have to get in touch with that frequency to feel the moment, to be grounded, and centered. What makes it hard to connect with the frequency is the distraction caused by the noises in the surroundings. Aside from your core frequency, everything inside you – tissue, vertebrae, organ, muscle, Etheric field, and chakra, has a resonating frequency.

Sound healing helps you become more aware of the symphony inside of you. Through the use of methods, such as toning and vibroacoustic massage – a form of massage in tables with speakers, you will find it easier to maintain a healthy flow of music from deep within.

2. Healing comes from the force behind all things found in the universe and not something that you do. Jonathan Goldman created a formula in 1992 that equates healing as a sum of frequency and intention.

Shamans believed that intent is an indescribable and immeasurable force connected to everything that exists. They refer to it as a universal mind, consciousness, soul, spirit, or source. Its practitioners believe that miracles happen when people become in harmony with the spirit. People align themselves to this universal power through intention.

Everyone has an intention in every action whether you were conscious about it or not. In sound healing, the sound carries this intention to bring back the harmony to your mind, body, spirit, and emotions.

3. Every sound has a harmonic structure. One note from a playing instrument is composed of several notes playing in harmony. The harmonics that constitute a sound are mathematical multiples of the root frequency. They prove that everything is connected and there is a unified field every person is always connected to. Through sound healing, it gets easier to become more aware of this connection.

Sound Healing Principles

Sound healing helps you to connect to a supreme being and your core by following these principles:

1. Entrainment

This principle, discovered by a Dutch scientist, Christian Huygens in 1665, states that when two or more oscillators in the same area are pulsing at about the same rate, they are pulled together and locked in while pulsing at the same rate.

For example, birds fly together during migration. They glide and flap their wings at the same time. They conserve energy by flapping their wings according to the group's rhythm. The bird in front creates a pocket air of turbulence that the other birds use to their advantage to boost the resistance of their flapping wings.

In the human body, the notion is applied when one part of the body is out of tune. Sound healing works by bringing back the balance without the need to take medicines or undergo a surgery or operation.

2. Resonance

This healing technique believes that every organism has its own vibratory rate. Different objects in this universe have a unique resonant frequency that sets them apart from one another. Every cell, bone, and organ in the body has its resonant frequency. Together, they act as the instruments in an orchestra to form a composite frequency. The body experiences something different when one instrument did not work.

Modern medicine utilizes Lithotripter, a machine that employs sound waves to break up the gallstones and kidney in the human body. It sends a specific sound frequency to the stones for an hour or two. In most cases, this will only require one session and can be done without any anesthesia. The stones are efficiently broken and pulverized before getting mixed with urine for the body to get rid of them. The goal of science is to eventually use the resonance principle to get the bodily organs in harmony to avoid surgery and drugs.

3. The healing power of voice

Toning requires the creation of sound with an elongated vowel for a long duration. It helps your breathing to become deeper and for the body to get oxygenated and stimulated.

The elongated vowel sounds, Aaah, Eeee, Eye, Oooo, and Uuuu, are non-specific and non-local. You can recite them while directing the vibration to the body part you wish to address.

You will feel a connection when you tone along with other people. It also offers other benefits, which include the following:

- Energizes your body
- Makes you feel calm and relaxed
- Releases your repressed emotions and stress
- Improves your posture and breathing
- Makes the vocal muscles stronger
- Stimulates the muscles of your digestive system

Toning also has a neurochemical effect on the body. It aids in releasing the endorphins in the brain by boosting your immune system. This is also an effective tool in addressing various sleep disorders, such as insomnia. In the medical field, it helps in reducing the patient's tension before undergoing CAT scans and MRI. It also helps in releasing psychological stress before undergoing surgery and in decreasing the respiratory rate and blood pressure of cardiac patients.

4. Chant

The practice, commonly called kirtan in India, is done by saying words, syllables or phrases over and over again. Chanting is done until the practitioner relaxes, which makes it easier to find inner peace.

It can be as simple as repeating the sounds in any way you are comfortable with. You can begin by chanting the OM sound. Focus on what you want to achieve or what negative energies you want to get rid of. Inhale and as you release your breath, chant the OM sound repeatedly in a loud manner. Inhale and continue chanting as you breathe out. As you go through the process, you will gradually decrease the volume of your voice until it sounds almost like a whisper.

Continue the process until you are repeating the chant silently wherein you no longer move your tongue and lips. Focus on the sound until it leads you into the realm of infinite possibilities. Repeat chanting OM silently at times when your mind wanders. Keep the pose for 15 minutes.

Here are some samples of the chants you can use to focus on your Chakras:

- LAAM – First Chakra, located at the base of the spine
- VAAM – Second Chakra, located in the sacral region
- RAAM – Third Chakra, located at the navel area
- YAAM – Fourth Chakra, located at the heart
- HAAM – Fifth Chakra, located in the throat area
- KSHAAM – Sixth Chakra, in between the eyebrows
- OM – Seventh Chakra, located at the top of the head

Here's a list of the toning sounds you can use to address specific areas of your body or to achieve a specific purpose:

- UU-AH-EE-MM – Gives a boost of energy and helps in keeping you awake
- MM-EE-AH-UU – Relaxes your body, especially during bedtime
- Nnn – For the ears
- Wooo – For the bladder and kidneys
- Mmm – For the sinuses
- Shhh – For the small intestine and liver
- Eemm – For the eyes
- Sssss – For the large intestine and lungs
- Lmm – For the nose
- Ma – For the heart
- Paam – For the stomach
- Mam – For the reproductive organs
- Haa – For the diaphragm
- Yaa Yu Yi – For the jaw
- Kaa Gaa Gha – For the throat

5. Rhythm

A human heartbeat follows the rhythm of the music. Your breathing rate decreases when you hear a slower tempo playing. For example, Pachelbel's Canon has a similar rhythm to the resting heartbeat rate, which is 64 beats per minute. Upon hearing the music, your brain wave pattern changes from Beta to Alpha. In music therapy, patients listen to slow classical music to improve their metabolism and make the nervous system calmer.

6. Drumming

The brain rhythm slows down when it hears repetitive drumming that leads you into a trance-like state. Healing happens when the practitioner and the client get out from the conscious awareness and venture into the realms of consciousness, a technique popularly used in Shamanic practices.

A reticular activating system or RAS is found in the brainstem that makes it possible to get affected when you hear repetitive drumming. The RAS alerts the brain about the incoming sensory stimulation. The sound overpowers the other sensory channels in the brain. It leads to your consciousness exploring other kinds of perception as it suppresses the normal activity of the brain.

Sound Healing and Aura

The first energy field you will sense upon seeing a person is their spiritual aura. This aura is something that everybody has with the qualities that have been likely developed in their past lives. You were born with an aura, but you have to learn how to activate that aura and use it in this lifetime.

In sound healing, you have to focus on your spiritual qualities and set aside your current psychological state. You don't deal with emotional problems head-on because doing so will only give too much importance and energy to the problems. You have to rise above the emotional level of consciousness to make it easier for you to understand what you are going through on a deeper level.

The process allows you to focus on your personal history, qualities you were familiar with but choose to ignore most of the time. These qualities emit certain colors shown in your outer aura.

These colors include the following:

- Blue signifies wisdom, love, perception, and intuition.

- Red signifies willpower, courage, leadership, and independence.

- Violet signifies dignity, truth, vitality, action, integrity, and rituals.

- Orange signifies beauty, balance, rhythm, and harmony

- Green signifies adaptability, mental power, impartiality, and instinctual power

- Yellow signifies patience, tolerance, precision, and logic.

- Rose pink signifies service to others, devotion, directness, and loyalty.

Meditation helps beginners in finding their unique quality color and meaning. Sound affects your energy fields. Sound healing operates within the laws of attraction, truth, love, and karmic cause and effect.

A part of the wider law of attraction states that lower vibration draws in a higher vibration. A second law states that higher vibration helps in bringing the lower vibration up to its own level. A third law follows the order in spiritual healing and the fourth law works by moving the energy in an upward manner once freed and transformed.

The fastest-moving energy in a human body is spiritual energy. You can easily draw it out whenever you need it to turn the vibrations from your emotional blockage into a lower frequency. The blockage comes from your old belief structures, the pent-up thought patterns, and emotions that formed vicious cycles.

To break the cycle, you need a higher understanding and a higher vibration. The blockage can resist consciousness, so you tend to carry them every day like excess baggage causing unwanted stress and tension. Through sound healing, your consciousness experiences a boost in energy that activates a temporary opening.

With activated energy, your consciousness follows the sound formed by a higher vibration. It observes the activation process. With the combined healing power of sound and the fast spiritual energies – truth, compassion, and love, your consciousness go through the process called consciousness growth. At this point, the consciousness learns to transform your old beliefs from a mental level and energy is freed once done.

If the process is accomplished through energy exercises or meditation, you will likely hear a popping sound that signifies the dissolution of a vicious cycle. The process is not easy since the energy fields are connected to the other levels of consciousness.

Effects of Sound

To maximize the benefits of sound healing, you have to tap the five important factors that determine the effects of sounds:

1. The receptivity of the receiver and being open to everything that might transpire during the process

2. The musical components used in the healing process

3. The attraction level of the person performing the healing session

4. The energies present while healing is going on, including people, time of day and year, and place.

5. The quality of the source of sound or the musical instruments used to facilitate the process.

Sound has multiple effects. First, the effect will depend on your background and how you respond emotionally to the sound. Sound will penetrate through the energy blockage and activate some of your subconscious memories. These memories range from visual scenes, karmic memories, emotions, sounds, and etheric-sensual. When you are ready, these memories will be brought into your consciousness. The healer will use different levels of sound until the vicious cycle is broken.

By releasing energy blockage, you will become more prepared for more changes and it also implies a change of attitude. Your aura and the aura of the healer will blend into a deeper level that will lead to the development of openness. The deeper the level that you can work with the healer, the more efficient the healing process will become.

Aside from the memories, sound healing can also help you in reaching the deeper levels of consciousness. This will give you a vision of what you want to become in this life, your dreams, and ambitions.

Sound healing is not a substitute for medicine. It heals the levels of your being that medicines cannot penetrate. It harmonizes the different areas of your being to make you feel complete. You will not readily feel the effects of the sound healing process. It takes about 24 to 36 hours after the treatment before you realize the changes.

Music has an important role in sound healing. By learning about what inspired its creation, the music will affect the different layers of your consciousness:

- Spiritual level – soul
- Upper astral – love, peace, serenity, joy, and compassion
- Lower astral – painful emotions
- Upper mental – intuition
- Lower mental – the level of intellect affected by the lower astral
- Collective layers – spiritual and collective memory

The five-element tool will come in handy to benefit from sound and music healing. Here's a look at the five elements and their role in the sound healing process:

1. Earth

In music, you will hear the earth quality in musical structures used as the foundation of any piece of song or music. When you play an instrument while your earth structure is imbalanced, the sound will lack security and confidence.

Some samples of the associated instruments with the earth element include sound bed, deep drums, deep voice of Tibetan singing monks, okarina, gongs, log drum, gong drum, ribbons of bells, didgeridoo, tampura, flowerpots, and electric or double bass, Indian surbahar, and cello.

2. Water

In music, this element is expressed on how the changing rhythms adapt to the sound – from the performance to the emotions it emits from the performer and listener. This element is associated with musical instruments that include clay pot drums, talking drums, and the Irish bodhran. It will also help to participate in trance-like rituals to re-establish your connection with the water element.

3. Fire

The element is expressed in music in a dynamic manner. This is done by playing a gong, drum or cymbals. You can also use your own voice to practice playing louder and softer sounds. You will need certain elements of the other areas to control fire in a productive manner. For fuel and strength, you will need the container that the earth element provides. You will need the water element to extinguish the fire and the air element to stimulate it.

Some of the musical instruments associated with the fire element include cymbals, woodblock, temple blocks, singing bowls used in a percussive manner, overtone flute, claves, kokiriko gekko, rattles, crystal bowls, horns, wooden clap, saxophone, trumpet, and Indian shanai.

4. Air

In music, the feeling of this element is brought about by the striking chords and the big movements of a melody, compels your body to dance and raise your hands. Flutes and strings are some samples of the instruments of the air element. To get a sense of fulfillment and joy, you'll need to find the kind of instrument that best describes who you are.

Some of the musical instruments associated with the air element include Japanese singing bowls, sound bed, tubular bells, hang, koto-monochord, flutes, tambura, glockenspiel, aeolian harp, bar chimes, harp, zither, birds song, synthesizer, violin, Indian sitar, and hammered dulcimer

5. Space

This element is heard in music used in meditation, overtone chanting, the Tibetan singing bowls, Gregorian chant, and use of gongs. It is also common for recording studios to use the reverberation and echo effects in their music.

Uses of Sound and Music Healing

There are two distinct areas of sound healing: the utilization of sound for medical purposes and the use of music for learning, relaxation, and productivity. Different techniques and musical instruments are used to facilitate the healing process, but the human voice is said to be the most powerful among all the instruments.

Sound healing is used for different purposes, which include the following:

1. Pain Alleviation

Sound is used in the birthing process using a wide range of songs that help in making the birthing process smoother and less painful for the mother. The technique is also used in the dying process where music and sound are played to aid to a beautiful death.

Many doctors around the world utilize sound therapy before, during, and after an operation procedure. The technique has shown a substantial reduction in the amount of anesthesia used in the practice.

2. Voice Analysis

It utilizes multiple systems to provide a blueprint of what's going on inside your body. The frequencies in the voice provide a map of the different aspects of your being – emotional, mental, spiritual, and physical.

Voice analysis can help in detecting the ailing organs in the body and the presence of any signs of diseases. These health issues are addressed using music and specific sounds.

3. Therapeutic benefits of sound

The importance of sound in healing is now being used in many complementary and integrative healing centers. Their services include relaxation techniques, reduction of hearing sensitivities, stimulation of the nervous system and brain, auditory biofeedback, and stress management. They also use sound and music to correct learning problems and making the auditory tonal processing better.

4. Uses of sound in the medical field

The medical field, despite the continuous technological advancement, is utilizing sound in healing. Sound is utilized in various techniques, including sound massage, sound surgery and the use of sound inside the body. Ultrasound has been used for many years in breaking up plaque on teeth and kidney stones.

There are ongoing studies to find out more about how the cell opens up to receive energy once the resonant frequency of a cell is found. The cell explodes when the resonant frequency's volume is raised. Medical practitioners utilize certain non-invasive medical techniques to destroy diseased cells without side effects. One sample of this technique is the use of highly precise tones in the targeted organs of the body.

The experts are now geared towards finding more options on how sound can heal. It follows the basic notion that people only need to accept and learn how to use their power to heal themselves with the aid of sound and music.

5. Learning how to connect with one's spirit and raise consciousness through music and sound. Sound healing allows you to discover your inner thoughts and desire, including what makes you happy and contented.

Chapter 15 - Vibrational Healing

It follows the concept that everything that surrounds you vibrates. The human body works with several rhythms, such as:

1. Cranio-sacral pulse – the pressure of the liquid in the brain and spinal cord that pulses 8 to 12 times per minute.

2. Brain waves – The normal rate when you are awake is 18 to 22 cycles per second.

3. Breath – an average person breathes 14 to 16 times per minute.

4. Stomach – contracts every 3 minutes.

5. Heart – resting heart rate is 60 beats per minute, heart rate after doing average activity is 72 beats per minute, and the normal heart rate is 60 to 70 beats per minute.

6. Gastrointestinal tract – contracts one time per minute.

7. Body temperature – changes from day to night.

The practices done during a healing session, including sound and music, affect the rhythms. You'll have up to 87 heartbeats per minute when stressed and about 57 heartbeats per minute when relaxed.

Here are some samples of the instruments and techniques used in sound healing:

- Vocal expression – chanting, singing, toning, and laughing
- Relaxing and therapeutic music
- Self-healing
- Healing facilitated by a sound healer
- Different musical instruments

Like many kinds of alternative medicine, sound healing doesn't have the same effects on everyone. Your healing depends on many factors, including the techniques used and how open you are about the process.

Here are some samples of the known benefits of sound healing:

- Enhances your immune system
- Corrects the body's imbalances
- Improves brain function
- Helps in giving you a more positive outlook in life
- Makes it easier for you to deal with problems and other challenges in life

- Helps you understand your emotions on a deeper level

- Tunes the auric field and your physical state to resonate in harmony with your surroundings

- Removes the feeling of emptiness and makes it easier for you to feel whole

- Improves mood and sleeping pattern

- Reduces headaches and migraine attack

- Shrinking of ovarian cysts

- Reduced inflammation and improved joint function

- Helps in healing bunions and kidney stones

- Modification of the heart rate, blood pressure, breathing depth, and breathing rate

- Deep relaxation and stress alleviation

- Relieves anxiety and depression

- Triggers the release of endorphin responsible for pain reduction and enhanced mood

- Allows the body to heal on its own

Overall, sound healing makes you happier and healthier. It improves your mood, outlook on life, energy, and wisdom.

The Other Aspects of Sound Healing

For sound healing to work, you have to trust sounds and let them into your consciousness. Only then will they be able to penetrate your core and dissolve the blockage causing your illness and depression.

Here are some vital tips on how to maximize the benefits of the process:

1. You can use recorded music in sound healing, something played using single or only a few instruments.

2. Lie down or sit during the process. You have to be comfortable without falling asleep. Wear loose clothing and take off your shoes.

3. The left side of the brain or the intellectual side takes up to 20 minutes to calm down. Do not hurry the process. The right side of the brain will naturally take over and when it happens, you'll become more aware of the healing process.

4. Perform a relaxation exercise before the healing process. You can do slow and fluid movements along with soft and deep breathing, which will help in improving your overall body contact.

5. Consider the process as your "me time". Disengage from anything that will distract your thoughts.

The Effects of Sound

It will take up to 36 hours or more to feel the effects of sound depending on the sound used in the process. It goes deep into the energy fields surrounding your body and leaves traces. Sound affects your psycho-energetic system in many different ways.

The rhythm of a deep hand drum, for example, affects the lower part of the body – from the pelvic area to your feet. It emits emotional and mental reactions. If the instrument was intentionally played to make you feel inspired, the effects will become visible in your outer aura. You may feel and realize the effects of your dreams. You will also develop inner changes without being aware that it is happening.

Sound with penetrative effects in your etheric energy field comes from hard percussion instruments, such as gongs, bells, Tibetan bowls, cymbals, or bells, glass, and tubular bells. For a more potent effect, the instrument has to be played using a hard object made of hard rubber or wood.

The sounds from the instruments go deep into the two layers of the etheric in your body – the light ether and chemical. To prevent any blockage, it will help if you'll perform the right energy awareness exercises along with the penetrative sounds.

The etheric energy field is not exclusive to humans. Everything around you – animals, objects, plants, air, planets, has it. The shape of an instrument affects the sound form and helps in realizing the resting center found in your core.

The sound form next to the instrument used is recognized as a physical phenomenon, which is felt like a density or pressure. Its energy form spreads and extends along with the shape and could sometimes be sensed at a distance. You will feel the instrument quality on a spiritual level.

A musical instrument has a memory of how it was played and who handled it. Through time, it will accumulate different levels of energy. This is the reason why it takes several playtimes before a new musical instrument can develop its full potential.

Chapter 16 - Healing Instruments

There are many musical instruments used for healing. They represent one or a combination of the five phases of energy change, which include the following:

1. Earth – clay instruments associated with structured thinking, spleen, and the stomach

2. Metal – normal or tubular bells associated with depression, sadness, and lungs

3. Water – drums linked to fear and the kidneys

4. Wood – instruments made of wood associated with will, anger, and liver

5. Fire – stringed musical instruments associated with the heart and happiness

Here's a comprehensive list of the instruments used in sound healing:

String Instruments

They gravitate to the air element. The strings that produce low notes will settle towards the bottom of the torso and the types that produce high notes will keep your attention to the chest area. In traditional Chinese medicine, these instruments are used in treating heart-related problems.

1. Guitar

It plays a perfect chord by simply striking the strings and without an elaborate left-hand technique. You can hear water with the changing flow of the sound of the guitar. The earth's qualities are attracted to its rhythmical base. The air element is drawn when the instrument is played in a melodic manner.

2. Violin

Its sound affects the body along the lower ribs in between the heart chakra and the solar plexus. It draws the air element by opening up the upper half of your chest. The sound will emit the feeling of inspiration, especially with the way your shoulders and arms move.

3. Harp

The sound helps a person to go into deep relaxation. It calms the nervous system and opens your mental field. The massively generated notes due to the 6 octaves of strings a concert harp has make this an instrument of angels. The sound feels as if you are being lifted, which no other instrument can make.

4. Sithar

The complex technique of how it is played attracts strong air. You will hear the sympathetic strings resound every time you play a note in this melodic instrument.

5. Sound bed

This therapeutic instrument will require you to lie down in a hollow table, which is actually a large monochord. It has about 50 strings beneath the table tuned according to the patient's needs. The sound bed and the monochord affect the senses by making them sharper and they also soothe the nervous system. The bed will move you towards the element of space. It also emits a motherly-like sound that will draw you towards the qualities of the earth. You'll feel drawn to the fire element when the sound bed and monochord are played using mallets.

6. Tampura

This instrument has four strings tuned to two identical fifths, octave, and tonica. It establishes an earth sound, or a drone background used in Indian classical music. It has similarities with sithar but it cannot play melodies. To produce a range of overtones of air, fire, and space, a string of cotton is inserted on the end of its string. The sound it emits is both reassuring and calming.

7. Cello

When played in lower notes, your focus will be drawn towards the water area or your pelvic and hips and fire area or your navel. When you play it in a freestyle manner, you will develop sensitivity to its sound and proper intonation.

Drums

Drums activate the water and earth elements.

1. Clay Pot Drums

They help in directing your focus to the belly area. They create a soft and low pitch when the hole is slapped using your hand.

2. Ocean Drums

The instrument has numerous tiny metal marbles inside the double frame drums. By rolling the drums in different directions, you will hear a sound similar to the waves on the beach. It helps in calming babies as the sound will remind them of the blood moving inside their mother's aorta while they were still unborn.

3. Water drum

This instrument produces soft percussive sound when the upper calebasse is knocked with a soft mallet. Press the upper bowl near or far from the water to create varying pitches.

4. Talking drum

Place the instrument under your armpit and squeeze to produce varying pitches depending on how hard you squeeze it. You can also play the instrument using a mallet or your fingers. This drum produces a soft watery sound.

5. Slid or log drum

This rectangular closed box made of wood instrument is more of a xylophone than a drum. The cavity emits a warm sound. You can play it using a hard material to attract earth and fire qualities and play using soft mallets to attract air and water.

6. Tabla

Considered as the most popular Indian percussion instrument, the smaller type activates the mental and fire aura while the larger drum attracts water qualities.

7. Bodhran

You can play this tunable instrument with your hand for a softer tone and to create a sound with more water and air. You can also play this using a double-edged wooden beater to create a harder tone.

Small Percussion

1. Indonesian Kokiriko Gekko, Wooden Claps

They create a dry and sharp sound that attracts the fire area.

2. Chicken Shake, Maracas, Rattles, Chakchas

They emit sounds that loosen the etheric and get rid of the energy blockage. They help in making you more alert and in stimulating your nervous system.

3. Rainstick

When used while seated, it creates a relaxing sound, especially when placed near the back, shoulders, or neck.

4. Claves

The instrument, made of a pair of short hardwood sticks, produces a dry, awakening, and sharp sound when hit together. It attracts the earth element when played with regular pulsations. In traditional Chinese medicine, it is used to tap a person's fire element.

5. Tempelblocks, Woodblocks, Wooden bells

When hit with hard mallets, these tuned instruments produce a sharp and dry sound that brings you towards heightened consciousness when played during meditation. Use your bare hands in playing the instruments to create a warmer sound.

Tuned percussion

1. Crystal Singing Bowls

Rub or bang the bowls with different mallets to create a penetrative sound used for healing.

2. Mouth Harp

This old instrument can induce trance. To make different sounds, change the size of the cavity of your mouth, position of your tongue, or the style of your breathing.

3. Bass xylophone bars

They offer the most beautiful and warmest sounds among any wooden instruments.

4. Boom Whackers

The instrument made of short tubes of plastic is played by slapping them on your thigh to make a sound.

5. Flowerpots

They are lithophones that produce beautiful earthly sounds.

6. Lithophones

They produce a pure sound that invokes the power of the sky. The sound is not earthly but more on cold, brilliant, and dry.

Keyboards

1. Piano

The instrument also attract water, fire, space, air, and earth qualities depending on the piece that you are playing.

2. Waterphone

This new instrument can create unfamiliar and new sounds.

Wind Instruments – Flutes

1. Pan Flute

The instrument is easy to play. Every note has its own bamboo tube and it emits a smokey sound. It comes in different forms, such as a double row, straight row, and bent.

2. Overtone Flute

The instrument doesn't require any fingering technique and can be easily played by people of all ages and even those with disabilities. You can make varying sounds depending on how strong or soft your blow is.

4. Didgeridoo

The original instrument was made of wood from the eucalyptus tree. Once you learn how to play this right, it can help in improving your grounding and it also increases your awareness of the earth element. You need to do a circular breathing technique to play the instrument.

5. Bullroarer

It has a low roaring sound that draws the solar plexus. Whirl the string attached to a piece of flat wood around your head to create a sound.

6. Ocarina

Considered as one of the oldest flutes, this instrument made of clay emits a damp and warm sound. The warm tone and simple melodies will help you in connecting with your feelings.

7. Irish Whistle

This metallic instrument has six holes that can play a full musical scale. You will need more than one whistle to produce sounds of different keys.

8. Low Whistle

This instrument made of aluminum can be played with a range of subtlety. You will need to play it in front of a microphone to hear it clearly.

9. Saxophone

Its sound draws your attention to your stomach and sternum. The sound also draws you closer to light, warmth, and fire.

10. Bird's Voices

Various instruments that emit songs of different birds are now available. The sound will remind you of nature and has calming and soothing effects.

11. Conch

Considered as one of the oldest instruments and is played by blowing in its opening. It is made of a sea shell with the tip cut off. The sound it emits is haunting and reverberates in places, like a cave, rocky walls, and church. To create varying sounds, you will need to change the tension of your lips.

Metallophones

1. Table Tubes

The instrument made of a set of tuned tubular bells arranged in a frame is played using a medium felt ball mallet.

2. Glockenspiel

This metal instrument is a cousin of the wooden xylophone. The best type among its kind is said to be the ones with lower tones and resonators.

3. Gongs

Gongs vary in size and sound but all of them create a powerful sound. The instruments are played with sensitivity in sound healing. It offers healing benefits to people with an oversensitive solar plexus zone.

4. Barchimes

It has several small metal chimes arranged in a declining order and hung on a horizontal piece of bamboo. To emit a sound that will draw your mental aura and nervous system, play the instrument by gliding any object or your hand along with the chimes.

5. Tubular Bells

The sound of the bells expands quickly up to a point when you will get confused where the sound is coming from. The sound lingers in the room for an extended period, a common characteristic of most metallic percussion instruments. When used to attract the element of space, the sound allows the expansion of the mental aura. It helps you in overcoming your vices, fears, and worries.

6. Windchimes

The instrument will create sound when hit by the wind. It will create a reinforcing effect when placed above the points where the energy lines meet.

7. Cymbals

It creates a powerful sound that brings out your fire quality, especially helpful to people with hypersensitive solar plexus. You can practice playing the cymbals at your own pace. Listen to how your body reacts to the sound and continue playing in ways that it affects your core. Do not play it too loud or else the sound will hit the nervous system directly and might cause a fright.

8. Small cymbals and bells

They come in pair that when hit together, create a metallic, penetrating, and sharp sound. They are capable of activating the space and air elements. You can activate the healing powers of the instruments by placing them above an acupuncture point. They have the ability to calm the energy, activate, or dissipate depending on how they are played.

9. Singing Bowls

The sound depends on the kind of singing bowls you play. They come in two basic forms – the traditional Himalayan singing bowl and the steel bowls from Japan, China, or Korea. The steel bowls sound sharp, clear, and straight. The Himalayan bowls produce a wavering sound.

You can play these bowls with the tip of your finger or by using the top mallets. To create a long constant sound, you can rub the bowls with a wooden beater. The sound makes a pleasant impression and helps you in finding your center.

Most Popular Instrument for Sound Healing in Buddhism

Tibetan singing bowls, also called Himalayan bowls, have long been used by Buddhist monks in their meditation practices. The instrument is also popularly used for healing by wellness practitioners, such as yoga therapists, massage therapists, and music therapists.

These singing bowls are categorized as a bell. The vibration of the bell when played, result in a deep and rich tone. Aside from the healing effects, these Tibetan singing bowls are also used to achieve deep relaxation.

The vibrations produced by the instrument is said to be beneficial in giving the energy system of the body its needed balance. It also harmonizes the cells and reduces stress.

To use the singing bowl for healing purposes, hold the mallet and press it in a circular motion at the bowl's rim. Use your arm instead of your wrist in accomplishing the motion. Slow down once you hear a clear and bright tone produced from the process. The other ways of playing the instrument include striking the bowl in a gentle manner before starting with the circular motion and performing the circular motion against the bowl's outside belly.

If you want to purchase the Tibetan singing bowls for healing purposes, look for high-quality materials capable of producing more resonant sounds. You can get them at specialty stores for new age products, music shops, yoga studios, certain meditation centers, and online shops.

Conclusion

I'd like to thank you and congratulate you for transiting my lines from start to finish. I hope this book was able to help you understand the Buddha's sample and what you can do to follow his lead towards enlightenment.

The next step is to try different meditation practices, including proper exercises and breathing. All these will help you understand yourself better and all the things that surround you.

I know you could have picked any number of books to read, but you picked this book and for that I am extremely grateful.

If you enjoyed this book and found some benefit in reading this, I'd like to hear from you and hope that you could take some time to post a review. Your feedback and support will help this author to greatly improve his writing craft for future projects and make this book even better.

I want you, the reader, to know that your review is very important and so, if you'd like to leave a review, all you have to do is click here and away you go. I wish you all the best in your future success!

Thank you and good luck!

Harini Anand

Buddhism:

Discover Ancient Strategies For Beginners or Advanced To Achieve Lasting Happiness, Mindfulness & Calm Stress
In The Modern World

Table of Contents

Introduction

Chapter One: An Overview of Buddhism

Chapter Two: The Schools of Buddhism

Chapter Three: Buddhism- Other Concepts

Chapter Four: Buddhism - Ancient Techniques in the Modern World

Chapter Five: Meditation, Yoga, and Buddhism

Chapter Six: Daily Life and Buddhism

Chapter Seven: Buddhism and Karma

Chapter Eight: Buddhism for Kids

References

Introduction

We live in a world that is full of competition, suffering, and pain. Everyone wants to become successful and great. Thanks to the competitive nature of modern society, no one can sit down for a while and relax. Everyone is afraid that if they relax, they will be thrown out of this competition. The human body is a marvel of nature, but it is not made for continuous use. Our body and mind need time to reset and relax.

One of the major problems of this competitive modern world is stress. It is impossible to find a person who is not stressed about something. Everyone, right from little kids to retired elderly, is living a stressful life nowadays. Little kids are stressed about their school and friends, adults about work and politics, the elderly about their purpose and existence in general. Being stressed about things is normal; in fact, many people proclaim that they perform really well when they are stressed about something. But being stressed all the time can wreak havoc on your mind as well as body. Stress can lead to various mental and physical disorders, many of which are life-threatening.

Stress is often accompanied by anxiety. The number of people suffering from anxiety disorders is on the rise since the last couple of decades. Anxiety is harmful to your personal, professional, and social life, as well. People who suffer from anxiety disorders often cannot perform well. Many great and highly talented artists could not achieve and fulfill their potential just because they suffered from anxiety. Stress combined with anxiety can break a person completely and shatter his dreams and plans.

While there are many different treatments and methods available today that can help you tackle anxiety and stress, but many of these involve medication. These medicines are costly and are often unavailable. They also have many harmful side effects. This is why many people who suffer from these problems often become discouraged and lost.

But don't worry; it is possible to get rid of these problems without medications with the help of Buddhism. Many people have now started looking at Buddhism as a way to attain a peaceful mind and a tranquil life. But understanding Buddhism is not easy. It is one of the most ancient religions and schools of philosophy in the world, which has deep-set roots in ancient Indian cultures. A lot of people have left Buddhism before because they could not understand it leading to confusion and frustration. If you are one of those people, congratulations, you have finally unlocked the secret of understanding, Buddhism is a simple and lucid manner.

What makes this book one of the best books on Buddhism is the fact that it can be read by anyone. While specifically meant for beginners, this book is also useful for people who understand Buddhism and have practiced it for a long time. This book is easy to understand and contains all the necessary information that is required to begin your path towards Buddhism. This book has been prepared by consulting many reputed sources regarding Buddhism and simplifying the vast knowledge contained in Buddhist scriptures. It breaks down the complex concept of Buddhism and deconstructs it so that even the most novice reader can understand its principles and doctrine.

This book is recommended for everyone who wants to gain a clear yet concise understanding of Buddhism. It covers all the basics of Buddhism in sufficient detail. Buddhism is a brilliant way of living life as, unlike other religions, it forces you to look for the source of your problems inside you. This introspective quality of Buddhism is often compared to modern-day psychology. Thus, it can be safely assumed that Buddhism is based on science. This book provides you with different codes of practice, which, if you incorporate in your life, can change it for good.

Buddhism has become really popular in the modern world. Many famous thinkers, rationalists, entrepreneurs, etc. are Buddhists. For instance, Leonard Cohen, Orlando Bloom, Steve Jobs, Jack Kerouac, Allen Ginsberg, Penelope Cruz, Jet Li, Courtney Love, Richard Gere, George Takei, Sharon Stone, Naomi Watts, Tina Turner, and many other successful people are Buddhists. Many of them credit Buddhism to be one of the reasons why they are successful.

The success of the above-mentioned people is not due to some divine intervention; rather, it is due to the various practices and exercises that are prescribed in Buddhism. These exercises are mentioned in detail in this book. Like the above-mentioned people, if you incorporate these exercises in your daily life, you too will start noticing positive changes in yourself, your life, and the atmosphere around you as well.

Stress is a slow killer. It doesn't just affect your personal life, but it can also ruin the lives of people around you. Stress is also bad for your professional life. But the worst thing stress can do make your life unlivable. People who are stressed and anxious all the time hate their lives because they cannot find peace in it. Such people often start using drugs and may even contemplate suicide as well. If you are one of such people who feel that their life has no pleasure or peace, you need to act right now. Choosing the path of Buddha can change your life for good. It will allow you to feel peace and pleasure once again.

Don't worry; you do not need to become a Buddhist to enjoy its fruits. Buddhism is a flexible philosophy that can be incorporated into your present beliefs as well.

Wake up and start waking on the path laid by Buddha now! Good luck!

Chapter One: An Overview of Buddhism

Before moving on to the various practices of Buddhism, it is crucial to understand its basics. This chapter will try to answer all the basic questions that you may have about Buddha and Buddhism.

What do Buddhists Believe?

This is a difficult question to answer, as Buddhism is not an organized religion like the Abrahamic ones. Buddhism is often said to be a living organism composed of many different religions, sects, and ideas that live together like a huge family. Buddhism developed over hundreds of years in many different parts of the world; the growth hasn't stopped. Each sect, group, and often individual interprets Buddhism differently.

While all the sects of Buddhism are different in some way, all of them are linked to each other by the tenets and practices laid down by Buddha, an Indian prince who changed the course of the world. Buddha lived in India sometime between the fourth and sixth centuries BCE and taught many different things, which later became the basis of Buddhism. Buddha was not his real name and was given to him when he became enlightened. Buddha means 'awakened one.' He was able to release himself from the cycle of samsara, i.e., the cycle of pain and rebirth. Buddha attained enlightenment and found unconditional and everlasting happiness. Nothing could disturb it, including illness, old age, or even death. Buddha preached and taught about this path throughout his life to help others achieve the same freedom from samsara.

Buddha preached that suffering and dissatisfaction, illness, old age, and death are all important and inseparable parts of life and are unavoidable. However, suffering is our own creation. Suffering is a result of clinging and attachment. We desire things to stay or be in a certain way, and when they do not remain so, we suffer. Buddha preached that every action and idea has consequences, forming a never-ending chain. This is often called the chain of karma.

It is crucial to understand that we are the creators of our suffering. Similarly, with efforts, we can end this suffering as well. Every person on this Earth has the capacity to exit the cycle of rebirth and suffering.

People who are not born into a Buddhist family often pick up Buddhism through various methods. Learning about the teachings of Buddha and understanding and witnessing the practices of Buddhism is often a gateway for people to Buddhism. Conversations with Buddhists, meditation, and even books like this can help you start your study of Buddhism.

While many major schools and sects of Buddhism offer formal conversion or transition ceremonies, they are not crucial. Your practice, faith, and dedication towards the teachings of Buddha make you a Buddhist. In formal ceremonies, the inductee is taught 'Trisharana' or the 'three shelters.' A person can take shelter from the vicissitudes of life in these three shelters. These shelters are Buddha (the physical embodiment), the Dhamma (the teachings), and the Sangha (the community). These three together are also called as 'Triratna' or triple gems or jewels.

Is Buddhism a Religion, a Philosophy, or a Way of Life?

Buddhism is one of the most complex practices in the world, and it is difficult to define it. Buddhism can be defined as a combination of philosophy, religion, and a way of life. It depends on the practitioner and the student how he or she interprets it. It is possible to study Buddhism in a purely philosophical way, as well.

Many practitioners think of Buddhism as a religion. As mentioned earlier, Buddhism is considered to be a living family of religions with different philosophical sects and aspects. One of the major things that people find attractive about Buddhism is its deep philosophy. Buddhism does not ask you to believe in things blindly; rather, it asks you to investigate your mind, reality, and reason. It is one of the few religions that promote critical thinking as well as reasoning. This is due to its philosophical base.

Buddhism has an end-goal, which is to find a release from the cycle of pain and rebirth. This end-goal makes Buddhism a form of religion. Buddhism offers a path to escape from this cycle with the help of ethics and different practices. Other elements of Buddhism can also be considered to be religious. Each sect and school of Buddhism has developed different rights, rituals, books, etc. They express their devotion to Buddha in many different ways, as well.

Certain characteristics of Buddhism do not match the typical ideas of religion. For instance, there is no divine revelation in Buddhism. Similarly, practitioners are not required to read scriptures and attend regular services. The scriptures are not considered to be the absolute truth, like, for instance, the Bible or the Holy Quran. Buddhism does not encourage a leap of faith and makes you question everything.

Practitioners rarely get into debates regarding the true nature of Buddhism. For them, Buddhism is just a way of escaping the world of pain. Often Buddhism is compared with western notions of religion, which is why people find it phony and unreal. Buddhism is concerned with meaning and not doctrine.

Who was Buddha?

Buddha, before becoming Buddha, was an Indian prince named Siddhartha Gautama. Born in Lumbini, Nepal, Siddhartha lived around 2600 years ago in the northern region of India and Nepal. Siddhartha was a prince and thus a warrior. He was born in the Shakya clan to King Shuddhodhana and Queen Maya. Buddha is often known as Shakyamuni, which means the Sage of Shakyas.

There are many legends and stories associated with the birth of Siddhartha. According to some legends, the birth of Buddha was prophesied by a great sage who told his father that the child would either grow up to become a 'Chakravathi' or the king of the world or will become a world-renowned spiritual leader. Shuddhodhana was shocked to hear these words and did everything in his power to stop his son from becoming spiritual. He surrounded and showered Siddhartha with luxuries, privileges, and all the joys of the mortal world and sheltered him from all the harsh realities outside the palace. Siddhartha thus grew up to be a pampered prince who did not understand pain and suffering. He was married off to an intelligent princess called Yashodhara, who soon bore him a son called Rahula. When Rahula was still young, the prince managed to escape the palace and witness something that changed his life forever.

Siddhartha witnessed the truth of life when he escaped his palace. While riding in a carriage, he saw a sick man in immense pain. In his next ride, he saw an old, tired man. In the third ride, he saw a funeral procession and understood that death was inevitable. These three encounters were his first experience of the inevitable suffering of human beings. On his next ride, Siddhartha saw a mendicant meditating and realized that he could to find a way out of this cycle of suffering.

Soon after these encounters, Siddhartha, at the tender age of 29, left his palace, wife, son, and all the materialistic pleasures of this world and set on a quest to find the true meaning and release from the cycle of suffering. He studied, meditated, met with many people, and fasted for many years. He soon realized that exiting the cycle of pain was possible only with the help of the 'middle way.' Extremities of any sort would not help him to escape samsara. A person who indulges in extreme material pleasures is similar to a person who indulges in extreme physical denial. Siddhartha realized that the only way to end suffering was the 'middle way,' which could be achieved by training your mind. He then decided to meditate under a Ficus tree (Peepal or Bodhi tree) in a small town called Bodhgaya in north India. For 49 days, he meditated and received many insights into the nature of reality, and finally, after a long struggle, he became enlightened. The existence of Prince Siddhartha vanished, and Buddha emerged. For the next 45 years, Buddha preached and taught the path of freedom that he had realized under the Bodhi tree.

Siddhartha's life of spirituality was not an easy one. Soon after leaving his palace, he spent around six years practicing and studying under different teachers. These teachers had many different methods of meditation, often extreme and sometimes inhumane. While these meditations helped him get away from the palace, he understood that these were otherwise useless- he could not achieve his goal, which was freedom from the samsara.

According to Buddhist traditions, the first people Buddha taught were his five companions, spiritual seekers. Siddhartha had practiced severe self-denial with them and had then abandoned the practice.

These five seekers met Buddha near Benares in India and tried to avoid him, for they thought that he had gone back to the life of luxury. However, soon, they realized that the old Siddhartha had vanished and had become Buddha. Buddha then taught them the 'middle path' and said that neither self-indulgence nor self-denial could help them in their goal. This is the Middle Way or the Maddhyama Marga. Later Buddha taught these men the foundational bases of Buddhism, including Chatura Arya Satya or four noble truths and the Ashtanga Marga or the eight-fold path. Thus, the Sangha was born, and Buddhism began.

Over the next 45 years, Buddha managed to reach out to thousands of people from every walk of life.

People from all castes, creeds, class, gender, etc. became students of Buddha. Even murderers and hardened criminals were accepted in the Sangha. Prince Siddhartha's family, including his son, wife, and father, too, joined the Sangha.

Many of Buddha's students became enlightened and spread his message. Sariputta, Moggallana, Mahakasyapa, etc. were some of his star students. Mahakasyapa is said to have organized the First Council of Buddhism after the death of Buddha. In this council, 500 enlightened monks gathered and discussed and collected Buddha's sermons.

According to certain texts, women were not allowed to join the monastic communities in the beginning, and only men were allowed to become bhikkhus or monks. Buddha's stepmother, Mahapajapati, and a council of 500 other women approached Buddha and requested him to grant them permission to join. Buddha's disciple Ananda too, requested him to grant women permission to join the sangha. Women were soon allowed to become bhikkunis. According to some sources, this story is false, and women were allowed to join sangha right from the beginning.

Buddha's Death

Buddha's death is considered to be as important as his life. After 45 years of teaching, Buddha passed away at the age of 80. He was surrounded by a large group of students when he died smiling. This event is also known as Mahaparinirvana. Buddha had escaped samsara and was free from the cycle of death, birth, and suffering.

According to early Pali texts, three months after the Mahaparinirvana, around 400 BCE, the First Buddhist Council took place. Here around 500 senior, enlightened monks gathered and discussed the teachings of Buddha and planned how his teachings should be preserved.

Seventy years after Mahaparinirvana, another council was held. In this council, certain disputed rules regarding bhikkhus and bhikkhus were discussed. Here the sangha underwent dramatic change and got divided into two branches. One of these branches wanted to uphold all the traditional rules of Buddha's teachings, while the other wanted to move on with time and relax certain rules.

It is said that a third council was held during the reign of Emperor Asoka, one of the most celebrated rulers of India. Emperor Asoka became a Buddhist around 250 BCE after witnessing a massacre. Emperor Asoka is responsible for spreading Buddhism across the subcontinent- even Asia. The third council was held to remove corruption from the sangha. Heretics were banned from the sangha as well. Many essential components of the Buddhist scriptures were discussed and formalized in this council. In the third council, Emperor Asoka decided to send teaching missions around the subcontinent to spread the word of Buddha. These emissaries took Buddha's teachings to Sri Lanka, Myanmar, Himalayas, etc. In later years Buddhism spread over East and Southeast Asia and beyond.

Origin of Buddhism

The origin of Buddhism is a complex and sometimes controversial topic. In this section, let us have a look at its inception and history.

Buddhism is followed by more than 300 million people around the world. Yet, Buddhism is quite different than any other religion as almost all sects of Buddhism deny a supreme deity. For Buddhists, the teachings of Buddha hold the supreme position. The earliest form of Buddhism was thoroughly based on the teachings of Buddha. Here it was believed that through proper moral code, efforts, dedication, and action, anyone could achieve enlightenment. This form of Buddhism is still practiced (albeit in a slightly altered form). This form of Buddhism is called the Hinayana or Theravada Buddhism. Theravada means the Way of the Elders. This form is practiced in most of Southeast Asia.

Another prominent school of Buddhism is the Mahayana or the Great Vehicle. Its inception can be traced to the first century CE. In this Buddhism, Buddha became a deity, and soon other past and future Buddha's as well as Bodhisattvas were added to the pantheon. Bodhisattvas are enlightened people who postpone their nirvana just so that they can help others on the path of salvation. Mahayana Buddhism is popular in Central Asia and Far East Asia.

Another form of Buddhism developed in the seventh century CE were different practices, doctrines and esoteric dogma got mixed with Buddhism. Necromancy from Hindu beliefs got added to Buddhism as well. This form of Buddhism is called the Tantrism or Vajrayana Buddhism (the Diamond Path). It became extremely popular in the Himalayan regions, and soon, female Bodhisattvas were added to the already expanded pantheon of Buddhism. It is here mandala, and similar cosmic patterns were added to Buddhism. Many local beliefs, shamanic, and sometimes terrifying deities were added to Buddhism, and a new religion was born. Unlike other forms of Buddhism, in Vajrayana, a spiritual teacher or guru is essential to guide on the path of nirvana.

Thus, the origin of Buddhism is convoluted. You will find out more about the schools of Buddhism later in this chapter.

Buddhist Texts and Scriptures

Many religions of the world have particular scriptures that are considered to be holy and the word of God. However, there are no particular or specific texts that are considered to the ultimate Book of Religion. This is due to the fact that Buddhism is a living family of many different spiritual and philosophical systems. No single set of scriptures is considered to be authoritative by all the Buddhist sects and groups. Each Buddhist sect has its own textual canon that it follows.

Theravada or the Way of the Elders Buddhists follow the Pali canon. This canon contains some of the oldest Buddhist texts. This canon is known as the Pali canon because many of its books are in an ancient Indian language called Pali. These scriptures are known as Tipitaka, which means Three Baskets. These include the 'Sutta Pitaka,' the 'Vinaya Pitaka,' and the 'Abhidhamma Pitaka.' Sutta means sutras, which are the discourses of Buddha and some of his major students. The Vinaya Pitaka contains a code of discipline for the monks, and the Abhidhamma Pitaka contains a detailed study of the origin, nature, and the interaction of psychological and material phenomena. These texts are dated sometime between the third and the first century BCE.

East Asian Buddhist sects present in Japan, Korea, China, and Vietnam follow the Chinese canon. The texts present in this canon can be dated back to the first century BCE to the fifth century CE. There exists a lot of overlap between the Pali and the Chinese canons. Doctrines and methods are the distinguishing features of the Chinese canon. Another canon that often overlaps the Chinese canon is the Tibetan canon. The Tibetan canon contains two parts, the Kangyur or the word of Buddha and the Tengyur, the later commentaries. Tibetan canon also contains various tantric rituals and descriptions.

Certain branches of Buddhism like to base the practices on certain treatises or sutras only. For instance, Nichiren Buddhism is based around the Lotus Sutra and chanting its title is an integral part of the practice. Another branch, the Pure Land Buddhists, practice the three sutras that are focused on Bodhisattva Amitabha or Amitabha Buddha, i.e.,

Buddha of Infinite Light. This Buddha is supposed to reign over 'the pure land.' This pure land is often referred to as the Buddhist heaven by these practitioners.

Buddhism and Reincarnation

Reincarnation is an integral part of Buddhism, as Buddha believed that any living being is caught in the cycle of samsara. In this cycle, a living being is born, then he or she dies, and ultimately is reborn. To escape this cycle of samsara and pain is enlightenment.

According to Buddhist texts, people are reborn because of desire and clinging. As said earlier, desire is also the root cause of suffering. So ultimately, desire and suffering are the reasons behind samsara. Buddha believed that every clinging adds a brick to the bridge of the next life.

Buddha said that when, where, and how a person will be reborn solely depends on the karma or the credit that he or she accumulated in his or her past life. This means our deeds in previous and this life affect our next life. He believed that even at the time of death and later, we could make certain choices that can affect our next birth, whether positively or negatively. Buddhists believe that the attitude of mind at the time of death is crucial. If we are calm, focused, and pleased while dying, we will be born in good circumstances. Thus, preparing yourself for death through meditation forms an integral part of the Buddhist practice.

There are many different ideas about what happens at and after death in Buddhism. These ideas differ from tradition to tradition. For instance, many branches of Buddhism believe that chanting certain parts of some scriptures and holy mantras can help the dying in the next life. Many Buddhist texts also name and describe various realms like heaven and hell. In certain scriptures, these are thought to be the creation of the dying mind.

Many secular and modern Buddhists do not believe in reincarnation and rebirth. Such Buddhists mostly focus on the secular aspects of Buddhism, including meditation and mindfulness. Many secular Buddhists compare themselves with the early Buddhists, as they did not believe in God and similar principles as well. Yet, there is a huge difference between the two- the modern do not believe in reincarnation and new births while the early Buddhists did believe in these.

Understanding the basics of any philosophy or religion is crucial as it reduces confusion. In the next chapter, let us have a look at different sects of Buddhism that are currently practiced in the world.

Chapter Two: The Schools of Buddhism

In the last chapter, different schools and sects of Buddhism were introduced briefly. In this chapter, let us have a close look at some of the most prominent schools of Buddhism.

There are a variety of schools or sects of Buddhism thanks to its inclusive nature. The two principal forms of Buddhism are Theravada Buddhism that is prominently present in Cambodia, Sri Lanka, Thailand, Myanmar, Laos, etc. and the Mahayana Buddhism, which is dominant in China, Japan, Taiwan, Mongolia, and Korea. A version of the Mahayana Buddhism, often known as the Tibetan or Vajrayana Buddhism is dominant in Tibet and surrounding Himalaya region. The practices and doctrines of all the branches of Buddhism may be different; however, all of them are focused on helping the practitioner to follow the path of enlightenment. Almost none of the Buddhist sects focus on conversion except the Nichiren Buddhism in Japan.

The three main branches of Buddhism developed over a long period of time. Each of these has its own spiritual ideals and characteristics. Hinayana or the Lesser Vehicle is often called foundational Buddhism. It is the precursor of the Theravada school. This school emphasizes enlightenment through monastic life. Not many people follow this school now. In fact, the word Hinayana was coined by the Mahayana sect and is seen to be a pejorative. Mahayana Buddhists call it a difficult path and thus a lesser path because very few people can follow it.

Many sects believe that you need multiple lives to reach enlightenment except Vajrayana Buddhism. The Vajrayana or the Tibetan Buddhists believe that it is possible to achieve enlightenment in a single life without having to accumulate enough good karma in past lives.

The three major branches of Buddhism are not mutually exclusive, and they often overlap. However, their different practices and doctrines have made Buddhism and Buddhist art a complex structure.

Foundational or the Hinayana Buddhists believe that enlightenment can only be achieved by monks and that too through their own efforts. Mahayana and Vajrayana, on the other hand, believe that everyone can become a Buddha with the help of Bodhisattvas. Due to this, Mahayana and Vajrayana Buddhists often have many shrines dedicated to these Bodhisattvas and Buddha's. They also form an integral part of their art.

As said earlier, the oldest form of Buddhism (for the common people) is called Theravada. In this form, the practitioners strictly adhere to the teachings of Buddha and often lead a life of meditation. Practitioners believe that only a few people can reach nirvana with ample efforts. In this form of Buddhism, initially, Buddha was not represented in human form; instead, various symbols and icons were used. At the beginning of the first century, under the able rule of Kushana kings, Buddha began to be presented in human form. Around the same time, Mahayana, a new branch of Buddhism, arose. For Mahayana Buddhists, Buddha is much more than a teacher and a human being; he is a savior god. They believe that Buddha appeared on this earth in the perfect human form so that he could guide and help people achieve nirvana.

Theravada Buddhism

Theravada Buddhism is also known as the Buddhism or doctrine of the elders. It is considered to be the oldest out of all three prominent schools of Buddhism. It is also the most orthodox out of the three. Theravada practitioners believe that their doctrine is the closest to what Shakyamuni Buddha taught and preached. Their practices, beliefs, and doctrines are based on the recollections of Buddha's teachings, which were collected by Buddha's companions. These companions are known as Elders. They were the senior-most and highly respected monks. Nowadays, Theravada is predominantly practiced in Thailand, Sri Lanka, Myanmar, Laos, Cambodia, and certain parts of Vietnam. A lot of practitioners can be found in India as well.

Theravada was not the only school of Buddhism that existed after the death of Buddha. In fact, around 18 prominent schools of Buddhism practiced their religion and philosophy in harmony. Many other schools of Buddhism disappeared with attacks from various other religions.

For the followers of Theravada Buddhism, the enlightenment of the individual, spirituality, pure deeds and thoughts, self-discipline, etc. are important. They think that monastic life and following the rules of ancient Vinaya is essential as well. Theravada Buddhism prescribes specific roles and rules for monks and common people. In Theravada Buddhism, each person is responsible for her or his own nirvana. It also believes that only a monk can attain nirvana.

Theravada Buddhism Beliefs

Theravada Buddhism holds many beliefs that often overlap with other forms of Buddhism. In Theravada Buddhism, the three Noble Virtues are as follows:

- Dukkha or Suffering, pain, and pursuit of desire.

- Annica or the temporary state of being and all things

- Annata or the illusion that is known as reality

Theravada Buddhists believe that everything is temporary, and if you get attached to material things, it will only lead to unhappiness and suffering. It will also interfere in spiritual matters. Annica teaches that nothing is permanent. If you try to focus on states of mind, experiences, objects, materialistic pleasure, it will only lead to dukkha. Annata understands that there is no point in considering these things important and necessary.

Theravada Buddhism does not allow practitioners to worship any living or nonliving objects. The offerings of flowers and fruits in shrines are not considered to be an object of worship; rather, they are seen as symbols of impermanence. Similarly, chanting is only the reminder of the teachings of Buddha, the Dhamma, and the Sangha.

According to Theravada Buddhists, Gautama Buddha was a human being and not a divine figure, a deity, or a legend. He experienced the same sufferings and pains that all of us experience. What made him unique was that he wanted to transcend beyond this pain and suffering. It is said that Buddha took a vow in front of the first-ever Buddha that he would reincarnate many times and finally become a Buddha. Theravada Buddhists believe that the death or Mahaparinirvana of Buddha is his escape from the human world.

Mahayana stresses on becoming a Bodhisattva. Buddha never gave any explicit instructions on how one should become a

Bodhisattva. All the information regarding is collected in many sutras; however, these sutras were written after Mahaparinirvana. When he was alive, Buddha majorly focused on how to end suffering in one's current life and achieve "Arhatship." Theravada Buddhists thus believe their practices to be purer and closer to what Buddha preached.

Buddha referred to himself as Arhat multiple times, which has led to a lot of confusion in scholars and practitioners as well. Arhat in Pali means 'perfected person' or a person who has achieved Nirvana. Buddha calling himself an Arhat implies that he was no different than his enlightened students. What made him different was that he had mastered everything that is associated with enlightenment. This is why Mahayana Buddhists often believe that total enlightenment should be postponed until one becomes perfect.

Most of Mahayana's knowledge is based on the Lotus Sutra, which was taken from the Nagas by Nagarjuna. Nagarjuna is considered to be the second greatest master after Buddha himself by many. Many people also believe that Nagarjuna was, in fact, a new Buddha who was born to clarify any doubts that the past Buddha might have left. You will find more information regarding Nagarjuna later in this chapter.

As said earlier, Mahayana Buddhists stress on becoming Bodhisattva. This stress was the main reason behind the strain between Mahayana and Theravada Buddhist schools. Avalokiteshvara is considered to be the highest Bodhisattva who stalled his enlightenment just because he wanted everyone to be enlightened first. Many Mahayana shrines are dedicated to Avalokiteshvara.

Mahayana Buddhism has many different sects, practices, and philosophical schools under its shelter. A said earlier,

Mahayana is more popular and widespread than other forms of Buddhism throughout the world. It includes many different and modern forms of Buddhism, including Soka-Gakkai and Zen.

Mahayana means a great vehicle because Buddhist philosophy compares itself to a vehicle that will carry people from the world of pain and suffering. It's known as greater because, unlike other schools, Mahayana is all-encompassing (according to the followers).

The main reason why Mahayana became so widespread and popular was that it allowed the monks to travel more freely. Along with this, the concept of Bodhisattva, which was similar to many local religions and pantheon, was easily accepted by the people.

Mahayana Buddhism Beliefs

Mahayana Buddhists believe that there exist many different kinds of heavens, hell, and nirvana. Bodhisattvas enjoy an exalted status in Mahayana because they help others in achieving nirvana by stalling their own.

Mahayana Buddhism tenets are comparatively vague and 'universal' than the strict codes of Theravada Buddhism. They believe that anyone can achieve nirvana. They love philosophical discussions and are often seen debating and discussing various topics. They worship many male and female deities along with a large pantheon of gods, Bodhisattvas, and Buddhas.

For Mahayana Buddhists, Buddha was a magical and divine figure who was born on the earth to help mankind. The

Supreme Buddha became an omniscient force like a creator God.

Differences Between Mahayana Buddhist and Theravada Buddhists

The distinction between Theravada Buddhism and Mahayana Buddhism is often confusing because they overlap a lot. In this section, let us have a close look at the differences between these two branches of Buddhism.

Mahayana practitioners believe that they have just expanded on the beliefs of Theravada Buddhists and that their doctrines are still based on the teachings of Buddha. The Theravada followers believe that Mahayana is a corrupted form and also view it to be too easy. Theravada Buddhists firmly believe that only your own efforts can help you achieve salvation, while the Mahayana Buddhists think that faith and help from Bodhisattvas can help them achieve salvation.

The concept of Bodhisattvas is where the Mahayana doctrines and Theravada doctrines differ vastly. Mahayana Buddhists believe that there exist many Bodhisattvas as well as many Buddha's. Theravada Buddhists believe that there was just one Buddha and Bodhisattva, Buddha himself.

Tantric Buddhism

Tibetan, Tantric, or Vajrayana Buddhism is a branch of Mahayana Buddhism, which has become a full-fledged tree in its own right. It began with the Tibetan Buddhist monks around the early seventh century CE. Tantric or esoteric Buddhists accept the tenets prescribed by Mahayana monks but also added different forms of mediation guided by gurus and masters. These meditations often involve magical words, mantras, symbols, and practices that are said to speed up the process of achieving enlightenment.

Tibetan Buddhists believe that with ample compassion and meditation, people can achieve nirvana in one single life. These practices and beliefs developed parallel to Hindu practices and beliefs. Due to this, many different and new deities appeared in their pantheon. These deities are of different genders and are represented in different gestures, poses, expressions, etc. Certain deities are also wrathful, and they represent protection. Another major idea in Esoteric Buddhism is the concept of five celestial Buddha's. These five Buddha's each represent a direction, and the last one represents zenith.

It is often called a syncretic mix of Mahayana doctrines with local pantheistic religions and Tantra. The Bon religion has had an immense influence on Tibetan Buddhism. All the activities such as public practices, prayers, etc. are organized and handled by monasteries and temples. Lamas are considered to be the religious heads of the Tibetan Buddhist communities.

Tantrism is a highly ritualistic religion that originated in India. It believes in esoteric philosophy along with magic. Many different sacred shapes, chants, techniques, etc. are used in regular practice in this school of Buddhism.

As said earlier, the ancient Bon religion has had an immense influence on Tibetan Buddhism. For instance, Tibetan Buddhist practices like shamans, dispelling demons, pleasing gods, different mudras, mantras, yantras, and the practice of secret initiation have all been taken from the Bon religion. Mudras are ritual postures; mantras are special words; yantras are special symbols such as the mandala, etc. A lot of symbols, images, objects, etc. of deities worshiped in Tibetan Buddhism have been borrowed or derived from Tantrism. Many of the practices and techniques associated with this school of Buddhism were passed down orally.

The inception of Tantrism can be traced back to 600 CE in India. It was based on texts that are known as Tantras. According to Tantrism, all human conditions, states, feelings, etc. are connected, which means desire, anger, love, hope, etc. are all similar. According to many scholars, Tantrism is a complex combination of Buddhism and Hinduism. It combines Buddhist philosophy, with local folklore and legends and incorporated Hindu gods in its teachings. The erotic and charged Hindu ideas were mixed with authoritative and static teachings of Buddha to form Tantrism.

Why did Buddhism get Divided?

There are many theories behind why Buddhism broke into many factions. According to one theory, a couple of centuries after the death of Buddha, the atmosphere of sangha started heating up over politics. The members could not decide who would run the sangha and whether anyone should run it or not. Another controversy regarding certain rules pertaining to monks created a strain. A handful of Arhats made some decisions that angered a significant number of monks who resented how a small number of Arhats could influence the affairs of the monastery. Disgruntled, the monks and many other disciples worked for many years to lower the status of Arhats, and instead, the Bodhisattva was brought forward to be the ideal.

Mahayana branch of Buddhism still follows most of the original teachings of Buddha, but many of these teachings have undergone a lot of interpolation throughout the years.

The Chinese Mahayana, which is most dominant in Taiwan, is considerably similar to the older Mahayana sect, while the Mahayana of Vietnam, Japan, and Korea are later developments. The Mahayana of Tibet is so different than the original Mahayana that now it is considered to be a different branch of Buddhism itself.

Nagarjuna

In the modern world, many people follow the Mahayana way of Buddhism. It is perhaps the most prominent form of Buddhism that is extant today. It is, therefore, necessary to have a deeper look at Mahayana. To understand the development of Mahayana and its philosophy, it is necessary to study its greatest teacher (after Buddha) Nagarjuna. In this section, let us have a brief introduction of Nagarjuna and his work.

Nagarjuna was born around 150 CE. He is often regarded as the second Buddha about whom the first Buddha prophesized. Nagarjuna did clarify a lot of things and created the Heart Sutra.

Nagarjuna is considered to be the most important Mahayana philosopher and thinker. He, along with his disciple Aryadev founded the Madhyamaka school of Mahayana Buddhism. Nagarjuna also developed the Prajnaparamita sutras. According to a legend, he brought these texts from the Nagas or divine snakes. He also wrote many treatises on Rasayana and was the head of the Nalanda University for many years.

Not a lot is known about the life of Nagarjuna, and whatever information we have is from legends, accounts, and sometimes myths written about him in China and Tibet many years after his death. According to certain legends, Nagarjuna was born in

South India and was an advisor of a Satavahana (an ancient Indian dynasty) king. According to other sources, Nagarjuna was a Brahman from the Vidarbha region in the western state of Maharashtra in India.

Nagarjuna Writing and Philosophy

A large number of important Buddhist texts are attributed to Nagarjuna; however, many of these claims have little to no evidence to back them up. Even today, a huge debate continues regarding his contribution to Buddhism. However, everyone agrees that Nagarjuna definitely wrote the Mulamadhyamakakarika (Fundamental Verses on the Middle Way). According to other sources Nagarjuna wrote Sunyatasaptati (Seventy Verses on Emptiness); Mulamadhyamaka-karika (Fundamental Verses of the Middle Way); Vyavaharasiddhi (Proof of Convention); Yuktiaika (Sixty Verses on Reasoning); Bodhicittavivaraa (Exposition of the Enlightened Mind); Vigrahavyavartani (The End of Disputes); Catustava (Hymn to the Absolute Reality); Vaidalyaprakaraa (Pulverizing the Categories); Bodhisabhara (Requisites of Enlightenment); Ratnavali (Precious Garland); Suhllekha (Letter to a Good Friend); and Pratityasamutpadahdayakarika (Constituents of Dependent Arising).

Nagarjuna was well aware of many sects, religions, Sravaka philosophies, etc. that existed in his times. He was a scholar of gigantic merit. He was mainly focused on the concept of Shunyata or emptiness.

Other Schools of Buddhism

Zen and the Ch'an Sect of Buddhism

The Ch'an sect, also known as the Ching'T'u sect, is often described as the faith of wisdom. It inspired the Zen school of Buddhism in Japan. Ch'an stands for meditation. Its four main principles are:

- A special transmission outside of the doctrines

- The written word is not an authority

- Pointing at the heart of man directly

- Understanding one's nature and becoming a Buddha

The origins of this sect cannot be traced, as they are confusing and unclear. Some people believe that the early leaders of this sect were mythical/legendary, while others believe that they were real. Ch'an truly became a distinct sect when its sixth patriarch Hui-Neng spent around 15 years meditating in hills.

Zen Buddhism is a distinct version of the Ch'an School. It was brought to Japan from China in the reign of the Chinese Sung Dynasty around the 10th century by a Chinese monk called Huineng. Zen was not a popular sect in the beginning; however, in the 12th century, it became popular rapidly.

The aesthetics of Ch'an has had a great impact on East Asian art. Ch'an artists did not care for symmetry and figures present in the Sino-Indian tradition. For them trying to get as much as possible from each shade or line was essential. For them, art became a contemplative exercise, and for the viewers, it turned into a form of meditation.

School of Pure Land

The School of Pure Land, also known as the School of Pure Thought in Japan, is another Chinese school of Buddhism that has many practitioners all over the world. Its inception can be traced back to 500 CE. It started as a form of worship of Amitabha Buddha, Buddha of the Western paradise. What makes this form of Buddhism different than the Ch'an School is that it focuses and strongly recommends idolatry. The School of Pure Land is not as strong as the Ch'an School in China; however, it has significant practitioners all over Japan.

In the School of Pure Land form of Buddhism, the Mahayana belief of Bodhisattvas and Buddha is taken further. They believe that the Bodhisattva can help people attain nirvana who otherwise would have never succeeded in doing so. The importance of Bodhisattvas and numerous Buddha's is seen through a variety of descriptions of them in Pure Land shrines as well as caves.

According to certain scholars, the School of Pure Land started in India; however, as the oldest surviving texts of this sect are in Chinese and not in an Indian language, this claim cannot be proven. Others believe that it was founded by Hui Yuan, a Chinese monk. While the beginning of this sect cannot be traced, its presence and growth in China were considerable. When it started growing popular in China, Bodhisattvas were given Chinese names, and the arts and aesthetics changed as well.

Thus, these are some of the most prominent and studied sects and schools of Buddhism that are currently extant in the world. As it is clear that while the sects differ on many counts, the teachings of Buddha still form the basic core of all of them, thus uniting them under the name of Buddhism. Many different practices have risen from the above-mentioned schools. Some of these practices have adopted the secular aspects of Buddhism to preach mental and physical health.

Chapter Three: Buddhism- Other Concepts

Buddhism is a complex philosophy with many concepts that may confuse beginners; in this chapter, let us have a brief look at some of the major and important aspects of Buddhism.

Mind

The mind is a complex concept in philosophy and science. Western scientists are still confused about the function and nature of mind and consciousness. Even the existence of the mind is debatable. Buddhism, however, believes that the mind exists and explains it extensively. These explanations still stand true after 2000 years. In this section, let us have a look at these explanations.

As said earlier, the mind is a complex concept. The Pali word for the mind cannot be directly translated and compared with the English word mind as the intricacies and details get lost in translation. To understand the concept, we need to look at the different parts of the mind that are explained in the suttas.

According to the suttas, the mind consists of the following parts.

- Citta

- Mano

- Vinnana

These three are the crucial components that one needs to study and understand while looking for nirvana. Let us have a look at all the above concepts one by one.

Citta

Citta is often translated as the mind in English; however, at some places, it is also translated as the heart. For instance, in Dhammapada, at some places, 'mettacitta' is translated as a loving heart. An entire section of the Dhammapada called the Cittavagga is concerned with Citta, which proves how crucial the concept is for Buddhism.

So what does Citta mean?

Citta is a mind that has a certain quality. For instance, you may come across words such as cittapassaddhi meaning serene mind, mettacitta meaning loving heart, cittasaṅkhāraṃ meaning conditioned the mind, vimuttacittaṃ meaning released mind, ariyacittassa meaning noble mind and anāsavacittassa meaning taint-less mind, in Buddhism. Thus it is clear that citta can have quality. Citta indicates the mental state.

Mano

The next crucial word related to the mind is mano. Citta is slightly easier to translate; however, translating mano in English is difficult.

One can find words like dummano or unhappy mind, attamano or delighted mind, sumano or glad mind, manopadosa or ill-willed mind, manovitakka or thoughts, manopubbangama or something that is directed by the mind, manobhavaniyassa or the respect for the mind, manosoceyyam or purity of mind, manoduccaritena of bad mentality and manosucaritena or right efforts in Buddhist scriptures.

The Relation between Mano and Citta

All three concepts of the mind are related. It is possible to find the relationship between Citta and mano in the Mahaparinibbana sutta. It shows how everything has a cause, and the feelings that we get from an object or event are ultimately related to the cause. These feelings affect our citta/mind. This is known as dependent origination.

Vinnana

The third word that is associated with the concept of mind is vinnana. Vinnana is often translated as consciousness in English. Consciousness is based on manovinnana or the senses of the mind. The rise and fall of vinnana, the relationship of vinnana, and other parts of the mind all are explained in detail in many Buddhist suttas.

Using the above three concepts, the concept of mind in Buddhism can be explained as follows:

Consciousness is based on stimulus, and if the stimulus is removed, the consciousness is lost. This is the first aspect of the mind. Our consciousness leads to various mental impressions. These impressions are part of mano. Mano and vinnana both have an effect on the overall condition of the mind. This overall state is known as citta.

Liberation and the Mind

The vinnana aspect of the mind is often unsatisfied. By observing and understanding this dissatisfaction, one can achieve liberation. When you are not attached to the vinnana, the mano will not function. When the mano ceases to function, the citta will automatically stop changing. Thus the citta is dependent on mano, and mano is dependent on vinnana. It is impossible to kill or take away vinnana; however, we can alter all three states with efforts and by following the path of Buddha.

The Four Noble Truth

The Four Noble Truths or 'Char Arya Satya' can be called the essence of Buddha's teaching. These four truths are mysterious and often confusing for many. These four truths are dukkha or the truth of suffering, samudaya, or the origin of suffering, nirodha, meaning that dukkha can be ended, and magga or the path to end dukkha. In simpler terms, suffering exists in the world, it has a cause, it can be ended, and there is a way to bring about its end. While suffering is often considered negative by many people, in Buddhism, it is a pragmatic concept that looks at the world from a realistic point of view and tries to correct it. In Buddhism, pleasure is not a tabooed concept; however, it does consider it to be a fleeting and temporal concept. It believes that if a person shows an unquenchable thirst for pleasure, then it will only lead to unhappiness. Nothing is certain in life except illness, aging, and death.

The Four Noble Truth contains the summary of many other teachings of Buddha and thus forms the crux of his philosophy.

According to Buddha, dukkha is inevitable, and one of the only truths of life. Dukkha is often translated as pain, suffering, etc. It is a Pali word that means pain.

Dukkha is a significant philosophical concept in Buddhism. It is closely related to pain and suffering; however, it goes beyond them. It is also related to dissatisfaction, unfulfilled desires, etc., but ultimately, dukkha as a concept can have many meanings. The feeling of dissatisfaction, too, can arise from a variety of reasons, including impermanence, pain, vulnerability, etc.

Impermanence or anicca in Pali has a close connection to dukkha. It is often referred to in Buddha's teachings. It is impermanence that drove out Siddhartha out of his palace in search of truth and enlightenment. Impermanence in Buddhism can be anywhere between cosmic to microscopic. At the cosmic level, Buddha says that the universe is gigantic, and it is always evolving and breaking down in repetitive cycles right from the beginning of time and will continue to do so forever. On mortal levels, impermanence refers to the inescapable nature of mortality and how we are bound to sickness, aging, and death. Our body can die, it can disintegrate, and it can be destroyed as well.

Understanding of this impermanence allows us to understand the universality of dukkha. Buddha says that dukkha is omnipresent and is felt and experienced by everyone.

Karma

The concept of Karma is common in many Indian philosophical schools. It has also found a comfortable place in popular culture in the West. Many people think that karma means preordained fate; however, this is a myth. Karma is nothing but the good or bad deeds that people do during their lifetime. Karma is often translated as 'credit' in South East Asian nations. Good actions can either be genuinely positive actions such as charity, meditation, generosity, etc. or they can also be actions devoid of negativity. Bad actions are negative in nature. They include stealing, lying, killing, bringing unhappiness to others, etc. The weight of karma depends on many different things, they include: whether the action you did of repeated and done frequently, whether it was an intentional action, whether you regret the action, whether you did a bad action towards a person who had done a good action for you, whether the action was performed against an extraordinary person etc. Good actions beget good karma, while bad actions lead to bad karma. Along with these two, there is another form of karma, which is known as neutral karma. Neutral karma has no benefits or cons. It is gained from activities such as eating, breathing, sleeping, etc.

The Cycle of Rebirth

In Buddhism, the cycle of rebirth is controlled by karma. According to Buddhism, a person can be born in one of six different planes available. The people who did good actions get reborn in one of the three positive realms. The people who did mostly bad actions in their lifetime are sent to one of the remaining three, negative realm. The positive realms are named after demigods, gods, and human beings. The gods and demigods love the gratification; however, they can also be jealous. The realm of man or human beings is the topmost realm. It is the highest realm of rebirth. While this realm is not as attractive as the ones with demigod and gods, it is still safe and conflict-free. The three negative realms are animal realm, ghost realm, and hell itself.

The realm of man is also at the top because it allows people to devote their lives to the pursuit of nirvana once again. This is impossible in other realms. If the number and types of living things are to be taken into account, it is easy to say that getting a human birth is rare and should be celebrated.

Buddhism and Happiness

Buddha believed that the way of happiness begins by understanding the cause of suffering. Suffering forms a crucial part of Buddhism. No wonder many people reject Buddha as a pessimist. Thinking of Buddha as a pessimist is misguided and wrong. Buddha was concerned with suffering and pain, not because he liked them; it was because he wanted to understand them. As a doctor, Buddha looked at suffering clinically, and he wanted to treat it. The medicine that Buddha found for suffering was summarized in his teachings. However, like every other illness, the illness of suffering or dukkha can only be cured when the patient follows the advice of the doctor. If the path shown by Buddha is followed properly, you will be able to understand pain and suffering.

The treatment for suffering is a complex medicine. You need to practice mindful thoughts and actions daily. You need to concentrate on your feelings, emotions, and experience. One of the best ways to do this is by meditation. Many people think of meditation as a way of escaping or getting detached from the world. This is a myth; meditation is not an escapist's paradise; rather, it is a complex way of training the mind not to dwell on things, whether past or future. The present is far more important than the future or the past in Buddhism.

The way we act, live, and behave is a result of what we think. Our existence is firmly rooted in our thoughts. Our thoughts and actions can control our feelings and our fate, as well. For instance, if you speak or act negatively, you will feel pain.

As said earlier, suffering is a crucial concept in Buddhism, but happiness is the nucleus around which Buddhism revolves. Almost all the contemporaries of Buddha described him as 'ever-smiling.' Even the ancient and current portrayals of Buddha almost always depict him with a mysterious and mystique smile. It is not the smile of a celebrated man; neither is it the sign of a man indulged in hedonistic ways. Buddha's smile is far subtler because it comes from a deep understanding of the world. It comes from equanimity or the peace of mind and happiness.

Many people believe that happiness can only be begotten from materialistic pleasures. This belief has become even more prevalent in the current consumerist society. Buddhists, however, look for happiness in a very different place. In Buddhism, true happiness can be achieved with the help of knowledge and practice. While you may receive momentary pleasure from hedonistic activities, however momentary pleasure does not equal to true happiness. True happiness is equanimity or peace of mind. This peace of mind can only be achieved by detaching yourself from needs, desires, passions, and other factors that produce dukkha or suffering. If you can achieve such a mental state, then you become free and reach a state of transcendent happiness.

Buddha believed that mental dysfunction has its roots in mind. This is why Buddha encouraged his followers to seek 'tranquility' along with 'insight.' He believed that these mental qualities would lead his followers to nirvana. You will find more about this in the Eightfold Path. Ultimately Buddha believed that the right mindfulness, right efforts, and right concentration could lead everyone towards happiness.

In one of his sermons, Buddha compared the mind to a wild horse. In his Eightfold Path, Buddha asks his followers to practice the 'right effort.' In this, he advises them to clean their minds of unwholesome and negative thoughts. Once this cleansing is done, one can achieve true tranquility with the help of positive thinking. This is a continuous and ongoing effort that is accompanied with meditation and mindfulness. Let us have a brief look at mindfulness now.

Mindfulness

Mindfulness is considered to be one of the most important teachings of Buddha. It has had widespread influence and is now practiced by many non-Buddhists as well. It also finds an important place in modern psychotherapy, along with the popular culture. Buddha believed that right mindfulness was necessary for every aspect of our lives. This allows us to see things for what they really are. He wanted his followers to 'take things slow' and observe things. He encouraged them to develop a keen sense of attention, along with awareness. According to Buddha, the following are the four foundations of mindfulness.

- Contemplation of the body

- Contemplation of feelings

- Contemplation of states of mind

- Contemplation of phenomena

In simpler words, mindfulness is experiencing every little moment with openness and freshness. Buddha believed that with proper mindfulness, everyone could free themselves from cravings and passions.

Meditation

There are various different practices that come under the Buddhist concept of meditation. Right Concentration holds a special place in Buddhism. It is one of the major practices, which form the basis of many other, far more complex meditations, and practices.

According to Shakyamuni Buddha, Deep Meditation has four stages of concentration. These stages are as follows:

- First Stage: In the first stage, the mind slowly starts becoming pure and calm. All negativity is slowly drained from the mind.

- Second Stage: In the second stage, all activities of the mind and mental hindrances disappear. A feeling of bliss fills the mind.

- Third Stage: In this stage, the mind slowly starts becoming empty. The feeling of bliss disappears, leaving behind a faint sense of happiness.

- Fourth Stage: This is the last stage of concentration in deep meditation. In this stage, the mind truly becomes empty, and even the fleeting sense of bliss disappears. A feeling of total peace and emptiness descends on your mind. Buddha called this state a state of deep happiness.

Compassion

Buddha is well known around the world for his compassion and love. He preached the truth, but he also saw compassion because he believed that true happiness could only be gained when others are happy as well. Buddha not only preached this but also adhered to it strictly, in life as well as death. It is believed that Buddha achieved nirvana just because he wanted to teach the way of transcendence to others. It is also said that one of Buddha's followers poisoned him accidentally. Buddha did not get angry with this follower; rather, he said that the meal was one of the two most blessed meals that he had ever had in his life. The first blessed meal was the meal that he consumed to break his fast under the Bodhi tree, which showed him the way to nirvana, and the second, poisoned meal, which would lead him to the way of Mahanirvana.

Ultimately, the path to attain a deeper form of happiness is difficult because you need to face the fact that life is considered to be full of dukkha in Buddhism. Buddhism is closely associated with the mind and its various conditions, including emotions, feelings, etc. It believes that only by understanding the mind properly, one can achieve true happiness.

Buddhism in the Modern World

Buddhism is rapidly becoming one of the most prominent and popular faiths around the world. There are numerous Buddhist centers and shrines in European nations, South America, Africa, North America, Australia, etc. Buddhism has spread around not only in the western capitalist societies but also in socialist nations. Even in small nations like Poland, there are more than five thousand Buddhist practitioners. Why is it so that a thousands years old religion is suddenly gaining such widespread attention all over?

The appeal of Buddhism can be traced to its rational and scientific attitude. In Buddhism, you are taught to critic things. As Buddha said, "Never believe in anything that I preach just because you respect me, go ahead and test it, analyze it as if you were shopping for gold." This non-dogmatic approach is quite compatible with the psyche of the modern people.

Many current prominent leaders of various Buddhist schools, such as the Dalai Lama and others, have been invited to talk and discuss matters of great importance with eminent scientists. They have discussed the nature and essence of reality, along with many other things. Buddha preached that all our sufferings and problems are a result of not understanding the true nature of reality. This confusion leads to pain. If people had an awareness of who we are and why we are in this world etc. it would not create problems and confusion. Thus Buddha taught his followers to cultivate a questioning, inquisitive, curious nature. Many Buddhist leaders have proclaimed that if scientists prove that something that Buddha preached or followed is a superstition or incorrect, they would gladly drop it from their practice and instead take up the new scientific proof and preach it. This kind of approach is rarely seen in other religions, which makes Buddhism attractive.

The all-accepting and curious nature of Buddhism is not a new thing. Teachers and monks adapted Buddhism to the culture of each new society they visited, which facilitated its spread. Similarly, modern teachers are more than ready to assimilate, adapt, and adapt to new things. Ultimately, rationality is a crucial point in Buddhism.

Buddha taught many different methods of preaching, teaching, and learning because he had many different students who came from many different cultural, social, economic, and otherwise backgrounds. He knew that people would change even more in the future, and only one form or method of teaching would work. For example, we love eating different types of foods and wearing different types of clothes. Instead, imagine if we had only one type of food available, we would soon get tired of it. Similarly, it is possible this one type of food may or may not appeal to everyone. This is why Buddha taught many different methods according to the wide spectrum of tastes of people. Ultimately the objective of Buddhism is overcoming problems with our efforts and realizing our potential.

Buddhism is one of the few, or perhaps the only religion in the world that emphasizes a rational approach, critical thinking, and scientific attitude, and aptitude. Buddha believed that a person could not be truly wise until he or she develops logic and rationality. Buddhism presents a clear picture of how various experiences in life happen and how a person should deal with them in a way that will not cause anyone pain. Buddhism teaches followers to question things. It tells them that they should never accept a thing on its face value before thinking about it. It strictly promotes critical thinking and vehemently opposes blind faith. Nothing is to be considered sacred until you yourself test it out. If the results positive, only then a person is allowed to believe it.

Nowadays, consumers have become smart, and they do not purchase anything until they examine it properly. For instance, nobody likes to buy a car without test-driving it. Similarly, you should never accept something without testing it. This includes the philosophy of life and religion, as well. Do not make a life-changing choice without check whether it would suit your lifestyle or not. This is why a lot of people in the 21st century are moving on to Buddhism. As said earlier, in Buddhism, scientific inquiry is a must. This sits well with modern times- a fact that has made Buddhism so popular all around the world.

In certain Western nations such as Switzerland and the USA, psychology is considered to be a significant subject. Many Buddhist teachers present Buddhism through the lens of psychology in these nations. In nations that focus more on devotion and preaching, such as Latin America and Southern Europe, the teachers preach a devotional version of Buddhism. People who love chanting mantras really like the devotional method of preaching. In the Northern European nations, however, the teachers preach in a far more intelligent way.

Thus the style of preaching changes according to the nature of people and cultural demands.

Many nations in Eastern Europe live in abject poverty and violence. Such people find the presence of Buddha soothing in their lives. They believe that Buddhism can fill the empty space in their lives. Buddhism teaches people that working hard and making efforts can really help. It also makes people enthusiastic and appreciative of their lives ad work.

Thus Buddhism can adapt easily to the mentality and culture of people wherever it goes. Yet, it never forgoes the teachings of Buddha. The principles are never changed — only the approach of presenting them changes.

Chapter Four: Buddhism - Ancient Techniques in the Modern World

Buddhism is one of the oldest religions in the world, and it has undergone a lot of changes and evolution throughout this time. One of the most prominent things about Buddhism is that it's highly adaptive. It's flexible, and thus, it changed and adjusted itself according to the place and time. This is why there are so many different versions of Buddhism currently being practiced in the world. While these branches of Buddhism are different, most of their core principles remain the same. These principles are ancient, yet they are still relevant to modern times. In this chapter, let us have a look at these principles and ancient techniques of Buddhism.

The Noble Eightfold Path

The Noble Eight-fold Path consists of the following eight parts:

- Samma Ditthi: Right understanding and vision

- Samma Sankappa: Right thoughts and ideas

- Samma Vaca: Right speech

- Samma Kammanta: Right actions

- Samma Ajiva: Right livelihood

- Samma Vayama: Right efforts

- Samma Sati: Right mindfulness

- Samma Samadhi: Right concentration

Almost all of Buddha's teachings are related to the Eight-fold Path in some way. He often explained the path in many different words and different ways according to the need of his followers. While the methods may have been different, but the essence of those many thousand discourses scattered in the Buddhist scriptures is found in the noble eightfold path.

The eight-fold path is to follow as per the capacity of the practitioner. It is possible that you may not be able to follow certain parts of the path at first; however, with constant efforts, you will be successful in your endeavor. You do not need to follow the eight-fold path sequentially; instead, you can do it according to your capacity.

The eight-fold path is essential as it promotes and perfects the three important concepts of the Buddhist discipline. These three concepts are

- Sila or Ethical conduct

- Samadhi or Mental discipline

- Panna or Wisdom

Let us have a close look at all the eight divisions of the eight-fold path and their categories one by one.

Ethical Conduct (Sila)

Sila or ethical conduct is based on the concept of universal compassion and love. In this love, every living being is included. Many scholars fail to focus on this concept and often discuss Buddhism and the teachings of Buddha in a dry and academic manner. It should be noted that Buddha taught people because he believed in 'for the good of all, for the happiness of all, because of compassion for the world.'

As per the Buddhist doctrine, a person can be perfect only when he or she posses a balanced nature with Karuna (compassion) on one side and Panna (wisdom) on the other side. Karuna or compassion stands for charity, love, tolerance, kindness, and all such noble qualities related to feelings and emotions. These qualities are traditionally associated with the heart. Panna or wisdom stands for all intellectual and mental qualities. Thus, Buddhism preaches a total balance of the heart and the brain. If anyone of these two is neglected, then the person is imperfect. For instance, if you possess only the qualities of the heart, you will become a kindhearted fool. Similarly, if you develop only the intellectual qualities, then you will become a stonehearted person who will only care for his own selfish interests. It is thus necessary to develop both these sides equally. Buddha believed that wisdom and compassion are inseparable and should stay like that.

Let us now have a look at the parts of the Eight-fold path that come under the Sila section.

Right Speech

Right speech or sometimes translated as right words includes abstaining from lying, slander, backbiting, etc. In the right speech, people are advised to avoid using language that may cause enmity, hatred, disunity, and disharmony among people. You should not be rude, harsh, malicious, and impolite. You should not abuse others and should avoid gossiping and indulging in useless chatter. All these forms of speech are incorrect and should be avoided. When you successfully abstain from these, you will only speak the truth in a simple, pleasant, gentle, and benevolent way. You will only speak things that you find useful or meaningful. You should always speak carefully with ample consideration of the place, time, and situation. Buddha believed that if you do not have anything good or useful to say, then you should keep your silence. Nothing is nobler than silence.

Right Action

The right action governs our conduct. It promotes honorable, moral, and peaceful conduct. Under this part, you are not allowed to steal, destroy life, be dishonest, or have illegitimate sexual relations. You are supposed to help people live an honorable and pleasant life.

Right Livelihood

Right livelihood means that you should not obtain your livelihood from illegal activities. It also means that you should indulge in trades that can cause others harm. This includes selling poisons and intoxicating chemicals such as alcohol, trading in weapons, killing animals, etc. Cheating is strictly banned in Buddhism. Buddha believed that everyone should earn their livelihood in an honorable way. If your means of livelihood are harming others, then it is recommended to introspect and change your job. Buddhism is strongly opposed to war and believes that trading weapons are an unjust and evil way to earn money.

Thus these three factors constitute Sila. Buddha wanted life to be harmonious and happy for everyone. He believed that such a life could only be achieved with proper moral conduct, as advised in this section. You cannot achieve spiritual bliss until your moral base is strong.

Mental Discipline (Samadhi)

The next section is Samadhi or mental discipline. In this section, three more factors of the eightfold path are included.

They are the right effort, right mindfulness, and right concentration. Let us have a look at them one by one.

Right Effort

According to Buddha, you should use your energy to prevent evil and do good. He believed that with efforts, one can get rid of unwholesome thoughts, evil ideas and can destroy them forever. The right effort also includes developing once positive ideas and a wholesome state of mind.

Right Mindfulness

In this, one needs to be aware and attentive about the Kaya, Vedana, Citta, and Dhamma. Kaya means the activities of the body, vedana stands for feelings, citta means the activities of the mind, and Dhamma means conceptions, thoughts, etc.

Mindfulness is often achieved with the help of many different breathing exercises. One such exercise is the anapanasati or concentrating on breathing. There are many other ways of being mindful such as many different forms of mediation etc.

One needs to pay close attention to the feelings and sensations that they feel. These sensations can be pleasant, unpleasant, or even neutral. All these are interconnected, and they rise and disappear within them like flames. You should try to keep your mind free of everything. You should be aware whether your mind is deluded or not, whether it has hatred or not, whether it is lustful or not, whether it is concentrated or distracted etc. Paying close attention to your feelings, and being aware of them is essential in Buddhism.

One should understand how things, thoughts, and ideas appear and disappear. People should also understand the nature of these objects.

You will find more about mindfulness later in the book.

Right Concentration (Dhyana)

The last factor that comes under mental discipline is the right concentration. Right concentration is essential because it leads to Dhyana or trance. In the first stage of Dhyana, all ill feelings such as worry, languor, lust, doubt, and restlessness are destroyed. Only happiness and joy remains. In the second stage, all intellectual activities such as thoughts and ideas are suppressed, and only tranquility remains. In the third stage of Dhyana, the active feeling of happiness disappears; however, the overall aura of peace remains. In the final stage, the whole mind becomes empty, and even the sensation of happiness disappears. The mind becomes totally blank and, the only equanimity remains.

Thus the mind is disciplined and trained carefully through right effort, right mindfulness, and right concentration.

Wisdom

The third section includes the remaining two parts of the eight-fold path, which are the right thought and right understanding.

Right Thought

The idea of right thought encompasses selfless renunciation and detachment. In this, you are supposed to extend thoughts of peace, love, tranquility, and non-violence towards all living beings. A noteworthy thing here is that the concept of love and non-violence is grouped under the banner of wisdom. This proves that Buddha believed that a person could not be truly wise until he or she posses these noble qualities. If a person has selfish desires, or his or her mind is full of violence, hatred, etc. then he or she is not wise.

Right Understanding

Right understanding means understanding and analyzing things as they are. The Four Noble Truths explain the reality of everything; thus, the right understanding means understanding the noble truths. Understanding the noble truth allows you to understand the Ultimate Reality. According to Buddhist principles, there are two kinds of understandings. One is our generic understanding related to memory, knowledge, etc. This kind of understanding is known as anubodha, which means knowing accordingly. This kind of understanding is not deep. The second type of understanding is called pativedha or seeing a thing in its true nature without any label or name. This is a real and deep understanding. This kind of understanding can only be achieved with the help of meditation and mindfulness.

From the above discussion of the Noble Eight-fold Path, it is clear that the way is an immaculate way of attaining nirvana. It is an adaptive path that can change according to the needs and requirements of the individual. It teaches the followers to become self-disciplined not only physically but also mentally, socially, and verbally. It focuses on the purification and development of the follower without involving any prayers, ceremonies, or even worship. It is truly secular in nature and has nothing to do with the popular notions of 'religion.' It is a path that can be followed by anyone to achieve true freedom, complete peace, and total spiritual, intellectual, and moral perfection.

The Three Jewels of Buddhism

The Three Jewels of Buddhism, also known as the Triratna, Three Gems,

Three Diamonds, etc. of Buddhism, can be considered to be the foundation of all forms and schools of Buddhism. These three are the core of Buddhism, and the follower is supposed to seek refuge in them. These three are Buddha, Dhamma, and Sangha. In this section, let us have a look at all these three Jewels one by one.

Buddha

Buddha is the first jewel of Buddhism. The word Buddha means 'one who is enlightened or one who is Awake.' While the word Buddha is often associated with Shakyamuni Buddha or the historical Buddha, in Triratna, it achieves a far more significant status. Here the word means everyone who has become enlightened and has achieved his or her full potential. These Buddhas are supposed to be the teachers of everyone. Them being teachers is as important as them being enlightened.

Nirvana, freedom from suffering, liberation, salvation, etc. everything comes only when you understand your own reality. Shakyamuni Buddha believed that no one could help you achieve nirvana; only your own efforts can help you do so. He preached that no magical way of enlightenment exists. It is not a secret, nor is it a gimmick. It won't come through meditation either. You need to incorporate a lot of things to reach enlightenment.

Buddha then stands for a teacher who can guide us and show us the path to enlightenment. Teaching should not be dogmatic. A teacher should provide his or her student's tools through which they can learn, study, and develop themselves.

It is, therefore, the historical Buddha believes that all followers should take refuge in Buddha. This forms the first line of the Trisharan (The Three Refuge): Buddham Sharanam Gacchami, which means I take refuge in Buddha. The nature of Buddha as a concept is secular. It does not mean that you need to take refuge in a religious teacher or preacher; in Buddhism, a Buddha or a teacher can be anyone, including your schoolteacher as well.

Dhamma

The second jewel is Dhamma or Dharma. Dhamma has a much different meaning. The highest meaning of Dhamma means the reality that helps us stay in a state of bliss. Dhamma is also our reality that we strive hard to understand completely. Dhamma also incorporates all the methods of teachings present in arts and science that can help up to become aware of our reality.

The qualities that we develop, the ethics that we follow, the practices that we undertake, which can lead us to freedom, all come under the concept of Dhamma. This is why some people consider Dhamma to be synonymous with religion. In Vedic Brahmanism, Dhamma, aka Dharma, also stands for duty and routines; however, Buddha freed the concept from these restraints. In Buddhism, Dhamma is the journey towards freedom.

When a follower is asked to take refuge in Dhamma, he or she is asked to take refuge in reality itself. Taking refuge in anything that is unreal is insecure, as it is temporary. Reality is not created by anyone, and thus, it lasts. Thus it can provide you refuge.

It is, therefore, Buddha believed that all followers should take refuge in Dhamma. This forms the second line of the Trisharan: Dhammam Sharanam Gacchami, which means I take refuge in Dhamma.

Sangha

The third jewel of Buddhism is Sangha or the community. Community includes everyone who seeks refuge in the three jewels and who are trying to achieve freedom. All such people in Sangha are evolving continuously and are walking on the path towards becoming Buddha. Sangha includes every Buddhist in this world.

This forms the last line of the Trisharan: Sangham Sharanam Gacchami, which means I take refuge in Sangha.

Thus the complete Trisharan is as follows:

Buddham Sharanam Gacchami

Dhammam Sharanam Gacchami

Sangham Sharanam Gacchami

All Buddhists throughout the world say this either in Pali or in their native language. Taking refuge in Buddha, Dhamma, and Sangha has multiple meanings. Taking refuge is not only a pious and meditative act; rather, it is also an act that restores your faith and energy. It allows you to have much-needed rest and serenity. Thus, the Three Jewels form the core of Buddhism.

Five Precepts

The five precepts (or Pancasila in Pali) are the five rules of training in Buddhism philosophy and practice. It is an essential system of morality that Buddhists are supposed to follow. This code consists of various ethical practices that all practitioners of Buddhism must adhere to. The precepts are rather simple and mostly deal with moral and ethical practices such as not lying, not killing living organisms, not stealing, not indulging in sexual misconduct, and avoiding intoxication. According to Buddhist practice, these five precepts are meant to help people follow the path of enlightenment. Certain Mahayana scholars refer to them as 'sravakayana' precepts, which are different from the 'bodhisattva precepts.' The five precepts are crucial to the Buddhism philosophy, and monks, as well as common people, are supposed to follow them. Many people compare these precepts with the ten commandments of Abrahamic religions and sometimes with the codes of conduct of Confucianism. In modern times many scholars believe that the precepts complement the concept of human rights and are universal in nature.

The Five Precepts are as follows:

Panatipata veramani sikkhapadam samadiyami!

(I receive the training-precept to stay away from killing living/breathing beings.)

Adinnadana veramani sikkhapadam samadiyami!

(I receive the training-precept to stay away from taking what is not mine or snatching what is not given.)

Kamesumicchacara veramani sikkhapadam samadiyami!

(I receive the training-precept to stay away from sexual misconduct.)

Musavada veramani sikkhapadam samadiyami!

(I receive the training-precept to stay away from false speech.)

Suramerayamajjapamadatthana veramani sikkhapadam samadiyami!

(I receive the training-precept to stay away from intoxicating products and substances.)

These are often recited in the presence of monks along with the Trisharan.

The five precepts were common to the overall religious atmosphere in the time of Buddha; however, Buddha found them important and thoroughly focused on them. The importance of the five precepts kept on increasing day by day, which is observed in the Buddhist scriptures. Ultimately, the five precepts became one of the main conditions of becoming a Buddhist. The nature of the five precepts changed with time and according to regions. For instance, in China and similar nations, the five precepts were developed into a sort of initiation ceremony, which a new follower must undergo to become a Buddhist truly. This was because, in China and similar regions, Buddhism had to compete with other religions. In other nations such as Thailand, where Buddhism had virtually no competition, no ceremonial or ritualistic aspect got attached to the five precepts. In such nations, people were thought to be born Buddhists naturally.

It is necessary to not only undertake the five precepts but uphold them as well. The Pali Canon teaches practitioners to compare themselves with others before hurting them. Buddhists are taught to believe in karma and compassion. These two factors form the basis of the precepts. Reciting and undertaking the precepts is a common Buddhist practice that is often done in monasteries, temples, and homes. In many Buddhist sects, it is also used in various ceremonies such as weddings where the Pancasila assumes the position of marital vows. People tend to uphold the precepts out of devotion towards Buddha and also the fear of bad rebirth.

These are often recited in the presence of monks along with the Trisharan. All the above sentences are loaded with meaning, and thus, they are often interpreted in various ways according to the need and requirements of the time, law, and place. For instance, the first precepts talk about abstaining from killing any breathing and or living being. Many scholars believe that this precept prohibits capital punishment along with suicide, euthanasia, and sometimes abortion. However, many Buddhist nations still use the death penalty in modern times. Buddhists generally believe in non-violence, which is often interpreted as opposing violence; however, many scholars disagree with this and believe that defense is not violence.

The second precept deals with theft. No kind of stealing is allowed in Buddhism. This includes physical objects and mental ideas, as well.

The third precept deals with adultery and sexual misconduct. Scholars believe that this stands for responsible sexual activities and commitment.

The fourth precept refers to dishonest speech. This includes malicious speech, gossip, lying, slander, harsh speech, etc.

The fifth precept advises practitioners to avoid intoxication. Intoxication is a loaded word and can refer to many things such as alcohol, drugs, etc. Almost all Buddhist sects and texts are against alcohol. The attitude towards smoking keeps on changing quite often, but in modern times, it is generally tolerated (for common people only).

In the West, the five precepts are considered to be major by many Buddhist organizations. Many meditations and mindfulness trainers incorporate the five precepts in their sessions, as well.

Buddhism: Stress and Anxiety

Stress is one of the most searched and talked about things nowadays. It is difficult to find a person who is not stressed today. Everyone is either anxious about something or worried about another. While it is true the world and life have become more stressful now, stress itself is not a new thing; people have felt and have tried to deal with stress since the beginning of time. In Buddhism, stress and getting rid of it is an important thing because stress often creates hurdles in the path of enlightenment. The question of stress and suffering is the nucleus of Buddhism. It was stress and suffering that made prince Siddhartha quite his pleasant life and went away in search of peace. Thus, Buddha, his teachings, and his followers have examined stress on many different levels and have provided us with many different perspectives as well.

The Experience of Stress

Stress is an extremely uncomfortable feeling that creates unpleasant sensations. Stress is often experienced in the form of anxiety and pretty. Some people also feel a claustrophobic sensation due to stress. Stress feels like a sea of pain in which you drown continuously without dying. You may feel overwhelmed by everything, and even the littlest thing can blow your fuse. Stress attacks your mind from all sides and corners it. If you are stressed, even the simplest activity such as brushing your teeth may seem like a Herculean task. A stressed person feels entrapped.

Stress affects our bodies and minds physically too. Our body gets tighter; some people also experience pain in muscles. We get edgy and afraid. Even the slightest irritation can lead to an uncontrollable fit of anger.

Many times when we are stressed, we try to find someone whom we can blame. We think that only some external objects can cause these feelings, and if we get rid of the object, everything will go back to normal. In rare cases, there might be a physical object, which you can and should remove immediately. However, stress is often due to internal situations and causes which cannot be discarded immediately.

The Buddhist tradition considers stress to be a part of life. It understands the reality of stress and how discomforting it is. It is acknowledged in the first noble truth itself, which makes it so difficult to accept. We often think that a little tweak and change in lifestyle will help us get rid of stress. For instance, you may think if you were wealthier, smarter, prettier, etc. all your problems would be solved automatically. But this never happens, they are not realistic, and you are not accepting your reality. It is unrealistic to desire for a stress-free life, which is why Buddhism focuses on helping you make sense of stress and learn how to deal with it.

Stress is often exaggerated by your mind, especially when it is not calm and is unbalanced. It is also exaggerated when your mind is preoccupied with things. Mindfulness and compassion can help you clear your mind and allow you to look at stress in an objective way. Remember, it is unrealistic to expect a stress-free life; you need to accept its reality. Instead of viewing it as an unbeatable foe, look at stress as a puzzle that can be solved with the right tools and moves.

Chapter Five: Meditation, Yoga, and Buddhism

Meditation and yoga have become quite popular throughout the world in recent times. Many people confuse them for the same thing; however, there are many differences between them. In this chapter, let us have a close look at meditation and yoga.

Meditation

There are many different forms of meditation that are advised in Buddhism, but before moving on to them, let us have a look at some questions related to meditation and Buddhism.

What is Meditation?

There are many different types and interpretations of meditation. Buddhist meditation, for instance, is the practice of exercising your mind. Every meditation in Buddhism starts with various practices that help you to become calm and concentrate on your mind only. Once you are calm and focused, you can start to investigate the truth of reality and develop insight as well.

One of the most common forms of meditation in Buddhism is breath meditation. In this form, you are supposed to concentrate on your breathing. You find the instructions for this form of meditation later in this section. As Buddhism is a family of sects, schools, and practices, different branches and sub-branches of Buddhism have different instructions and interpretations of mediation. Vipassana, a popular form of meditation, is supposed to have been taught by Shakyamuni Buddha himself. The Zazen, a form of mediation from the Zen school, is thought to be a stripped-down version of the above-mentioned breathing practice.

Why Meditate?

There are many different reasons why you should meditate. Every person has his or her own reason why they should meditate. The 17th Karmapa, a Tibetan Buddhist teacher, says that meditation can help us realize that we are full of compassion and wisdom. Meditation can also calm and relax your body and mind. But this calm and serenity are accompanied by the profound realization and a strange awareness of our existence. It can help you to cut through the entire chase, discard problems, errors, and misconceptions and instead form a compassionate and loving relationship with yourself.

Some people also meditate to cultivate positive traits. For instance, meditation can help you become courageous and steadfast. It can also increase your attention span and make you more focused. It also has positive results in your relationship. Many people have proclaimed that mediation made them more resilient.

While all the above-mentioned things are perfectly valid reasons for meditation, ultimately, Buddha preached mediation because he believed it to be a crucial tool to achieve nirvana.

What Challenges Will I Face While Meditating?

While there are no significant challenges or problems associated with meditation as such, people may still feel bad about certain things. For instance, many people believe that they can be either good or bad at meditation. This is false for meditation is as simple as breathing.

Many people are also confused about the timing and period of mediation. Buddhists believe that any time you spend meditating, whether short or long, is ultimately beneficial. Start with whatever feels comfortable and slowly increase the duration. Once you form the habit, you will find meditating relaxing and easy to do.

Some people also complain of physical discomfort while meditating. This is a common problem, and even the most experienced practitioners feel discomfort from time to time. With time the physical discomfort will go away. You can also use tools such as pillows to make yourself more comfortable.

Some forms of Meditation

Buddha believed that we should be able to meditate anywhere and in any position. Buddhist texts talk of standing meditation, sitting meditation, walking meditation, and lying down meditation as well. Ideally, you should be able to meditate while doing almost anything. Let us have a look at some of the most popular forms of meditation in this section.

Breath Meditation

Breath meditation is the simplest form of meditation, which makes it so popular. It is also considered to the base of many other forms of meditation.

Instructions

- If you have a meditation room, then move on to the second step, if you don't have one then find a calm and peaceful corner in your house and spread your yoga mat there.

- Sit down, your legs should be crossed, and feet should be flat on the floor. You can use a pillow or meditation cushion to support yourself.

- Choose a sitting posture. For instance, you can put your hands on your thighs (palm down). Sit upright and keep your posture straight. You should be dignified yet relaxed.

- Start focusing on your breath. Keep the attention light and slowly start dissolving in the space around you.

- Keep close attention to the thoughts that may arise while focusing on breathing. If you ever think that your attention has gone awry, just return to the breath slowly. This happens even with the most senior and experienced practitioners, so don't judge yourself for it.

- After the end of the stipulated time, slowly come out of your meditative state and relax. Try to keep the aura and sense of calm and openness stable — all it to remain present throughout the day.

Shamatha

Shamatha is a popular Buddhist practice that focuses on clarity of thought, calmness, and equanimity. It is also known as the Buddhist practice of mindfulness. The cultivation of the above-mentioned qualities can help you achieve deep inner peace. This practice is often combined with Vipassana practices. This combination can help you become spiritually away and insightful. Anyone can practice this meditation.

Instructions

- Sit in a meditation posture. You should be comfortable, and your knees and back should not hurt.

- Slowly pay attention to your breathing, however, only focus on breathing out. You should focus on one breath at a time.

- Acknowledge all the thoughts that come to your mind but don't engage with them. Let them float away gently. If you ever get confused or distracted, don't worry and just go back to breathing. This is also known as 'touch and go.' Whenever a thought arises, do not kill or ignore it, just let it float away.

Metta

Another popular method of Buddhist meditation is Metta. It is also known as kindness meditation. Many different forms of this meditation exist as well, but all of them begin with simple breathing exercises to calm your mind. Your mind should be receptive and settled else you won't be able to meditate properly.

Instructions

- In one of the most popular forms of this meditation, you are supposed to direct your wishes of kindness and wellbeing towards yourself.

- Slowly direct these wishes towards people that you love.

- After this, you are supposed to direct these wishes towards people about whom you are neutral.

- Later direct these wishes towards people that you despise.

- You are supposed to direct your feelings of love and compassion towards everyone equally. You may be angry with someone or may dislike them, but you still should be full of compassion for them. The feeling of love will dull the feeling of enmity. You will start feeling real compassion for the person, and your mind will be full of purity and devoid of any negativity. This mediation thus concentrates on benevolence and compassion.

Some people also chant mantras and holy prayers while performing this meditation. Things like 'May everyone is happy and calm.' 'May everyone achieve their goals of love.' etc. can be chanted to help you perform this meditation.

Once the period of metta practice is done, practitioners sit and experience the feeling of peace and tranquility for a while.

Contemplative Meditation

Another popular form of Buddhist meditation is contemplative meditation. In this, practitioners are asked to reflect on themselves in a contemplative and highly focused manner. One of the best-known forms of this meditation is 'The Four Thoughts the Transform Mind.' In this method, you are supposed to sit down and contemplate instead of wasting time on social media and other such useless activities. Let us have a look at these four thoughts:

- I possess the ability to devote my energy towards developing compassion, wisdom, and power to help others. I believe that this opportunity is precious because not all can have it. I vow to use it well and not waste it.

- I understand that life is a cycle of continuous change, and my golden opportunity may disappear. I have no time to waste.

- Everything that exists in this world exists for a reason. Every action that we commit has some sort of consequences. This is the truth of interdependence, and often our action may do a lot more harm or help than what we imagine.

- Ultimately we will be separated from the materialistic objects of this world. Everything that we loved and cherished will be lost forever. It is therefore recommended to focus our energy on being beneficial to society and develop the qualities of compassion, wisdom, and spirituality.

Guided Buddhist Meditation

Do you want to start Buddhist meditation, but don't know how? Are you confused about certain things that are causing problems with your practice? Then you should contact a Buddhist teacher and check whether they have guided meditation programs. Many institutes have specially designed meditation courses that are taught by experienced professionals.

If you do not have a meditation institute, you can also join a meditation class. This is a brilliant way of interacting with people and enjoying the benefits of being in a sangha.

Buddhism and Yoga

Yoga and Buddhism are two ancient Indian practices that have taken over the West. They have to lead to a revolution of physical as well as mental fitness. In the West, many people believe that Yoga and Buddhism are the same or are at least similar. While Buddhism and yoga both arose as sister traditions and have significant similarities, there are also a lot of differences in them that make them two distinct philosophies and practices. Yoga and Buddhism are both schools of Indian philosophy; however, they represent two opposite groups of the hermeneutics. Indian philosophy is divided into two groups called the Orthodox group and the heterodox group. The schools of philosophy that come under the orthodox group accept the Vedas while the heterodox do not accept it. The list of these schools is as follows:

Orthodox Schools: Vedanta, Mimamsa, Yoga, Samkhya, Vaishesika, and NyayaTrisharan

Heterodox Schools: Carvaka, Jain, Buddhism

As it is clear from above that Yoga and Buddhism fall in the opposite groups. Yoga believes and accepts the supremacy of Vedas (Hindu scriptures), while Buddhism and teachings of Buddha do not accept their supremacy. Buddha abhorred Vedic rituals and practices. Yoga believes in God, whereas traditional Buddhism either denies the existence of God or neither accepts it neither denies it.

In the West, the form of yoga that is prevalent is just one small part of the philosophy. The asanas or postures and the modern forms of yoga such as hatha yoga, Iyengar yoga, Ashtanga yoga, etc. all emphasize postures only and do not pay any attention to the philosophy. Such practices can be combined with Buddhism. Some of the benefits that regular asanas can have on Buddhism are:

Regular asana practice makes our mind and body sharp. It also helps us become disciplined, which is a big plus for people who find meditation difficult due to a lack of focus.

Asana practice makes our body flexible and strong. This allows a practitioner to sit and meditate for a long period. Asana practice can also help our posture.

Asana practice can also increase attention span and help people control their breathing.

Philosophically, Buddhism, and yoga share certain ideas; however, there are significant differences as well. Let us have a look at some of the similarities and differences in philosophies of yoga and Buddhism.

Similarities

- Both are ancient schools of philosophy from India.

- Both accept rebirth and karma.

- Both believe that we do not understand the reality, and it is distorted.

- Both believe that these distorted views cause problems such as attachment, desire, and anger.

- Both believe that these problems can be overcome by understanding the truth of reality.

- For preparing our minds to understand the truth, we need to concentrate and focus on the help of a code of conduct, ethics, and discipline.

- With ample training of the mind, a person can achieve nirvana/moksha.

All the above ideas are similar to each other; however, there exist many minor and major differences in the above concepts as well. For instance, moksha and nirvana may seem to be the same concept, but they are not.

Let us have a look at the major differences between these two philosophies.

Differences

- In yoga, the reality is considered to be 'Maya' or a non-existent illusion. In Buddhism, reality exists; however, our perception of reality is unrealistic, irrational, and often problematic.

- Yoga is a theistic practice where the creator Brahma is acknowledged, unlike Buddhism.

- In yoga, the final stage of liberation is the union of soul and Brahma. In Buddhism, mastering our own mind and getting rid of the negativity is the final stage. It does not involve any divine interception.

- While nonviolence, i.e., ahimsa, is practiced and promoted in both, yogis choose a more ascetic way while Buddhists follow the middle path. They are neither hedonistic nor ascetic.

Thus, incorporating the physical aspect of yoga in your daily Buddhist life is fine; however, you should avoid mixing the philosophical aspects as it may cause confusion.

Making Space in your Home for Meditation

Having a special room or corner in your home for meditation and mindfulness activities is recommended. The aura of the room will become positive. You will always feel optimistic when you will enter the room and will forget all your stress and problems for a while. It will not only recharge your mind but will also recharge your body.

There are no specific rules that you should follow while creating a meditation room/corner, but there are certain considerations that, if taken, can make your room the best place in your house. In this section, let us look at some tips that can help you transform a simple room into a paradise of peace.

1) Choose the corner/room

Your meditation room is supposed to make you feel tranquil and happy, so it is necessary to choose a room that has no negative memories attached to it. You should be able to walk into the room with a smile. It also needs to be quiet and away from noise and traffic. Your meditation room should get ample natural light. Avoid using too many artificial light sources. If you prefer dark while meditating, install ambient lights that will make the room serene while being dark.

If you do not like restricting yourself to rooms while meditating, you can also choose a corner in your yard and adjust it accordingly.

2) De-clutter

Once you have chosen your room, you should clean it thoroughly. An unclean atmosphere can get reflected in your meditation. If your room is cluttered, de-clutter it and throw away or donate anything that you do not need. Many people try and fail to meditate in their offices, as offices are too cluttered.

Keep your mediation room as simple as possible. If possible, just keep a few posters, a couple of yoga mats, rugs, a small table, and tools necessary for meditation.

3) A Green Touch

Plants and trees are the best gifts that nature has bestowed upon the earth. Add some natural elements to your meditation room. It will make it more beautiful and peaceful. Meditation deals with connecting your mind (and body) with your atmosphere and nature.

To add a touch of nature to your meditation room, you can add simple flowers, a couple of live plants, seashells, water fountains, etc. Plants that produce fragrant flowers such as jasmine are best for meditation.

4) Ambient Music

While music is often not a part of meditation, some people find it soothing and calming and allows them to meditate in a better way. Ambient music can especially helpful for people who live in noisy areas.

There many music choices, lists, and suggestions especially made for meditation available online. It is recommended to choose music without lyrics. Classical music is a great choice; however, you can also choose ambient sounds such as nature sounds, the sound of the sea, etc. Instead of making a playlist of sound, use a loop.

5) Aromatherapy

Meditation works not only on the mind but also on your overall body and senses. You can introduce pleasant and calming scents in your meditation room. These include chamomile, lavender, peppermint, natural jasmine, etc. You use essential oils, candles, frankincense, and similar products to create these smells.

6) Make it personal

If you are the only one who is going to use the mediation room, try to personalize it. If there are certain things that help you calm down, add them to your room. This may include statues of Buddha, some healing stones, bells, plants, chimes, crystals, or basically any other object that you love. But remember, do not overcrowd your room as it will distract you from your meditation.

7) Fresh Atmosphere

Along with aromatherapy, your room should have a continuous source of fresh air. Fresh air is essential for the health of your mind, body, and soul. It will keep you refreshed and active. If you normally meditate outside, then getting fresh air will not be difficult for you, however, if you meditate indoors, then select a room that is well ventilated. If your room does not have a fan, invest in a good quality 'silent' fan along with an air purifier. This will keep your room breezy and well ventilated.

8) Choosing a paint palette

The color of your room can affect your meditation, as well. Check out articles on color theory and how color affects your mood to know more about this. It is recommended to choose a color palette that matches the mood that you plan to achieve. Many people prefer pastels, while others believe that dark shades are more soothing- the choice is subjective to your needs and tastes.

9) Ambient Lights

Natural light, as said earlier, is best for mediation; however, it can become harsh at certain times of the day. To cut some light and keep the room cozy, you should install some sheer curtains. These will diffuse the light and keep it serene.

If your room has no natural light, then you need to use light fixtures. Keep the lights semi-bright and use shades and curtains to diffuse them.

If you choose to meditate outside, select a space that does not receive direct sunlight. It should be a shaded corner. If you don't have such a corner, invest in a good umbrella.

10) Good riddance gadgets

One rule that you must follow in your meditation room is getting rid of gadgets. No electronics should be allowed in your meditation room (except music player). Meditation allows you to get away from stress and anxiety for a certain period of time. Gadgets will hinder this process. Avoid having a phone, TV, video games, or any other similar gadget in your meditation room.

Chapter Six: Daily Life and Buddhism

Mindfulness

What is mindfulness?

There is no fixed definition of mindfulness; however, many people define it as a total and nonjudgmental awareness of the current moment. Mindfulness has multiple meanings because it is a state that cannot be expressed in words and can only felt. You need to practice mindfulness at least once to understand what it truly is.

The origin of the concept of mindfulness can be traced back to the Pali word 'sati' or the Sanskrit word 'Smriti.' Both of these words mean 'memory.' But these are literal translations; a precise translation would be 'presence of mind.' Buddha, once upon a time, said, "When we sit, we understand that we are sitting. When we walk, we understand that we are walking. When we consume food, we understand that we are eating." The quote may seem simple, but it points out how Buddha and his followers were always fully present for the act. Mindfulness is so potent that even when a practitioner gets lost in thought, he or she is aware of the fact that he or she has lost himself or herself in thoughts. Mindfulness is being conscious of everything that may arise in the present while concentrating on something. In mindfulness, you observe changes that happen. It is also a motion detector. For instance, a motion detector sits idle if nothing moves or changes, but it gets into the action as soon as something moves.

Similarly, in mindfulness, while concentrating on an object, if nothing moves (i.e., if no sensation, feelings, or thought arise), then the mind stays put. But as soon as one of the above arises, the mind gets into action. Mindfulness is like a dartboard where the point of concentration is the bull's eye. But here, the bull's eye serves as an anchor and not the ultimate goal. In Buddhist meditation, you are not supposed to focus in such a way where everything disappears except your point of concentration.

Mindfulness can be compared to a dream catcher. A dream catcher captures all negative and bad dreams while you are asleep. Similarly, mindfulness captures every thought, sensation, and feeling that arises while 'meditating.' But, here, neither of them caught objects are labeled. You just acknowledge them, and then they are allowed to vanish. While practicing mindfulness, each sensation and feeling that rises comes to your mind automatically. You are supposed to acknowledge it once and then let it go away without thinking about it or judging it.

Mindfulness may seem quite difficult in the beginning. It is human nature to be judgmental. We always try to judge, guess, experience, and understand our thoughts. But in mindfulness, you just acknowledge them. Don't worry if you think that you cannot do this; once you understand mindfulness and start doing it properly, these things will come naturally.

Remember, you are not supposed to reject anything in mindfulness. Mindfulness accepts everything that enters your awareness with open arms. For instance, if you practice mindful walking and certain thoughts arise in your mind, do not reject them just because they interrupt your walking. Observe them, acknowledge them, and then let them go and slowly come back to your original activity. Bring your focus back to your walking. In the beginning, your mind may wander quite a lot, but with habit, time, and practice, you will be able to concentrate and focus without any problems for a long time. Your quality of mindfulness will improve, as well.

Mindfulness has many different 'qualities.' This makes it difficult to define. However, if mindfulness is analyzed with the help of these qualities, then it is possible to understand it as a whole.

Mindfulness is one of the core meditation techniques that has its roots deep-set in Buddhism. It has spread like wildfire all over the world. While this widespread presence of Buddhist practice is welcome, it has been disconnected from its roots. Mindfulness is a great activity, but it can be made much better by accompanying it with the original Buddhist wisdom and teachings. While this disconnection was necessary for the beginning for it to spread, it has been now observed that without the base of Buddhist wisdom, mindfulness has not unlocked its full potential. There are many profound ways to expand your mindfulness. Many simple things can be incorporated in your like to make your daily life more exciting and insightful.

Buddhist mindfulness is based around the 'Four Foundations of Mindfulness.' Most of the modern-day mindfulness practices come from the Satipatthana Sutta. It is believed that Buddha laid down the principles in the 4 Foundations almost 2500 years ago. Almost all of the Buddhist meditation techniques are based on these four principles. Each of the four points provides the practitioner with chances to develop his or her mind, which leads him or her to freedom, independence, peace, serenity, and happiness.

Let us have a quick look at these four foundations one by one.

1. Mindfulness of Physicality

Mindfulness of the physicality, aka Mindfulness of the body, is the first step of Buddhist mindfulness practice. The foundational technique of any mindfulness practice is the mindfulness of breathing. This is often followed by the mindfulness of eating, the mindfulness of chewing, etc. These are some of the examples of mindfulness of positions and movements. Along with physical movements and such, this mindfulness also concerns with our anatomy. This includes various intricacies of our body, such as our internal organs, bodily fluids, etc. While people do not like to talk about these things, Buddha believed that it is necessary to focus and contemplate on them as they allow us to become complete.

A simple meditation that is recommended for this step is as follows:

Sit in meditation posture and slowly concentrate on different parts of your body. This should include your hair, toes, nails, skin, wrinkles, etc. Imagine that you are smiling at each organ.

This mindfulness is essential because it allows us to understand that our body is not a single entity; rather, it is a homogeneous collection of different elements combined together.

Through this step, Buddha wants you to realize the conditioned, selfless, and impermanent nature of reality and things. Once you realize the truth of these, you will be able to let them go and realize the truth.

2. Mindfulness of feelings

This mindfulness is also known as the mindfulness of feelings in feelings. It is easy to understand and follow. It is the mindfulness of pleasurable, painful, and neutral feelings. We feel these feelings through our six sensory organs- the five traditional ones and mind.

This is a crucial stage because it deals with the 3 Poisons of mind according to the Buddhist teachings. These three poisons are hatred, greed, and delusion.

Mindfulness of feelings talks about them in the following manner:

All pleasing feelings lead to attachments, including lust and greed.

All painful feelings lead to problems such as fear and hatred.

All neutral feelings lead to delusion.

Acknowledging feelings will lead to confusion and ultimately suffering. But this does not mean that you should not feel anything at all. You are allowed to experience joy and other emotions, but you should attach yourself to them. Otherwise, these pleasurable moments can transform into suffering as well. Mindfulness can help you avoid these problems properly. It serves as a constant presence that stops us from becoming attached because it provides us with the clarity to understand the truth of reality.

With mindfulness, you feel joy, peace, and other emotions without getting attached to things. A non-attached emotion can lead to the greatest peace that one can experience.

3. Mindfulness of consciousness

Mindfulness of consciousness is also known as the mindfulness of the mind in mind. Buddhist traditions believe that there are 52 mental formations, which include emotions such as fear, joy, anger, excitement, etc. among other things. It should be noted that feelings are just one of the 52 mental formations. These are targeted in the second foundational step, while the rest are focused on in the third stage.

One of the best ways to start mindfulness of consciousness if by focusing on the coming and going of different emotions and states of mind, including fear, joy, anger, etc.

4. Mindfulness of mental objects

This type of mindfulness is also known as the mindfulness of objects of mind in objects of mind. The phrase may sound confusing, but objects of mind are nothing but our ideas, thoughts, and conception.

Perception plays an important role in shaping our reality. Perception can be compared to a television screen. Whatever that is transmitted on the screen is real; however, the image that you see on the screen is not. The image thus is an object of mind. It is not the real thing; rather, it is just a thought or an idea of our mind. This means that we do not experience the object; rather, we experience the image of the object. But this does not mean that the object does not exist. But our experience will always be layered with perception. These perceptions often distort the real experience, either positively or negatively.

The idea of this mindfulness is to allow you to move beyond the world of perception and understand the true experience. For instance, when we love someone, we often love the image of the person that we create in our minds. Once that image is shattered, we start seeing the true nature of the person. It then has a negative (or positive) effect on our attachment. In the practice of mindfulness, this is known as the '5 Hindrances'.

The 5 Hindrances are:

- Lust or sensual longing
- Dullness
- Ill will
- Restlessness and worry
- Doubt

These hindrances hold us back from understanding the truth and thus keep us away from true happiness. These can be defeated with the help of the '7 Factors of Awakening.' They are:

The Seven Factors of Awakening are:

- Mindfulness
- Investigation
- Energy
- Joy
- Tranquility
- Concentration
- Equanimity

Buddha preached that a person needs to cultivate these seven qualities if one wants to achieve true happiness. The first factor of awakening creates a chain effect where each factor is followed almost naturally.

Ultimately, in the practice of mindfulness, it is necessary to remove the 5 Hindrances and invoke the 7 Factors of Awakening.

What's the difference between mindfulness and meditation?

Mindfulness and meditation are both important practices recommended by Buddha. They are often considered to be the same, but they are different. Mindfulness is one of the many forms of meditation, which is why many people often use meditation instead of mindfulness while describing it. This may seem confusing to a beginner. What makes the whole thing even more confusing is that mindfulness is often described in various Pali and Sanskrit terms as well. To avoid confusion, it best to stick with well defined and simple words like mindfulness.

Mindful sitting is also known as sitting meditation. Nowadays, some people also call it mindfulness meditation. Mindful walking is called walking meditation and not mindful walking traditionally. This may increase the confusion of the already confused beginners, especially the people who are learning mindfulness without any guidance.

Meditation consists of many different and broad techniques, but all of them are concerned with the development of the mind. In simpler words, meditation can be defined as a mental technique that is used to make your mind focus on an object (either physical or mental). It is done to develop, grow, and maintain the mind. As said earlier, meditation is a broad concept, and it is possible to define it in many different ways. Many practitioners also say that meditation cannot be defined; it can only be experienced.

Why should you practice Mindfulness?

One of the major causes of our unhappiness, according to Buddha, is mindlessness. The only way to cure this unhappiness is mindfulness; for Buddha, mindfulness was one of the most crucial practices that could change a person's life forever. It was his idea that a person who cannot control his or her destiny is just surviving but not living his life. While there exist many practices that can help you control your mind and destiny, the Buddha believed that mindfulness was the easiest, most approachable, and peaceful method. He believed that mindfulness doesn't just help you to control your destiny, but also your mind and your body. Many Buddhists still believe that a mindless person is like a zombie. Mindfulness can make you alert and bring back you from the land of the zombies.

When you are mindless, you are not in complete control of your mind. The limiting beliefs that are present in everyone try to direct and control your life in such a way that your ego gets protected. Your ego does not care for your wellbeing or happiness; it only cares for itself. This leads to the rise of deep-seated anger and, thus, ultimately suffering.

Along with this, the outside world always tries to pull, push, and control you. Our mind reacts to anything that happens in our life. Mindfulness can allow us to stop or hinder these reactions to save us from suffering. Many times, due to mindlessness, we react in ways that hinder our mental peace and lead to suffering. Mindfulness can help you to prevent this.

Mindfulness can serve an anchor point for you. Almost all of us live our lives in a peculiar manner where we are present physically in one place, but mentally we are in another. We do not live the present; rather, we divide our attention between present, past, and future constantly. What many people do not know is that this leads to a lot of suffering and pain. We continuously want and desire things that we currently do not possess. Along with this, we also spend a lot of time thinking about things that happened in the past and regretting them. We have no control over the past, and thus regretting past things disconnects us from the present. It is as useful as crying over split milk. Living in our own imaginary palaces is often desirable, but it ultimately leads to suffering. It can lead to a variety of problems, including stress, anxiety, pain, suffering, lack of creativity, decreased productivity, etc. It also disconnects us from the present, where we become unable to give time to our loved ones. This again leads to suffering. Instead of enjoying a peaceful and calm life, we continue to live a life with a chaotic, confused, and hurt mind.

In Buddhism, mindlessness is often referred to as 'monkey mind.' All of us have experienced this in our life. Our mind is naughty, and it bounces around from one point to another all the time. It is uncontrollable and jumpy. Only mindfulness can calm our mind as t provides it an anchor point. It is true that your mind may resist the changes in the beginning; however, with time, you will be able to control it and tame it. Once you are able to control your mind, the path to true happiness will open.

Mindfulness and meditation have become so popular in today's world because we are always busy and always connected. It has become extremely easy for everyone to live in a mindless state of being. Mindfulness can help you to get rid of this mindless state without disconnecting you from modern amenities and facilities. This is why Buddhism is growing rapidly in developed and developing nations.

Mindfulness is a versatile practice. Anyone can do it, including adults, children, the elderly, women, men, athletes, students, scientists, soldiers, etc. It is one of the easiest and basic practices of peace, self-healing, and happiness. And all of this has proved by science as well! In the next section, let us have a look at the science behind mindfulness.

Mindfulness and Science

There are a lot of reasons why you should practice mindfulness, and science is just one of them. Science has already proved that meditation is good for our mental health, peace, and serenity, and it can also help in the development of focus and attention. Similarly, mindfulness has many scientific benefits.

Mindfulness has been studied in many scientific studies all around the world. Almost all of these studies have come out with positive results that prove that mindfulness works. Many medical centers, hospitals, schools, and even Silicon Valley has started using it in their courses and curriculum. Everyone is adopting mindfulness because it truly works.

Here is a small list of various benefits of mindfulness that has been proved by different scientific research. All these benefits can help you lead a comfortable and peaceful life. These benefits prove that mindfulness is a necessary practice in today's world. Without mindfulness, our lives become dull, chaotic, problematic, and full of suffering.

Benefits of Mindfulness

As said earlier, there are many benefits of mindfulness. Some of them include:

- Mindful eating can help you lose weight. It can encourage healthy eating habits. It is particularly useful for people who binge eat.

- Mindfulness can help you live longer by enhancing your ability to fight diseases. Yes, mindfulness can boost your immune system and metabolism.

- Mindfulness can decrease various negative emotions, such as pain, stress, tension, etc. While reducing these feelings, it simultaneously enhances and increases positive emotions such as peace, calm, and serenity.

- Mindfulness can help you fight depression. While it can't make it go away completely, it can still help you tackle some of the most severe symptoms.

- Mindfulness can also reduce the effects of PTSD or Post-Traumatic Stress Disorder.

- Mindfulness can increase the density of grey matter present in our brains. Grey matter is essential as it controls and affects functions such as learning, regulation, emotions, memory, etc.

- Mindfulness, as stated above, can help you focus. It can also enhance your attention span. Limited attention span has become a global phenomenon now. Mindfulness can tackle it to make you more attentive.

- Mindfulness is all about living in the present moment. Due to this, many people have reported that they feel more love and compassion. This can also help to improve your relationships.

- Mindfulness can make you more relaxed, at peace, optimistic, satisfied, and accepting of mistakes.

- Mindfulness is great for children and their parents, as well. It can dramatically improve your relationship with your children. Your parenting skills will improve, as well. The children who are taught mindfulness will learn new social skills and become more responsible, compassionate, bold, and friendly.

- Mindfulness can also be a crucial asset for students and teachers. Mindfulness can reduce behavioral problems and aggression in students. It can also enhance their ability to focus. It can also increase their happiness levels. For teachers, mindfulness can reduce negative emotions and can tackle depression as well. It can also lower blood pressure and reduce tension. Many teachers have reported gaining a new sense of empathy, thanks to mindfulness.

Thus it is obvious how mindfulness can change your life for good. If incorporated in your daily life, mindfulness can truly bring in many positive changes.

Practicing Mindfulness

While understanding the theory of mindfulness is important, what is more, important is practicing it. In this section, let us have a look at how you can incorporate mindfulness into your life. Before beginning mindfulness, try to get it under your skin and be comfortable with it. Remember the definition that we saw at the beginning of this article. This will help you remind why and how to do mindfulness practice.

To begin, start examining everything right from the beginning of your day. Try to form a habit of checking on your mind and yourself throughout the day. Randomly ask yourself whether you are present in the present moment or not. Many times it is possible that you may not be present even in the most complex or simplest of things.

We often do not pay attention to what we are doing presently. Binge eating is one of the best examples of this. People often binge eat to either kill time or hide their feelings. For instance, if you are feeling sad and want to avoid it, you start binge eating just to take away attention from the sadness. Soon, the sadness takes over, and you focus on it, but you continue to binge eat as well. This puts in lots of useless calories in your body. People continue to eat even when they are not hungry. Another example of mindless binge eating is while watching television. We get so engrossed in it that we forget that we are eating and mindlessly consume a lot of food. This practice has become a lot more common thanks to a variety of streaming services. These services do not have breaks, and thus you continue to watch and continue to eat mindlessly.

Now that we have covered the beginning of regular mindfulness practice let us move to some simple exercises.

Basic Mindfulness Practice

Sitting

Sitting is one of the most popular ways of meditation. In fact, for many people, meditation and mindfulness equal to sitting. In Buddhism, many different methods, poses, etc. of meditation have been explained. Many people believe that mindfulness is just another name of sitting and meditating. Such people do not understand the purpose of mindfulness or look at it as another gimmick.

You can only create new mental habits when you are mindful. This means if you want to create a new habit quickly, you should be mindful throughout the day. This may seem difficult at first, but with time, you will learn to concentrate and focus without losing your attention.

Walking

Walking is another simple mindfulness exercise. It can be done anywhere and anytime. Many people like walking mindfulness because it allows them to connect with nature while being mindful. But ultimately, it doesn't matter where you walk, etc. Once you start feeling even better, you can walk anywhere and practice walking mindfulness. It is advised to this exercise only when cars and other such things are not present. Walking meditation should not be used as an excuse for jaywalking. But as long as you are taking proper safety precautions and care, you can practice walking mindfulness anywhere. Just see to it that you do not cause other people any trouble.

Following the Breath

This is one of the most versatile forms of mindfulness, as you can do it anytime and anywhere. It is also seen to be an extension of the meditation practice yet; it still posses its own distinct style, which makes it stand out. To do this method, you just need to pay attention to your breathing. You should focus on breath-ins as well as breath-outs. Ensure that your breaths are light, easy, and even. While breathing tries to stay aware of what actions you are doing and where you are.

You should be able to feel the breath going out and coming in. Do not try to control your breathing; just focus on it. It is possible that all this attention will slow down your breathing a bit. Don't worry, just continue to focus on it and do not let your attention go haywire. Breathing is one of the most effective methods of practicing mindfulness. Using breathing as an anchor is easy because it is always present and available.

This method is a brilliant stress buster that allows you to push the pause button for a while. If you are a beginner to the world of mindfulness, then it is necessary to practice it at least 3-4 times a day. This will help you to form a habit of mindfulness. Once the habit is formed, you can change your schedule according to your time, needs, and requirements.

Other Activities

As said earlier, you can practice mindfulness almost anytime, anywhere. Some basic activities where you can practice mindfulness include painting, drawings, brushing your hair, cleaning, doing the dishes, gardening, crocheting, etc. As these activities can be done passively, they are quite easy to do in mindfulness. Practicing mindfulness while talking to people is not impossible, but it is difficult, especially for beginners. With time you will develop enough focus and concentration to do it comfortably.

To practice your mindfulness, just pick up any of the above-mentioned activities and begin. In the beginning, keep the pace of the activities on the slower side. This will make practicing mindfulness easier. Always be 100% committed to that task that you have chosen. Without focus and dedication, mindfulness will prove to be unnecessarily difficult. For instance, if you are washing the dishes, then washing the dishes should become the most crucial thing in the world. You need to be so mindful of the activities that you should feel that the only reason you are doing the dishes is that they should be done. There should be no motive behind the act. If any motive or feeling arise, acknowledge them and let them go. If you continue to do things for motives, then you won't be able to practice mindfulness.

Buddhism in Your Everyday Life

Whenever someone utters the word Buddhism, many people still picture East Asian men dressed in orange, maroon, and yellow robes, sitting down, meditating or chanting mantras peacefully. Some people also think of Buddha beads and serene bell sounds. Some people also think of different planes where suffering does not exist, and only peace and tranquility rules. While all these ideas are different aspects of Buddhism, you should forget that millions of common people follow Buddhism as well. Buddhism is all about spirituality and choosing the middle way, which means not all Buddhists, leave their households, and become monks. It is possible to achieve nirvana while staying and doing your day-to-day life chores as well. In this section, let us have a look at how you can incorporate Buddhism in your day-to-day life or how a Buddhist lives his daily life.

People who research and approach Buddhism are normally haggled, frustrated, and angry at their lives. Such people believe that Buddhism can help them become serene and peaceful. They wish for balance and escape from the chaos that their life has become. There exists a common misconception that to achieve peace in Buddhism, you need to enter another realm. This is false. According to a Buddhist scholar, "A person may walk in space, another might walk on water, yet, the person who walks on earth will always be the greatest.' This explains why Buddhism is often known as the religion of the middle way. The above quote means that you should not detach yourself from your world and discard everything. You cannot lock yourself inside your house just to seek peace. This is not the right way to seek peace. Isolation is not recommended for everyone. It can wreak havoc on not only your mind but your body as well.

Allot Time for Meditation

If you want to be mindful and compassionate, you need to give it some time. Without practicing, you can neither be mindful nor compassionate. Everyone should possess a form of self-awareness so that our minds and bodies can spread out kindness and compassion in the world. Meditation should as natural and as regular as eating. We consume food for physical energy, while meditation can provide you with mental and spiritual energy. If you ever feel that you are too busy to meditate, then you need to check your schedule. A quick practice of mindfulness hardly takes more than a few minutes.

Let us assume that you are a very busy person. Check your schedule if you get any 10-40 minutes break. 10-40 minutes of meditation and mindfulness practice are more than sufficient for extremely busy people. You can also add a small session of about five minutes after having your breakfast. This will keep you fresh throughout the day. Never multitask while meditating. If you do, then the effects of meditation become zero. Avoid thinking about things like your work, bills, family problems, domestic issues, violence, etc. Try to keep your mind as clear as possible. Meditative music can help your mind to become empty quickly. It is true that emptying your mind, in the beginning, will seem difficult; however, with time and practice, you will be able to do it without any problem.

Morning Schedule

Many people have a bad sleep schedule, which means they sleep late and wake up even later, often feeling miserable instead of relaxed and calm. Most of the people wake up in a hurry feeling lethargic. Many times our tardiness creates chaos. If we get stuck at traffic, the chaos and our suffering increase. People get stressed because they do not get any time to do anything properly and peacefully. Ultimately this reflects negatively on our work as well. This creates a sort of phobia in our mind for mornings. The best way to tackle this is by sleeping early and maintaining a proper sleeping schedule.

Mornings are one of the best times to meditate and practice mindfulness. When you wake, take some time out of your busy schedule and practice mindfulness or meditation for some time. This means that you will have to wake early. To wake early, you will have sleep early at night. For this, you may have to forgo some social media time, etc. Social media is one of the most mindless things that you can do as it is addictive and useless. People spend hours together doing nothing or gaining nothing but scrolling down their feed. It is necessary to learn time management. Time management is a skill that can prove beneficial in almost all walks of life.

It is recommended to begin your day with green tea and meditation. Do some breathing exercises and chant mantras or sit down and meditate silently. Meditation opens your mind and makes you more compassionate. These feelings stay with you throughout the day. Even five minutes of early morning meditation can help you defeat stress and pressure of work. Remember, the motto of Buddhism is to spread peace and be at peace as well.

Chanting Mantras

Many schools of Buddhism prescribe different mantras that you can recite or chant to calm yourself. Many theistic schools of Buddhism consider these mantras as prayers dedicated to

Bodhisattvas and Buddha's; however, others agree that mantras are atheistic in nature and can be chanted by everyone.

Stress is one of the main culprits behind suffering. When we are stressed, we suffer a kind of breakdown. We grow hateful and start hurting others and ourselves, as well. We often become villainous and start spouting hatred. In such situations, it is necessary to remember why we exist. According to Buddhism, we exist because we want to spread compassion and peace. Even when you feel stressed, try to keep your calm and maintain a positive attitude. Chanting mantras can help you tackle stress. Whenever you feel stressed, start chanting mantras slowly and in a low voice. Always remember the teachings of Buddha and the way that he preached.

Helping Others

Dharma teaches you a lot of things. One of the greatest things that it teaches practitioners are helping and guiding others. You cannot be happy unless other people are happy as well. Everyone needs to work simultaneously to rid this world of pain and suffering. The world is full of misery, and selfishness just adds to it. If we do not help others, we, in turn, will not receive help either. Many Buddhist visit elders, homeless people, jails, soup kitchen, etc. to help and volunteer. You should also help your colleagues, family members, friends, and even the people that you dislike. Treating everyone equally in a fair and justified manner is essential to the teachings of Buddhism.

Remember, Buddhism is not just a religion; rather, it is a philosophy of living your life. Shakyamuni Buddha left the material pleasures of his palace; similarly, we too should surrender our pride and ego. You do not need to leave your day-to-day life, just change it and be mindful about it. Think of yourself as a gardener who plants the seeds of love and compassion. Our world is full of sadness and despair, and the only way to change it by spreading faith, hope, and friendship. Slow down a bit and observe things around; there is no need to rush. Never succumb to the desires of the materialistic world. The society is money-driven, but you should run after it. Spreading love and compassion should be your ultimate goal.

Clearing Your Mind

Meditation is often used to clear and cleanse your mind. Meditation has many different positive aspects. One such aspect is a clear and peaceful mind. Normally, our mind is hyperactive, and it continuously jumps from one point to another. As said earlier, the Buddhists called this monkey mind. People fail to think clearly because our mind continuously bombards us with ideas, thoughts, feelings, and other random things. This often confuses it, causing a lot of problems. This is why learning how to empty your mind is necessary as it can allow you some peace and serenity to think clearly. When the mind is empty, you become less scattered. A sense of self-direction is felt. It allows you to respond to things in a mature and sensible way. You become free of the complex web of thoughts.

For an untrained person, thoughts are automatic and uncontrollable. These people believe that it is impossible to control your mind. This is false, as it has been proven by Buddhism and modern-day psychology that it is possible to teach your mind and influence it. There are many different ways to do this. Most of these methods are related to mindfulness and meditation. Buddha believed that controlling one's mind is essential for enlightenment. Using proper concentration, attention, and focus, you can train your mind and refine it. Let us now have a look at some of the popular methods of training your mind.

Meditation 1: Focus the Mind

For this method, find a calm and secluded place. You should be able to meditate without any distractions for a long time.

Find a comfortable sitting posture and close your eyes.

Focus your attention on any one thing. It can be imaginary or real. Many people use their favorite colors to focus their attention.

Keep your eyes closed and picture the color. If you cannot picture it, try to imagine an object of the same color. For instance, if you are trying to imagine the color green, you can try imagining fresh grass. Once you get the color, stop thinking about any other thing and focus on the color only.

Other feelings, thoughts, and ideas will intrude while you are focusing. Like mindfulness, acknowledge them and then let them fly away gently.

When a sense of calmness comes over you, open your eyes.

This meditation is easy to do and can be done at almost any time of the day. You can also do it wherever you are. In the beginning, you may find it difficult to focus on something for more than a couple of minutes, but with practice and time, you will able to increase the length of your focus and meditation minute by minute. Find your own rhythm and adjust your medication schedule accordingly.

Meditation 2: Beyond Thought

In this method, you are supposed to control your mental chatter. For this, once again, find a serene spot where you can sit or lie down comfortably.

Close your eyes, and once again focus on a color. You can also focus on your breathing or any other object that you want. The object is not important; only the focus is.

If any time an idea or a feeling arises in your mind, acknowledge it gently and then let it subside on its own. Do not pay it any further attention. Return to your meditation at once.

Once again, when another thought arises, acknowledge it, and then disengage yourself from it. Once disengaged, return to your meditation immediately.

Your goal in this form is to stay focused all the time. In the beginning, many thoughts and feelings will arise, but with time your stream of concentration will become more focused. It will become clear, and your mind will become empty. Continue meditating until you feel a sense of inner peace.

Meditation 3: Clearing your Mind

After finishing the above two meditations, you are ready for the third one. You need to practice a lot to focus your mind on something for several minutes without any disturbances. Keep your mind empty of all thoughts.

Try to think of nothing. Your mind should be like to avoid.

In the beginning, do this for thirty seconds only. Slowly increase your time with the help of the above two exercises.

Practicing regularly is essential; try to do it for at least 15 minutes every day.

You may find this step a bit difficult in the beginning, but with time it will seem effortless and natural.

Chapter Seven: Buddhism and Karma

Karma or Kamma in Pali means 'doing' or 'action.' It is an essential concept in many ancient Indian philosophies and teachings. In the Buddhist tradition, karma stands for the action, which is guided by intention. This, in turn, leads to future consequences. These consequences are important as they determine your next birth in the samsara or the cycle of rebirth.

The Buddhist Understanding of Karma

Karma and Karmaphala (the result of karma) are both basic concepts in Buddhism. They are crucial as they explain how our actions keep us chained to the cycle of rebirth. The Buddhist path, which is explained in the Noble Eight-fold Path, can help us escape this cycle.

Rebirth

Rebirth is another common concept that is present in many schools of ancient Indian philosophy. In Buddhist traditions, birth and death occur six times, consequently in successive cycles. These cycles are controlled by avidya, trsna, and dvesa, meaning ignorance, desire, and hatred, respectively. Rebirth is a cyclic entity. This cycle of rebirth is called samsara. It has no beginning, nor does it have an end. You can either continue to be chained to this cycle forever, or you can escape (liberate) using the Buddhist methodology.

Karma and the cycle of rebirth are closely related, as it is karma that decides the fate and facts of the next birth. In the Buddhist tradition, any deed done deliberately through physical, mental, or vocal capacity is karma. This karma, as said earlier, will have some sort of future consequence.

Karmaphala

The results or future consequences of karma are known as karmaphala. Karmaphala literally means the fruits of action. All actions lead to some sort of reaction or results; however, in Buddhism, karmic results are different. Karmic results are the result of the intention of the action along with the moral quality of the action. Karma is more concerned with morality and ethics. It does not concern itself with the relationship between actions and their consequences; rather, it focuses on the moral quality of these actions and their results.

According to the theory of karma, good moral karma will lead to positive rebirths, but negative moral actions will lead to unwholesome rebirths.

Karma is a complex philosophical idea that has been confusing scholars and laymen alike from centuries. For instance, the question of how and why karma leads to rebirth still remains unanswered. Buddhist traditions preach the doctrines of no-self and impermanence, but it also preaches that idea of rebirth. These two ideas are contrasting; however, they have not been reconciled and are still preached simultaneously. There are many reasons behind these contrasting and seemingly confusing aspects of Buddhism, especially in the context of Karma. Buddha was not concerned about philosophical discussions and debates; he was more focused on people becoming enlightened and happy. Often in many Buddhist texts, when a follower would ask a question to Buddha, he would go silent.

In the early days of Buddhism, there exists no explicit theory regarding karma and rebirth. While Buddhism was based on these principles, they were not handled critically. It is also believed that the theory of karma could have arrived in Buddhist schools due to interpolation with other religions and faiths. In early Buddhism, it was believed that desire, ignorance, and cravings lead to rebirth.

In late Buddhism, the idea of karma changed. It was believed that intentional actions are controlled by kleshas or bad emotions, cetna and/or volition, and/or tanha or craving. These intentional actions create tendencies and impressions in our minds. These are known as seeds. These seeds mature and then ripen, which is karmaphala. Thus, to defeat karma, you need to overcome your kleshas. This will break the chain of karma and will stop the cycle of rebirth. You will not be reborn in any of the six realms once you break this cycle. If you are interested in understanding the philosophy of karma in-depth, you can refer to the twelve links of dependent origins. In the twelve links of dependent origins, the whole complex, and theoretical frameworks of karma, rebirth, samsara, and karmaphala are explained properly.

Complex Process

As said earlier, the theory of karma is a complex process. In Buddhism, the theory is not deterministic as such; rather, many circumstantial factors and phenomena are added to it. This is different than the other shamanic religion that developed around the same time, i.e., Jainism. Unlike other Indian religions, the concept of karma is neither rigid nor mechanical in Buddhism. It is fluid, flexible, and dynamic. Buddhists believe that not all present conditions are the result of karma. This is shockingly different than many other interpretations of karma. They believe that there exists no straight relationship between an action and the result it will have. The effect of karma or karmaphala is not determined by the karma or the action itself; rather, it also depends on the nature of the person who committed the action and the situation and circumstances in which the action was done.

Many people often confuse karma with predestination and fate. In Buddhism, karma is a secular concept. Karmaphala is not a form of a judgment given by an almighty God or being. It is considered to be a natural process. Certain actions that we committed in the past are reflected in the experiences that we gain in the present. But how we respond to these experiences is not predestined, yet our response too will have some results in the future. Unjust and bad behavior will lead to unfavorable karmaphala. But unlike other religions and schools of philosophy, you can choose to avoid unjust behavior.

Freedom from Samsāra

The most important factor regarding the doctrine of karma and karmaphala is how to escape it. You are supposed to put all efforts in this direction. Karmaphala is a complex topic. Acintita Sutta, one of the important Buddhist texts, says that the result of karma is one of the four non-understandable subjects. These subjects cannot be comprehended, understood, analyzed, and conceptualized with the help of reason and logic. It serves as a warning to people who try to analyze karma 'backward.' This means that people often tend to think that the unfavorable conditions that they are facing presently are perhaps due to their bad actions in the past. Buddhism avoids such explanations and rather tries to stick to the most important factor of karma, as said above. The ultimate goal of Buddhism is to escape from the cycle of rebirth or the samsara. Focusing on good deeds will let you have a good rebirth, but it will not help you to achieve nirvana.

Within the Pali Suttas

As per the Buddhist tradition, Buddha achieved complete insight into the workings of karma and samsara when he became enlightened. He realized that one could not escape from karma and its result once when the deeds are done, however, many sects and branches of Buddhism believe that it is possible to get rid of bad karma with certain rituals and practices.

According to the Anguttara Nikaya (a Buddhist text), the karmic consequences can be experienced in either this life or the next life. Former will allow you to see the connection between your karma and its results; however, the connection becomes far less obvious and apparent when the results happen in the next life.

According to the Sammyutta Nikaya, there is a difference between present karma and past karma. In the present, a person not only creates new karma, but he or she also experiences the results of his or her past karma.

12 Laws of Karma

The 12 Laws of Karma are not laws per se; rather, they are lessons that help people to live a proper life. These laws are supposed to help you to make the required changes in your life and within yourself. They help you to get rid of bad karma and allow you to collect good karma. If you feel that the world around you is crumbling, it is because you yourself are crumbling. Let us now have a look at the 12 Laws of Karma in brief.

1. The Great Law

The first law is a great law. It is also known as the Law of cause and effect. This law tells us that if we want something, we should embody them.

The message of this law is similar to the Law of Attraction. In simpler words, whatever you give out to the world, the world will give it back to you as well. This means if you want to love, then you cannot give out hatred.

2. The Law of Creation

According to this law, we need to be active participants in our lives if we want something that we desire. Waiting for good things to happen is useless. You need to work for things if you want them.

According to this Law, you need to look at things that are outside to understand what is going on inside you. For instance, if you think that your life is going haywire and that you do not like it, then you should introspect and see whether there is something wrong inside that needs to be changed.

3. The Law of Humility

This law is considered to be quite important in Buddhism. In this law, you are supposed to learn to accept the truth of reality before trying to change it. For instance, if you constantly blame others for causing problems in your life without checking the truth behind your problems, then you will never be able to change it or get rid of the problems either.

4. The Law of Growth

This law says that you ultimately have control over yourself only, and if you want to see a change in the world, you need to change yourself first. Focusing on your development instead of trying to change or control others will ultimately help you achieve the desired results.

5. The Law of Responsibility

It is necessary to remember that you are the source of what happens throughout your life. What happens around you is, in a way, a mirror to what is happening inside you. This means you are responsible for all the nastiness, the hatred, or the pleasantness that is present around you.

6. The Law of Connection

The Law of Connection can help people to remove bad karma from their life. In this law, the connection between your past, present, and future is emphasized. It teaches how you can control your present to manipulate your future and also remove the bad energy from the past.

7. The Law of Focus

This law says that focus and attention are essential if you want to achieve something in your life. It is always better to follow a single thought instead of spreading yourself too thin. If you have multiple goals, set your priorities straight and work on them one by one.

8. The Law of Giving and Hospitality

This law talks about the connection present between practice and belief. It believes that the lessons that we learn in our life are often tested.

9. The Law of Here and Now

Buddhism is all about accepting the truth of your reality. You are supposed to live in the present, and if you cling too hard to your past, you will not be able to move forward. This law believes that you should always live in the present while caring for the future and the past, as well.

10. The Law of Change

This law addresses the fact that the universe only gives you things that you desire for. According to this law, history will continue to repeat itself in a loop because you have failed to address something fundamental. If you see that things have changed suddenly around you, then it is because you addressed this fundamental issue and are now moving towards growth.

11. The Law of Patience and Reward

This law says that to achieve great success, you need to be persistent, patient, and dedicated. You cannot achieve something without any effort. Immediate results are rare; you need to work hard if you want to be successful.

12. The Law of Significance and Inspiration

According to this law, whatever you do contributes to your life and the world around you. Even if you do the littlest positive thing, it will be reflected back towards you. You may sometimes feel insignificant in this gigantic world, but you should remember that you matter. Your absence would change the universe significantly.

Thus, this was an in-depth chapter about various beneficial practices and aspects of Buddhism. Karma and karmaphala are very important and at the same time, very confusing aspects of Buddhism. These concepts often confuse esteemed scholars, as well. If you ever feel confused while practicing Buddhism or reading this book, just come back to this chapter and revise it.

Chapter Eight: Buddhism for Kids

Buddha preached thousands of sermons and ideas, out of which only a few were directed towards children specifically. There are only 3-5 sermons that target children specifically. Buddha preached thousands of sermons related to a multitude of subjects. Children have always been an integral part of all cultures, so it is quite a shock why Buddha did not preach more sermons for the children. According to some people, Buddha did not preach to children because he believed that to follow his path, it was necessary to possess a sound, adult, and mature mind. Buddhism is about commitment, and Buddha believed that the children would not be able to commit to his ideas, code of conduct, and rules. Another theory indicates that perhaps centuries ago, children were firmly controlled by the family, and thus the family was supposed to imbibe the teachings of Buddha in them. This is how education worked in ancient Indian society anyway. Until a specific age, children were taught valuable lessons by their adults, and after becoming slightly mature, they were sent off to the household of a teacher. Some people also believe that thanks to the innocence and compassionate nature of the children, Buddha did not find it necessary to teach them Dharma as they already followed it anyway.

Buddha was a father himself. Prince Siddhartha had a son named Rahula. Rahula is Pali for 'shackle.' When prince Siddhartha realized the truth of existence, he left and abandoned all of his family and materialistic pleasure to search for the truth of reality. Fathers who abandon their children have been a typical trope in the literature of almost all cultures. Normally, these fathers are portrayed in a negative light. However, in the case of Buddha, this abandoning is positive. Instead of calling it abandonment, many people prefer to refer to it as renunciation. Buddha renounced his royal duties, material pleasures, his family, and his son because he wanted to seek unconditional happiness. He knew that while seeking this happiness, the above things would act as shackles. He also knew that if he were ever to succeed in understanding the truth of reality, he would be able to preach it to his family as well.

Rahula was seven years old when he was accepted as a disciple of his father. He soon began his training to become a monk. The discourse that is associated with Rahula is known as Rahula Sutta. In this discourse, Buddha instructed his son and taught him many things about the Dharma. Buddha stressed the essence of being truthful and how crucial it is for enlightenment. He told Rahula that if he ever wanted to find the truth, he should be truthful to himself. Later, Buddha explained our actions are mirrored by the world. This means that if we want to love from the world, then we need to give the world love. He then taught his son to analyze actions and ideas before acting upon them. If the idea would lead to a negative or harmful action, then he asked him to abstain from it. If it would lead to a positive outcome, then Rahula was allowed to continue with the idea. Once you are done with the action, you should again ask yourself whether the action that you did had a positive effect or negative effect. If it brought positive effect, then great, but if it didn't, and the effect turned out to be negative, then talk about it with someone and choose wisely next time.

Buddha understood the importance of learning from your mistakes and thus taught the same to his son. He taught Rahula how important it was to take responsibility for his own actions. He also preached to him the importance of compassion and how one can cultivate it. But along with these things, Buddha also taught Rahula about how causality works and the cycle of karma. He taught how things have future reactions, along with immediate reactions. Buddha also taught Rahula the basics of the Four Noble Truths. He told him how suffering is caused due to present and past actions and how we can avoid them and ultimately achieve complete freedom from the cycle of karma.

Buddha believed that teaching children spiritual practice could help them immensely. In the era of Buddha, the children were already surrounded by an atmosphere of spirituality and instructions. They had very few distractions. The cultural practices were different, as well. Due to the combination of all these factors, instructing children and asking them to practice meditation and mindfulness was simple. The times have changed now, and getting children to follow these practices has become difficult. Raising kids as Buddhists in today's time is difficult because of the number of distractions and the changed cultural practices as well. To inculcate Buddhist values in children, parents need to form a base first. Sometimes it will be necessary for you to start from scratch. Such parents can utilize the Rahula Sutta and many other teachings of Buddha. These will make their job comparatively easier. If the parents have been practicing Buddhism for a long time, then getting children interested in it will not be a difficult task. Children love to imitate their elders; if you yourself practice Buddhism regularly, children too will start following you.

Another method of getting children interested in Buddhism is through the use of cartoons, comics, animations, stories, movies, etc. You can try to make your lessons interesting, fun, and interactive for the children. Many East Asian nations have produced significant material on Buddhism for children. But remember, just preaching will not help you; you need to make children understand how important and useful the lessons of

Buddhism can be. You should make them understand how meditation, compassion, mindfulness, love, and other teachings of Buddhism can help them in day-to-day life. You can force a child to learn something, but you can never force him or her to love something.

H. Stephen Glenn, one of the most celebrated educators and parenting guides who wrote books, including the best seller Raising Self-Reliant Children in a Self-Indulgent World many times, said how Western parents are pioneers. But he believed that these parents do not understand the benefits of being a pioneer.

Parents all over the world learn the skills of parenting from their parents, elders, family members, neighbors, etc. We copy the skills and methods of others. Due to this, all of us have similar parenting skills and methodology. Another reason why these skills are similar is that all of us live in the same community. The community as a whole shares values, emotions, and goals. This is was highly common in the ancient, medieval, and to some extent, pre-world war world. But after the World Wars, cultural traditions changed. Many different factors changed how we lived, interacted with each other, etc. In a way, cultural harmony and the feeling of the community changed forever. The Depression, industrial boom, rapid rise of capitalism, continuous wars, cold war, the explosion of technology, and money changed our world forever. The role and methodology of parenting changed rapidly and drastically, as well. What was once a cumulative work, a task for the community, now became a solitary duty. Parents lost the support of their elders, neighbors, parents, experts, etc. and parenting became a struggle for the couple. The world continues to change, and instead of parenting becoming easier, it continues to become more and more difficult. This is why many parents focus on experimenting and trying new things for their children.

This pioneering aspect often leads to positive results.

The situation of parents and Buddhists in the modern world is similar. Modern Buddhists are trying to steer children away from the materialistic world as it causes suffering. Teaching Dhamma to children may be difficult, but with ample practice, children will surely grow to love it.

Buddhism and How to Raise Children

Parents all around the world are always confused and worried about whether they are raising their children right or not. Parenting is one of the most difficult tasks in the world because if you mess up, you end up ruining the life of a whole family. While many people have adopted different modern ways to raise their kids, some parents believe that going back to the ancients can help them become better parents. These parents look for ancient methods, principles, techniques, and skills that can help them improve. Many ancient teachers, including Buddha, have influenced people for generations and have helped them find the truth of reality as well. Buddha's teachings are universal and can be applied anywhere, anytime, and do anything as well. However, as said earlier, Buddha did not provide us with any specific sermons, advice, or techniques for parenting and raising children. As said earlier, there are many reasons why Buddha did not teach his followers how to raise children. But, parents should not be worried, because as said above, Buddha's teachings are universal, and thus you can use these teachings to improve your parenting skills. Let us have a look at some examples.

1) Authenticity

Buddha believed that preaching could only reach a certain audience. To reach out to more people, you need to act and show them how things can be changed. Children do not like listening to sermons. It is difficult to get a young child to focus just on words. Children, especially young ones, love to imitate. They copy our ways. Many children pick up the way their parents walk, talk, dress, and act in public. Children are naturally curious, and they love to question and check things. They are also good observers. So, for instance, if you preach the teachings of Buddha, such as, love, compassion, devotion, wisdom, etc. but act the opposite, children we see through you and will never learn or respect you. You cannot preach wisdom and act neurotically. Similarly, you cannot expect your children to be compassionate if you act selfish and self-centered around them. Your spiritual practice will not work on your children if you do not practice what you preach.

2) Personal Practice

To teach someone, you first need to learn. If you want to raise a smart, emotional, and social child, you need to set an example for him or her. You can set an example with your own practice. Mindfulness practice is a great way to develop emotional intelligence. In mindfulness practice, we are able to empty our minds so that we can be calm and peaceful. As mentioned in the previous chapters, while doing a mindfulness practice, if a thought occurs in your mind, acknowledge it and let it disappear on its own. Do not deal with it or engage with it. Mindfulness practice teaches you to be non-judgmental, and it opens your mind. It helps us connect with our fears and hopes. This practice is crucial in households with young children. It will allow you to share your life with them with ease.

3) Surrender

Parents need to learn how to surrender if they ever want to become good parents. You should be able to surrender everything for your child. Often you will be forced to surrender things like mental peace, tranquility, sleep, and many other crucial things. But as said earlier, a parent cannot be selfish. Children are curious, young, and immature; it is necessary to let them act like children. While discipline is important, you should never overdo it. If you cannot surrender yourself, then a sort of tug of war is formed between you and your children, which leads to constant struggle, pain, and suffering on both sides. Your children will try to compete with you and will try to break your ego as well. Children are human beings with emotions and feelings. As their parents, your duty is to nurture them and not manage them. If you want to raise good and successful children, you need to learn how to sacrifice. You need to forgo your desires and wants and shift the energy towards parenting instead.

4) Let Go

As said earlier, mindfulness is one of the best ways to connect with children. Children who practice mindfulness regularly learn a lot of things about themselves. They understand their dreams, their reality, their capacity, and their wellbeing as well. As parents, we often have dreams about the future of our children. Many times these dreams are actually our unfulfilled dreams that we want them to fulfill. But these are our dreams, and it is possible that the children may have different ideas and plans. With the help of mindfulness, you can create a space where everything is accepted with love and kindness. Children can express their dreams in this space without any fear or guilt. Letting go while parenting is essential. We cannot control the fates of others, including our children. They should be free to live their lives however they want.

5) The Mundane is Sacred

Children live in the present and are often engrossed at the moment. They do not understand or even know the doctrines, experiences, and facts of Buddhism. They also are not aware of the politics, social conditions, economics, etc. around them. For children, especially younger, their whole experience and life revolves around their house. This is why it is crucial to act early if you want to influence your children. Once your children become mature enough to leave the house on their own, your chances of influencing them decrease rapidly. Mindfulness can help you influence your children effectively. It can help you teach your children how to observe and appreciate things. It can really fertilize the young and still-growing minds of the children. The more you practice it, the better your children will become.

The principles of Buddhism can really bring a great difference in the lives of parents, their children, and their family. If your children are too young, it is recommended to start slowly, or else these practices may overwhelm them.

Conclusion

Buddhism is one of the most ancient schools of philosophy. It is a complex family of religions with many different beliefs, theories, and ideas. Yet, what makes it so popular even now is scientific and rational it is. No other religion in this world is as logical and rational as Buddhism.

We live in a world full of desire. As said earlier, desire is the root cause of suffering, so in a way, we live in a world of pain and suffering. Everyone has problems, and everyone wants to live a life full of peace and tranquility. But due to the constraints of modern life and the ever-growing competition, these things have become virtually impossible. Stress has become such an integral part of our lives that people complain of feeling stressed in dreams as well. Our beautiful dreamlike lives have turned into never-ending nightmares.

Buddhism is one of the best ways to tackle stress and anxiety. A complex collection of various sects and practices, Buddhism is highly adaptive and flexible. You can incorporate it into your daily life without disturbing your schedule. It can also be included in your religious practices thanks to its secular nature. As said earlier, Buddhism is a complex group of practices and beliefs, which is why it can prove to be difficult to understand. Many people find it confusing and befuddling. This book can help you get rid of all these confusions. I am sure that all your queries regarding Buddhism must have been answered in this book. This book is a simple but in-depth guide to Buddhism. It explains the principles of Buddhism in a lucid, simple, concise, yet clear manner.

One of the main features of Buddhism is its rational nature. It makes you introspect to understand that all your problems are created by you. To find true happiness, you need to understand this and solve these problems one by one. You can neither find the problems nor the solutions outside. This book can help you find solutions to these problems. It contains various codes of practice according to the Buddhist principle that can help you live an ideal and peaceful life.

This book has been divided into eight well-researched and in-depth chapters. All these chapters contain information derived, collected, and simplified from various resources. Chapters covering basic information regarding Buddhism, such as the life and death of Buddha, the rise of Buddhism, the various beliefs and practices of Buddhism, are covered in the beginning. As there are many different kinds of Buddhism currently being practiced in the world, a novice may get confused; for this purpose, a special chapter has been dedicated to various schools of Buddhism. Buddhism contains various special codes and teachings- these include the Four Noble Truths, the Three Jewels, The Eightfold Path, etc. all of these have been covered in detail in this book. These ideas are essential for any Buddhists, and thus ample attention has been given to them. A special section has been dedicated to the place and importance of Buddhism in the modern world.

Many people are confused regarding Yoga and Buddhism. A lot of people believe that these two are the same thing. A special section has been devoted to this confusion. Buddhism is all about karma, rebirth, and escaping the cycle of rebirth as these concepts can be quite confusing, especially for beginners. For this, these concepts have been covered in detail.

Meditation and mindfulness are two essential practices of Buddhism. Both of these have become so popular that they have entered popular culture in the West as well. Mindfulness has taken the world by storm. Everyone is talking about it and how it has changed their life for good. In this book, mindfulness and many different forms of meditation are covered extensively. A special section has been dedicated to the relationship between mindfulness and Buddhism and how, by incorporating Buddhist wisdom in mindfulness, can you make it more effective and potent.

A small chapter has been dedicated to children, their parents, and Buddhism. It will prove to be an asset for parents who are planning or trying to raise their children as Buddhists.

The promises that were made in the introduction have been fulfilled. This book not only provides you the theoretical aspects of Buddhism but also guides you through the practical aspects, including meditation and mindfulness. Mindfulness truly can provide you the inner peace that you have desired desperately. Mindfulness, along with Buddhism, can help you overcome stress and anxiety, as explained in the book. Truly it can change your life for good.

Buddhism is truly a life-changing experience, but if you are still confused about whether you should incorporate it in your life for not, then the best way to test the waters is by trying mindfulness and meditation. These two are perfectly secular Buddhist practices that can be practiced by followers of any religion. Follow these practices with complete dedication and efforts. I am sure that you will soon start noticing positive changes in your life.

Ultimately, it should be understood that Buddhism is like a never-ending sea of knowledge. It is impossible to cover it in a few chapters, or even a few books. Let this book be your guide to the path of Buddhism. Use this book as a starting point to enter the peaceful world of Buddhism.

In conclusion, let us once again take refuge in the Three Jewels of Buddhism.

Buddham Sharanam Gacchami

Dhammam Sharanam Gacchami

Sangham Sharanam Gacchami

References

https://tricycle.org/beginners/buddhism/what-do-buddhists-believe-happens-after-death/

https://tricycle.org/beginners/buddhism/what-happened-after-the-buddha-died/

http://factsanddetails.com/world/cat55/sub355/item1336.html

https://archive.artsmia.org/art-of-asia/buddhism/buddhism-origins.cfm

https://www.lamayeshe.com/article/what-mind

https://www.pbs.org/edens/thailand/buddhism.htm

https://tricycle.org/magazine/four-noble-truths/

https://www.pursuit-of-happiness.org/history-of-happiness/buddha/

Müller, M., & Maguire, J. (2002). Dhammapada: Annotated & Explained. Woodstock, VT: SkyLight Paths Publishing. (Translation by Max Müller, annotations and revisions by Jack Maguire.)

Smith, H. (1991). The World's Religions. New York, NY: HarperCollins, Inc.

https://studybuddhism.com/en/advanced-studies/history-culture/buddhism-in-modern-times/the-appeal-of-buddhism-in-the-modern-world

https://www.quora.com/What-is-the-concept-of-mind-in-Buddhism

https://tricycle.org/magazine/noble-eightfold-path/

https://www.beliefnet.com/faiths/buddhism/2005/04/the-three-jewels-of-buddhism.aspx

https://en.wikipedia.org/wiki/Five_preceptszhttps://www.lionsroar.com/the-middle-way-of-stress-september-2012/

https://www.lionsroar.com/category/how-to/

https://mindworks.org/blog/buddhist-meditation-techniques-practices/

https://www.quora.com/What-is-the-relationship-between-yoga-and-buddhism

https://studybuddhism.com/en/advanced-studies/history-culture/interreligious-dialogue/combining-yoga-with-buddhist-practice

https://freshome.com/2014/12/23/10-ways-to-create-your-own-meditation-room/

https://www.depressionalliance.org/12-laws-of-karma/

http://www.thelawofattraction.com/12-laws-karma/

https://en.wikipedia.org/wiki/Karma_in_Buddhism

https://tricycle.org/magazine/introduction-teaching-your-children-buddhist-values/

https://www.lionsroar.com/ask-the-teachers-23/

http://meditation.radiantdolphinpress.com/clearmind.htm

https://matt-valentine-nr5w.squarespace.com/blog/what-is-mindfulness-guide

https://buddhaimonia.com/blog/buddha-guide-to-mindfulness-practice

https://www.tibetanbuddhismconference.com/buddhism-in-your-everyday-life/

https://blog.sivanaspirit.com/bd-sc-buddhas-advice-raising-children/

How To Meditate:

Practicing Mindfulness & Meditation to Reduce Stress, Anxiety & Find Lasting Happiness Even if You Are Not Religious, a Beginner or Experienced

Table of Contents

Introduction

Chapter One: Finding Your Why/Purpose of Meditation

Chapter Two: Origins

Chapter Three: The Power of Mindfulness

Chapter Four: The Technique of Meditation

Chapter Five: Body scan / progressive Relaxation Meditation

Chapter Six: Loving-Kindness Meditation

Chapter Seven: Spiritual Meditation

Chapter Eight: Focused Meditation

Chapter Nine: Zen Meditation

Chapter Ten: Mantra Meditation

Chapter Eleven: Transcendental Meditation

Chapter Twelve: Guided Meditation

Chapter Thirteen: Dynamic Flow/Meditation in Motion

Chapter Fourteen: Prayer even if you are not religious

Chapter Fifteen: How to Establish a Consistent Meditation Practice

Chapter Sixteen: Stages of the Path

Conclusion

References

Introduction

Mindfulness has always been a big deal in human history. However, its importance in the frantic nature of the modern world cannot be overemphasized. In *The 7 Habits of Highly Effective People* by Stephen Covey, a particular statement popped out of the book and has always been on my mind. He used an illustration in which a person was driving so fast that his tires had to be punctured to gain his attention.

Stephen Covey used this illustration to explain how **you should not move through life so fast that your "tires have to be punctured" to get your attention.** In other words, you don't need a disaster before you start paying attention to important things in your life. Unfortunately, so many people are entrenched in the fast lane of life because of the pressure from work and other things. It is good to be ambitious in life to achieve your dreams but it should not be at any cost.

When I mentioned "disaster", I am talking about unfortunate events such as the loss of a loved one or a decline in health. It is so sad that a lot of people only realize how important their health is when they have terminal diseases or psychotic diseases. In the same way, some people never learn to value their relationships until they lose them either by death or divorce. Many people claim to be too busy to take care of their physical and psychological health but will be forced to pay attention to it when things go wrong.

Some also claim to have a schedule that is so busy that it prevents them from spending quality time with their loved ones. They will only regret when they lose these precious people in the long run. However, you can avoid getting caught in the web or running too fast in life by inculcating the habit of meditation. Mindfulness is not only beneficial to your health but also to your performance in your daily activities.

Mindfulness is a simple but powerful tool that will enable you to live a happy and fulfilled life. Many people chase money so long in their lives only to realize that what they really need is happiness and fulfillment. They think money will give them happiness and fulfillment but they realized that they were wrong eventually. I am not saying that wealth and happiness are mutually exclusive; I am only addressing your priority.

Mindfulness is the process through which you focus our mind on specific things. You are alert and conscious of events in your life and deliberate about making changes where necessary. Most people are victims and products of the circumstances in their lives. However, mindfulness puts you in charge of your life. It enables you to pay attention to the minute but important details that can transform your life.

Just the same way a car has to stop and get fuel to be able to complete a journey; you need mindfulness as a person. Only those who have experienced the vitality and freshness that comes from meditation can fully explain its power. You have to take out time mediate to make your journey in life smother. There is a limit to your level of effectiveness when you keep huffing and puffing. You need to relax your soul adequately and start afresh again to get new ideas and be reinvigorated.

There are a couple of times when your mind will go through some things but you are distracted by the matters at hand. Meditation gives you a bird view of your life in which you have all the angles covered. In mindfulness, you are in "flight mode"; your mind is the focal point as you lose sight of your body. It empowers you to realize how powerful you are and have a proper view of your potentials. The resultant effect of this realization is that you will no longer be anxious and afraid about facing your daily challenges.

The benefits of mindfulness are endless and you will learn more about them as you continue to read this book. Ultimately, the transformative effect of mindfulness will enable you to live and happy and fulfilled life. Therefore, this educative book was written and compiled to lead you through the process of living a fuller and happy life. You will learn all that you need to know about meditation beginning in history and how to go about it.

This book is a complete guide that will help you either as a beginner or veteran of mindfulness. No information was left out including the kind of clothes you should wear when practicing mindfulness. This book is the solution to both ignorance and misconceptions about meditation. There are benefits some people think they will get through meditation which are not actually true. You will learn more as you progress on this memorable journey.

You only live once and you need to commit yourself to anything that will add value to your experience as a person. You have made the right choice by reading this book because it will definitely add value to your life. However, how much value you will get from reading this book depends on your attitude. If you have a casual approach to the study of this book, you will get the kind of effect a casual study deserved – no effect.

I am sure that you have other things to do with your time before you decided to commit to reading this book. Hence, you have to be determined to get the best out of the study of this book. Ensure you study this book deliberately to improve the quality of your life. The adequate research that produced this book guarantees the high quality of its content. Hence, the ball is in your court to study your way into good health and a happy and fulfilled life.

Chapter One: Finding Your Why/Purpose of Meditation

Only an unreasonable person will participate in an activity that he or she does not have any reason for participation. I know you are not an unreasonable person and that is why it is very vital that I intimate you with the reason for meditation. Just like every positive activity in life, you will have reasons to be discouraged to continue this new path.

However, what will keep on motivating you are the benefits you stand to gain by consistent and deliberate practice of meditation. Hence, in this chapter, I will be taking you through the importance of meditation to your life both in the short-term and long-term. The understanding of these benefits will help you maintain your focus in the long run.

The Monkey Mind

The "Monkey Mind" is an eastern idea that originated from Buddhism. I know the idea of possessing the mind of a monkey sounds funny but the reality and implications are critical. The monkey mind refers to a state of mind that is restless, uncontrollable, indecisive, and confused. The truth is that we all have a Monkey Mind and you must learn to subdue it for optimal performance.

You have myriads of thoughts running through your mind all day. While you are thinking about your car, you quickly switch to your spouse or kids. You were trying to think about a party, and then you suddenly remember that your exams are coming up the week after the party. The list goes on and on and it is not every time that your thoughts are on different topics.

Sometimes, this to and fro swinging action of your mind is around different parts of the same topic. For example, you may be thinking about how to be a better parent to your kid and switch in no time to what you need to do for your first son when he is back from school. We all have to battle this state of being unsettled on a particular thought for long just like a monkey swinging from one branch of a tree to the other.

Each thought is like a branch of a tree. It may sound fun to you in your imagination of a swinging monkey enjoying its day. However, in reality in the human context, it impairs your performance. You need to be able to concentrate on a thought for a while to be able to make a decisive decision that will be beneficial in the long run. Hence, it is critical to know how to control your thoughts to improve your experiences in life.

Meditation or mindfulness is the remedy for the malady of a monkey mind. Meditation is a positive version of worry. Worry brings with it irrational fears of losing your job or inability to satisfy your spouse or be a responsible parent to your kids. You will end up becoming mentally drained and you will often find out in the long run that it was never worth it.

Hence, you will have to learn to decrease the volume of the chattering monkey in your mind to focus on ways of improving your life. There are many ways you can get better as a person but you will struggle to focus on them when your monkey mind is in full motion. You need to slow down and maintain perfect tranquility within yourself to make headway in your life. There is no better way to have that inner peace than the serenity of mindfulness.

Benefits of consistent meditation

There are many advantages you stand to enjoy when you inculcate the habit of subduing your monkey mind via meditation. Below are the benefits of consistent meditation:

Reduced Stress and Depression

According to the World Health Organization (W.H.O), over 300 million people of all ages over the world are suffering from depression. Depression is a major contributor to the problem of ailments all over the world. The W.H.O reckons that it is the leading cause of disability all over the world. At its peak, depression can make people commit suicide. There are various therapies to help people who suffer from depression but prevention is always better than cure.

Stress is another main malaise many people in the world handle. The nature of the modern world makes it impossible to totally eradicate stress. However, you can effectively manage your stress level to an acceptable degree. Various researches have been able to establish that mindfulness can mitigate the effect of stress and depression.

Fang Lu and his colleagues carried out research in 2019 among 500 Chinese intensive nurses. The research showed that mindfulness negates the effect of stress on emotional exhaustion including depression. Hence, mindfulness is never a waste of time. It is vital to cut down stress levels and prevent depression. Depression is a problem people of all age categories and social status face.

Hence, don't assume that the reason you are depressed is simply that you don't have enough money. When you practice mindfulness, you will realize that there are so many things in your life more worthwhile than money. Your worth will not be based on ephemeral things but enduring values like your relationships and contributions to the lives of people around you.

Increased Calmness and Clarity of Thought

Mindfulness offers your soul unparallel serenity and tranquility. Many people live life with such a frantic pace that makes them susceptible to making poor decisions. Whether you like it or not, you cannot deny that the best decisions you have made in your life were during moments when you were not under pressure. The problem is that people and circumstances around you will make it difficult to make decisions without pressure.

However, the ball is in your court because only you have the right to choose the way you want your life to go. If any person has an influence on the decisions you make in life, it is because you gave them that privilege. Hence, unless it is absolutely necessary, don't make a decision without thinking it through. Most critical life decisions such as your career path or choice of life partner should not be made at the spur of the moment.

Mindfulness offers you the clarity of thought that will enable you to make wise decisions. Many do not admit it but the calmness of mind it a critical attribute anyone can possess. Calmness and patience are strengths that many views as "sluggishness" in the modern world. However, that assertion is false in practice.

Fewer Mistakes at Work and in Your Social Life

The product of a calm and clear state of mind is quality decision-making. The resultant effect of quality decision-making is that you will make fewer mistakes in your private and social life. You will also reduce the error of judgment at work and that will improve your performance. You are an active individual who will have to make decisions about various aspects of your life every day. It is essential that you make the right decisions consistently.

I am not implying that you have to be perfect because that is impossible. It is not possible that you will not make mistakes at all in your life. In the words of Life is a long journey in which you will make mistakes and learn from them. However, every mistake will cost you. Sometimes the damage is minimal but there are times the damage can be devastating. Hence, you have to ensure you make fewer mistakes in your daily activities. You can take advantage of consistent meditation to offer you're the fulcrum to make quality decisions and reduce the rate of errors in your life.

Focus and Clarity of Purpose

Focus and clarity of purpose are vital ingredients that will enable you to achieve your dream in life. Experts reckon that a dream is not yet a dream until it is specific, measurable, achievable, relevant, and time-bound. Hence, you have not begun until you have that specific goal you want to achieve in life. It takes a calm mind and clarity of purpose to set specific goals you want to achieve in your life.

When you live life with your monkey mind getting the better of you, you will swing from one dream to the other. You will only do what seems to appeal to you at a particular time. Your dream will be nothing but a product of current trends and turn of events. You need clarity of purpose to have a dream but that is not enough to achieve your dream.

You will face various challenges that will make you want to back down from attaining your goal. You will have many reasons to give up because of various distractions. Hence, beyond the clarity of purpose, the focus is very vital for you to be able to reach your destination. Mindfulness enables you to have clarity of purpose and focus required to achieve your dream in life. Hence, mindfulness is an important practice for those who want to make the best out of their lives.

Happiness and Enjoyment of the Present Moment

There are many pursuits of people in life but we all ultimately just want to be happy. You strive daily to earn more money, be a better parent, friend, and spouse. However, these pursuits are a means to the ultimate need of man – happiness. Many people think that happiness is a product of circumstances when it is actually a deliberate choice you make.

One of the ways you can choose to be happy is to choose to enjoy the present moment. During mindfulness, you lose sight of fear and worry and focus on reasons to be happy. There will always be reasons to be sad but there are also reasons to be happy. Hence, your happiness depends on you. The inner strength you need to focus on the positive aspects of your life and be optimistic about the future comes from meditation.

Chapter Two: Origins

It is not out of place to wonder where mindfulness came from. There is nothing in this world that does not have a beginning somewhere and mindfulness is not different. The journey of the practice of mindfulness began in the East before finding its way to the West. In this chapter, we will be looking at the background of the practice of meditation. I will be tasking you through how it all began; the evolution, and current modern trend. The essence of this brief history is to help you appreciate the preservation of this practice all through human history.

Mindfulness in recent times has enjoyed widespread acceptance among nonreligious people in the West. Various religions from Buddhism and Hinduism have practiced mindfulness for thousands of years before it began to gain acceptance among people who do not practice Hinduism or Buddhism. Basically, the practice of meditation was made popular in the East by religious institutions but made popular in the West by individuals and institutions.

However, the practice of mindfulness in the West can be traced to Eastern Origins. Hence, it is safe to say that mindfulness is a practice that began in the East that also became popular in the West. However, it is important to note that mindfulness is not only a practice found in the two aforementioned religions – Hinduism and Buddhism. It can also be found in religions such as Islam, Christianity, and Judaism.

According to Trousselard and his colleagues (2014), some commentators in history argue that Hinduism and Buddhism should not take the center stage when it comes to mindfulness because it is also prominent in Islam, Christianity, and Judaism. However, it is impossible to deny that most modern practitioners of mindfulness in the West learned about it from Hindu and Buddhists tradition. Hence, the focal point of this historical background is Hindu and Buddhist traditions.

Brief History of Buddhism

Unlike Hinduism, Buddhism has a well-defined history. It was founded by Buddha (Siddhartha Gautama) around 400-500 B.C.E. It is believed that Buddha was born and raised in India. There are many similarities between Hinduism and Buddhism and Hinduism is believed to have influenced the upbringing of Buddha. Both Hinduism and Buddhism are concerned about *Dharma* and are both from the same region.

"Dharma" is a concept that is not easy to explain but has to do with the harmony of life with the natural order of the universe. According to Hacker and Davis (2006), Buddhism is not a subsect of Hinduism in spite of the similarities. A key difference between these two religions is that unlike Hinduism, Buddhism does not focus on the ancient writings of the Veda. The aim of Buddhism is to enlighten its followers. The path to enlightenment was what inspired Buddha to begin his search and Buddhism is the product of his findings and teachings.

There are many factions in Buddhism and it began even when Buddha was still alive. Various traditions of Buddhism include *Zen Buddhism* and *Theravada Buddhism*. Most people who do not practice Buddhism view it in the light of Tibetan Buddhism and an enlightened teacher of Tibetan Buddhism called the *Dalai Lama*. Zen Buddhism began in China during the Tang Dynasty and it was called the Chan School back then before it later developed into different schools.

Zen Buddhism places a premium on intuitive knowledge which is a knowledge that is not based on reality but a gut feeling. The most commonly accepted name of the old extant name of Buddhism is Theravada. The Theravada school base their belief and practice on the teachings of Gautama Buddha. Tibetan Buddhism as formed from the blending of Buddhism with Tibetan religion.

Just like many religions, there is a whole lot of philosophy in Buddhism. Mindfulness is more entrenched in Buddhism than Hinduism. In Buddhism, mindfulness is considered as the first step towards enlightenment. Enlightenment is the process of viewing your original mind without the use of your intellect. Western mindfulness owes a lot to Buddhism because most people who made the practice popular in the West were tutored by Buddhist teachers.

Brief History of Hinduism

Just like Buddhism, Hinduism is one of the widely accepted religions among the oldest extant religion in the world. Though it is called a religion in the West, in the East, they prefer to call it "a way of life" or "dharma". With over 900 million followers in the world, Hinduism is the third-largest religion in the world only behind Islam and Christianity. It is considered to be the oldest of all the oldest extant religion but without a clear history like Buddhism.

The reason for this unclear history is that Hinduism is a product of the blending of various religions in the regions that formed modern India. Therefore, apparently, there is no particular founder of Hinduism unlike Buddhism. In fact, no one called the Religion "Hinduism" until in the 1800s when British writers referred to Vedic traditions as Hinduism. Over 4000 years ago, the gem form of Hinduism was prevalent in the Indus valley - modern-day Pakistan. These traditions are now part and parcel of Hinduism.

The development of these traditions did not stop in Vedic writings 2500-3500 years ago. The devotion to common Gods and the rituals observed in Hinduism in the modern world are in these writings. Additional texts were written about 1500-2500 years ago and these writings are still relevant in the modern practice of the religion. These writings include temple worship as well as the concept of dharma which is also present in Buddhism. Islam became a major competition with Hinduism in recent times. However, the effort of 19th-century reformers ensured that Hinduism became identified as a religion that denotes the national heritage of India.

The 19th-century reformers achieved their aims and a benchmark for their success is the identification of middle-class Indians in particular with the religion in mid 19th century (Hatcher, 2007). The Indian independence movement further solidified the belief of Indians in Hinduism. Although it not as pronounced as Buddhism, meditation has been involved in the practice of Hinduism for years. Hence, it is not possible to talk about the history of mindfulness and not say anything about the history of Hinduism. Both mindfulness and Buddhism are indebted to Hinduism. Meditation is found in the discussions of Bhagavad Gita of Yoga as well as Vedic meditation.

Mindfulness and Yoga

Many people think mindfulness and Yoga are the same but that is not the case. Mindfulness is incorporated in Yoga practices but not the same as Yoga. Yoga is a broader practice that includes various aspects as well as mindfulness. However, mindfulness is an integral part of yoga practices. Historically and presently, there is a lot of overlap between Yoga practices and mindfulness meditation practices. Body scan, for example, is common to both mindfulness and yoga practices.

Gaiswinkler and Unterrainer (2016) measured "mindfulness" among people who practice yoga. The essence of this measurement is to examine the similarities between yoga and mindfulness practices. The result of the study showed that those who were slightly involved in yoga had a lower level of mindfulness than people who were regularly involved in yoga practices. The implication of this result is that there is a positive correlation between yoga and mindfulness.

The result also implies that some forms of mindfulness and some forms of yoga are aiming towards achieving the same objective. It is also interesting to notice that the origins of Hinduism coincide with the origins of yoga. Besides, mindfulness began to gain ascendancy and popularity in the West the same period yoga started becoming popular in the West. These seeming coincidences show that Hinduism, Buddhism, yoga, and mindfulness practices are intertwined and interrelated.

The Journey of Mindfulness from the East to the West

Jon Kabat-Zinn is credited with the biggest influence as regards bringing mindfulness to the West. He was the founder of the Center for Mindfulness at the University of Massachusetts' Medical School. He was also the founder of the Oasis Institute for Mindfulness-Based Professional Education and Training. He developed an eight-week program for reducing stress which he called "Mindfulness-Based Stress Reduction (MSSR)" program.

The MSSR program was developed at the Oasis Institute for Mindfulness-Based Professional Education and Training.

Kabat-Zin gathered his knowledge from various Buddhist teachers. These teachers include the influential and popular Thich Nhat Hanh. Thich Nhat Hanh is a popular figure when it comes to Western mindfulness practices. Hence, Kabat-Zin was given an Eastern foundation upon which he developed the MSSR program.

It was the integration of Eastern philosophies with Western Science by Kabat-Zin that made mindfulness popular in the West. There is another mindfulness-based therapy called "Mindfulness-based Cognitive Therapy" (MBCT). The MBCT is a therapy developed for the purpose of treating Major Depressive Disorder. The MBCT was inspired by Kabat-Zin's MSSR. For people who were only familiar with Western science but not Easter practices, Kabat-Zin's work became a reference point thereby increasing the popularity of mindfulness in the West.

The reason it took Kabat-Zin, a Westerner to popularize an Eastern practice in the West is because of the differences in perception in these two regions. An example of such differences is an individualistic worldview that is prevalent in the West and an Institutional mindset prevalent in the East. There were other people apart from Kabat-Zin who also played crucial roles in the popularity of mindfulness in the West.

Sharon Salzberg, Jack Kornfield, and Joseph Goldstein contributed to the popularity of mindfulness in the West. They contributed by establishing the Insight Meditation Society (IMS) in 1975. This foundation introduced and popularized mindfulness meditation to both clinical and non-clinical populations. There are many other institutions apart from the IMS that made meditation popular in the West but they stand out among the rest.

Positive psychology is an aspect of psychology that is focused on the happiness of man. Mindfulness is a crucial tool used by positive psychologists to develop therapies that will make life better for people. MBCT is one of such therapies and it has wide acceptance among psychologists as an effective therapy to treat various patients. Hence, mindfulness is more than just a practice but a scientifically proven method of improving the quality of your life.

More people in the West are embracing meditation as a practice to help them live a happy and meaningful life. There are scientific evidences that validate the claims of people who believe mindfulness helps people to make the best out of their lives. Positive results abound to the effect of proving that mindfulness is not a farce but the real deal. In the subsequent chapters, you will gain more insight into the power and method of practicing mindfulness.

Chapter Three: The Power of Mindfulness

So, far, we have been able to explore the importance or benefit of meditation in your life. We have also been able to examine a brief history as regards how mindfulness came from the East and became popular in the West. However, we have not discussed what meditation really is. What is the power of meditation? You know the benefits you stand to enjoy through mindfulness. More so, it should interest you to know what mindfulness is really all about.

In this chapter, we will explore the meaning of mindfulness as well as what makes it effective. We will also explore how you can become better as you practice mindfulness consistently as well as the importance of breathing in meditation.

What is Mindfulness?

Mindfulness is not all about being mindful which will literally mean to be careful or cautious. It is not a restrictive term for self-imprisonment or consignment as some think. Instead, mindfulness involves the training of your mind to bring it to a state of stillness. It is the process of making your mind focus on what it should focus on. So many times in life, you know you are being distracted and allowing your mind to wander just like a monkey jumping from branch to branch.

Mindfulness is a psychological process in which you deliberately bring your focus on the current situation. Being able to concentrate on the present moment is not an automatic process but something you achieve through training. It takes deliberate and consistent mindfulness practice before you can prevent your mind from wandering into the future or the past.

Thinking about the future is not wrong but you may worry and fear irrationally because of pessimism about the future. It is not also wrong to think about the past but it can bring with it guilt about things you didn't do well in the past.

Mindfulness is a derivative of *sati* which is a crucial element of Buddhist traditions. It is based on Tibetan, Vipassana, and Zen meditation techniques. Mindlessness is the opposite of mindfulness. Mindlessness can be explained by those moments when you eat and suddenly realize you have just a couple left. You have been eating but not enjoying the moment. It is a state of being on autopilot mode. It sounds like fun but it is dangerous.

An example of research that shows that most people leave their minds on autopilot is the research carried out by Matt Killingsworth. He created an app with which he derived opinions about what makes people happy the most. In a sampling of 15,000 people across different socio demographic variables, the result was outstanding. The result of the research showed that people are most happy when they mindful of the moment and are not happy when they let their minds wander about. According to experts, an autopilot mode is just like being in a dream where you are not aware of your present condition.

When you are on autopilot, you will not notice the beauty of the world around you. Life will lose color to you and everything seems to be passing away right in front of you. In this state, you are no longer living but merely existing. Mindfulness involves taking the steering wheel and be the one directing your thoughts and your life. Mindfulness involves maintaining a moment-by-moment awareness of what goes on in your mind, the way you feel, and the sensations in your surroundings.

The Power of the Mind

Your mind is such a crucial part of your life that you cannot afford to handle with levity. In the Book of Proverbs in the Bible, King Solomon counseled that you should guard your heart (mind) with all diligence because therein lies the issues of life. Your mind is the steering wheel of your life and you have to be the one in charge. The terrible thing about the mind is that when you are not in charge of it, it will be on autopilot mode. It is never static but dynamic and relentless. It can move from stillness to chaos within a short period.

You know you have so much potential but you are finding it to unlock your undisputed ability. The late Miles Munroe stated that the richest place on earth is not the oil wells of the Arabs but the graveyard. The statement is intriguing and awkward at the same time but the truth is not farfetched. He was referring to great potentials that were never discovered or utilized before the possessor died. So many bestseller books, record-breaking movies, revolutionary speeches, and great business ideas worth billions of dollars have died with many people.

Hence, I agree with him that the graveyard is the richest place on earth. You are still alive (obviously that is why you can read this book) and you still have so many opportunities to make the world a better place. However, you cannot change the world until you change yourself. You have to break free from some routines and begin new ones to change your experience in life. Every great thing that has ever been achieved on earth begins from the mind of a person or group of people. Hence, your mind is the most vital part of your life. The Buddha says it all:

"To enjoy good health, to bring true happiness to one's family, to bring peace to all, one must first discipline and control one's mind. If a man can control his mind, he can find

the way to Enlightenment, and all wisdom and virtue will naturally come to him".

The direction of your life depends on the direction of your mind. Before you take a step, your mind has conceived it. Hence, you can never be greater than what goes on in your mind. Circumstances in life tend to make you want to focus on negative thoughts and limitations you have. It is true that you have limitations and we all do. However, you have so much strength as well but you will never be able to harness your strength when you don't put your mind in order. Control your mind and you will be able to control your life.

That requisite control you need to avoid your mind being in autopilot mode is what meditation offers to you. Once your mind spirals out of control, you have lost the plot. People who give up on life and commit suicide got to that point they should never get to. They allowed their mind to spiral out of control. They allowed their thoughts to drive them to make a terrible irreversible decision. There are many things that can go wrong when you are not in charge and you should never let that happen. Thankfully, meditation is a gift from the universe to rescue us.

What You Practice Grows Stronger

The most important thing about meditation practices is getting started. Don't allow procrastination to deprive you of what you stand to enjoy via mindfulness practices. You don't need to be perfect to start. It is perfect when you decide to start. Every great thing begins with a step. Rome was not built in a day after all. Hence, what is more important is starting first and not being bothered about doing it well. The more you practice, the stronger and better you will become over time. According to Nicole Byer:

"What can cake teach you about life? That practice makes perfect, and if you try something once, it probably won't be perfect, and you have to keep working on it if you want to be good at it."

I need to sound a note of warning that mindfulness is not some kind of magic wand. Most people want something they can just do within a day or two and their lives will transform radically in a positive way. However, there is no such thing as that. It is an accumulation of little efforts here and there that ends up deciding what happens in your life in the long run. A great man is seen in his daily routines. It is little drops of water that ends up becoming an ocean with patience.

Hence, don't feel discouraged if it feels as if you are not getting concrete result within a few days of practicing mindfulness. I am not saying that you cannot get immediate results by practicing mindfulness. However, it is not always like that for everybody. The truth is that positive changes are already taking place in your life from the day you start practicing mindfulness. However, it may not be obvious to you yet. Hence, don't give up because you are not having your expectations met yet. Don't give up and you will be glad you didn't eventually.

Breathing

Breathing is an integral part of meditation. Meditation involves paying attention to your own breath. You need to set out time because an interruption is the last thing you need to practice "mindful breathing". 15 minutes is more than enough to do this daily. However, you can set out more time as you practice and reap the benefits. What do you stand to gain? You will have a reduction in stress, anxiety level and focus on what matters.

You don't have to practice meditative breathing only during the designated time. You can also practice it when you are feeling stressed and under intense pressure to cool yourself down. However, practicing meditative breathing during difficult moments is not automatic; it comes with practice. The more you practice it during periods when you are calm, the more you will be able to use it during tough times. During tough times, you can start by taking a very deep breath and hold it for like three seconds before you exhale through your nostrils. With mouth, you can make it four seconds.

Breathing during meditation is as simple as focusing on inhaling and exhaling. You can stand while doing this or sit down. You can also lie down as long as you are comfortable. There are differences here and there and you will discover what works best for you over time. A little trial and error initially will not do any harm. You can also close your eyes because it is easier to maintain your focus that way. However, if you don't want to close your eyes, you can simply look at the ground or stare into space.

As you breathe and try to focus on your breath, you will find your mind wander and distracted by your thoughts and body sensations. Don't fight it; just gently bring your attention back to your breath. Stay there for like seven minutes and get lost in your breath and your thought and then your breathing again. Before you stop, relax and observe your body and savor your effort and discipline.

Chapter Four: The Technique of Meditation

There are techniques involved in the practice of meditation. Failure to do it the right way will prevent you from getting the best result out of the practice. Whatever is worth doing at all should be given the requisite attention and effort to get the best out of it. Hence, when it comes to meditation, it is important you are conversant with important things as regards how to go about it. In this chapter, I will be helping you with the different ways you can meditate and still get similar results. You will also learn about what to wear and other beneficial information that will take you from a novice to a pro in meditation.

Different Ways to Meditate

There are different meditation practices and each one requires its own peculiar mental skills. Below are the different ways to meditate:

Concentration Meditation

Concentration meditation is important, especially for beginners. It involves focusing on a particular thing or point. You may focus on your breath or a particular word or mantra. You can also consider looking intensely at a candle flame or any other activity that can distract you from the thoughts on your mind. It is easier said than done for a beginner and you will need to be happy with the progress you are making. You may only be able to meditate for a few minutes initially before you are able to do it for longer periods.

Don't feel disappointed in yourself; be happy with the fact that you are doing all you can do get better. If you don't give up, you will be impressed with your level of improvement. This form of meditation is all about training your mind to focus instead of wandering from one thought to the other. Hence, you have to make up your mind about what exactly you want to focus on all through the period of meditation. Failure to decide what you want to focus on before you start meditating will lead to chasing various thoughts.

Don't overestimate yourself because your mind can become boisterous in no time. Therefore, to avoid fighting a needless battle with your thoughts, decide what you want to be the focal point of your attention while meditating. Ensure what you want to focus on is not vague such that your attention drifts away from it over time. It is always better to choose something physical like the flame of a candle rather than a thought. Focusing on a particular thought is feasible but it is not easy. Your best bet is something you can look at or listen to in order to get the best out of concentration meditation.

Mindfulness Meditation

Mindfulness meditation is not as rigid as concentration meditation. This technique of meditation involves actually allowing your mind to wander. However, this wandering is to the end that you can monitor every mental note as it arises. The intention is not to judge your thoughts or scrutinize them but to be aware of your thought pattern. It is more like being in the position of an eagle observing the activities of chicks on the ground except that you will never interfere at any point.

This observation of your thought pattern and tendencies will give a clear view of how your mind drifts so that you can know how to curb and direct it. Mindfulness meditation will let you see how you judge various experiences as worthwhile or useless. Mindfulness meditation will eventually help you develop an inner balance for your thought pattern in the long run. Some schools of meditation combine both the concentration and mindfulness meditation techniques. Whether it is mindfulness or concentration meditation technique, what matters is discipline and stillness to focus on the activities going in your mind.

Cultivation of Compassion

Cultivation of techniques is not a common meditation technique but it is nonetheless effective. It is a technique found among Buddhist monks. It involves a deliberate imagination of negative circumstances and recasting them in a positive light to cultivate compassion. This technique is not pessimism or an expectation of unpleasant events. Cultivation of compassion is about imagining negative events and how you will handle them in a positive way. Hence, this technique is all about being proactive rather than being reactive.

No one wants to experience unpleasant situations such as betrayal or a cheating spouse. However, such occurrences are part and parcel of life that happens to even the best of us all. However, you can choose to forgive people when you see their offenses as "frailties of human beings". When you see the offenses of people that way, you will be able to have compassion and forgive them. Cultivation of compassion helps you to prepare your mind for such terrible experiences and be strong in case they happen.

What to wear

The knowledge of what you should wear during meditation is as important as the knowledge of the techniques of meditation. In fact, knowing what to wear in itself is an important technique in meditation. What you wear lays the foundation and sets the tone for how much you will get out of your meditation. You have to be mindful of the effect of your cloth on people around you if you are meditating in a public place. The color of the cloth you pick also matters because it can either support or negate the purpose of your meditation.

Wear Comfortable Outfits

The first thing you need to consider when picking what to wear during meditation is the comfort of the cloth. You should wear an outfit that is comfortable and makes you feel confident. There is really no such thing as wrong clothing especially when you meditate at the comfort of your room. You can even meditate without wearing any cloth as long as you are alone in your room. However, you will have people around you, then, you need comfortable yoga pants, sweat pants, and tank tops.

Avoid Wearing Tight-fitting Clothes

You should avoid wearing tight-fitting clothes when meditating because they will hinder your breathing. Wear loose clothing that will enable you to breathe comfortably while mediating. It is important to note that wearing something loose does not imply that you should wear a gown or any other cloth that will get in the way. However, a flowing robe can be utilized. If you are feeling numb in your legs during meditation, it may be a sign that your clothes are too tight. Pants with elastic pants are good options because they offer no restriction regardless of the position of meditation.

Go for the Right Color

The color of your outfit also matters. Every color has its own energy. Hence, the purpose of the meditation will determine the color of your outfit. The color red stands for courage and strength and encourages physical activity. Yellow engenders intellect, happiness, and creativity. White is the color of virtue and protection while green encourages prosperity and healing. Therefore, if you have health challenges, you should wear green when meditating. In the same way, you should wear a yellow outfit if you are having issues with depression.

Other Tips

In case you want to go and meditate in a temple, you have to be courteous because there are often restrictions and rules you need to obey. Hence, to avoid the embarrassment of being asked to go back because you are not dressing appropriately, it is better you call someone who can give you accurate information as regards the dress code. Usually, the restrictions are usually around not wearing something too short and seductive.

You can also consider layering your cloth. Layering your cloth will ensure that you are comfortable regardless of the environment you choose to meditate. Initially, you may feel cold but you will feel warm later. If there is an air conditioner where you intend to meditate, you can use a hoodie or light jacket. You can also get some socks to avoid getting cold in case you have to be barefoot.

Meditating Positions

Whether you are sitting, standing, lying down, or kneeling, there is a way to go about it when meditating. Below are helpful tips that will help you with each meditation position:

Chair-sitting Meditation

Chair sitting meditation is ideal for meditating while at work or while travelling. The right position for chair-sitting meditation is to sit straight back in your chair with your feet flat on the floor. Your feet should form a 90-degree angle with knees and you may need to scoot to the edge of the chair to achieve this. Your sitting position should be such that your head and your neck are in line with your spine while sitting straight. For additional support, you can employ the use of a pillow. Place it under your hips or behind your lower back. As for your hands, just place them on your laps or on your knees.

Standing Meditation

In case you are not comfortable with sitting meditation, you can consider standing meditation. Standing meditation involves standing tall with your feet shoulder-width apart. Turn your heels slightly inward by shifting your feet such that your toes are slightly pointing away from each other. Bend your knees slightly when you are in a position. With every exhale, let your body root down through your feet. Have an image of the lifting of your energy through the crown of your head each time you inhale. Place your hands on your belly to feel your breath moving through your body for additional relaxation.

Kneeling Meditation

Kneeling meditation is ideal if you are somewhere you can kneel down comfortably. The advantage of kneeling meditation is that it makes it easy for you to keep your back straight. This meditation position involves bending your knees as you rest on the floor. Your ankles should be below your bottom while shins are flat on the ground. For additional support, place a cushion between heels and your bottom. This will help you to avoid straining your knees. If you feel pain while meditating in this position, you should try another position but you should not feel pain normally. To avoid putting too much pressure on your knees, root your weight back and down through your hips.

Lying-down Meditation

Relaxation and release of tension are easier with lying down meditation. This meditation position supports your body totally. This meditation position involves lying on your back while your arms are extended alongside your body. Turn your toes to the side while your feet are hip-distance apart. Modify the pose to support your lower back if you are not feeling comfortable. When lying flat, place a pillow underneath your knees to slightly elevate them.

Using essential oils

Essential oils have nutritional value but can also be used to good effect in meditation practices. Your serenity and sense of calm during meditation can improve greatly with the use of essential oils. Essential oils commonly used during meditation include Patchouli, Vetiver, Palo Santo, Cedarwood, and Atlas. These essential oils are considered grounding. Other essential oils such as Roman Chamomile, Clary Sage, and Lavender are considered to have the ability to enhance the state of relaxation as well as act as natural sedatives.

There are some essential oils that have the ability to enhance spiritual connection with the divine. They include Frankincense and Helichrysum. You can also combine different essential oils to create a blend of their abilities. For the purpose of blending, a candle diffuser or a room mist can be utilized. It is important to note that you should understand the contraindications and safety of every essential oil before you use it.

To create a relaxation blend, you can combine 3 parts of lavender with 2 parts Atlas and 1 part Bergamot. For an enlightening blend, go for a combination of Frankincense and Helichrysum according to the manufacturer's instruction. The combination of Frankincense, Sandalwood, and Bergamot will produce a good grounding blend.

To create a relaxation blend, you can combine 3 parts of lavender with 2 parts Atlas and 1 part Bergamot. For an enlightening blend, go for a combination of Frankincense and Helichrysum according to the manufacturer's instruction. The combination of Frankincense, Sandalwood, and Bergamot will produce a good grounding blend.

Chapter Five: Body Scan / Progressive Relaxation Meditation

Now that you know the way to go about different meditation postures, you are ready to know about the various types of meditation. There are various types of meditation such as Zen Meditation, Spiritual meditation, Mantra meditation among others. In this chapter, we will extensively discuss body scan/progressive relaxation meditation.

What is Body Scan Meditation?

When you hear "body scan", you can be forgiven to think that it involves the use of a machine to scan your body while meditating. However, surprisingly, body scan meditation is not that sophisticated. It is possible that you don't pay attention to the physical comfort you are experiencing in your body such as tense muscles, headache, shoulder and back pain as a result of the level of stress you are experiencing. Most times, these physical discomforts are linked to the state of your emotions.

The state of your mind can affect the way you feel physically. You can feel so alive and full of vitality when you have the right state of mind and you can have physical issues because of what goes on in your mind. Body scan meditation aims at helping you release the tension you may not even realize you are going through. This meditation involves focusing on parts of your body and the accompanying sensations. It is a gradual process in which you pay attention to your body parts from your head to your feet. It is a mental process in which you scan and bring yourself into the awareness of what is happening to your body.

This meditation will help you notice sensations such as tension, pains, aches, and any other general discomfort in your body. Body scan meditation does not make these negative sensations disappear; it will help you learn about them to the end that you will be able to manage them better. You can carry out this meditation either daily or even several times a day depending on your schedule and determination.

Benefits of Body Scan Meditation

There are many benefits you stand to enjoy from the practice of body scan meditation:

Release of Tension

This type of meditation is an effective remedy for stress and tension. You will find yourself being able to remain in a calm state as you let go of tension easily with this meditation.

Reduction of Inflammation, Insomnia, and Fatigue

Body scan meditation does not only help you release tension. There are other benefits to this type of meditation with scientific evidence. The practice of body scan meditation regularly helps to reduce inflammation, insomnia, and fatigue. According to research carried out by Woods-Giscombé and his colleagues in 2014 on "The Cultural Relevance of Mindfulness Meditation as a Health Intervention for African Americans: Implications for Reducing Stress-Related Health Disparities", meditation reduces stress which in turn leads to the reduction of inflammation, insomnia, and fatigue. Via body scan meditation, the cycle of physical and psychological tension is broken. Hence, you will be able to stay calm and relaxed with ease with the regular practice of body scan meditation.

Enjoy Every Moment

With body scan meditation, you will be able to subject your mind to enjoy the moment rather than be anxious and tensed. You will no longer go through life passively. You will be able to stop your monkey mind from being too restless and going wild. You will be able to train your mind to explore both pleasant and unpleasant sensations and learn from them. It enables you to travel through your body without the need to change or fix anything. You are like a visitor in your own body checking through the sensations and taking notes for future use.

How to Practice Body Scan/Progressive Relaxation Meditation

Now that you know the benefit of body scan meditation, it is time to know how to practice it. Just like other forms of meditation, body scan meditation is not difficult to practice. Below are some things that will enable you to be effective in the practice of this form of meditation

Ensure you are Comfortable

The most important thing in the practice of any form of meditation is to be comfortable. Meditation is to bring you comfort at the end of the day. Hence, if you start out uncomfortable, you are already setting up yourself to be frustrated in the long run. Comfort begins from the posture of your body and extends to your outfit. Just as I have mentioned in the previous chapter, you can practice meditation by sitting, kneeling, lying down, and standing. What matters is to find a posture that best makes you comfortable. It is not a crime to try different postures until you discover the one that is best for you.

As regards the outfit also, I have explained in the previous chapter that you should not wear tight-fitted clothing for maximum concentration. As much as you should be modest especially when you are practicing meditation in a public place, you should never sacrifice it for comfort. Hence, it is better you practice body scan meditation at home where you can be comfortable rather than go somewhere you will be restricted. It is always good to practice where there are other people to encourage you. However, always ensure you are comfortable.

Take a Few Deep Breaths

Slow down your breathing deliberately when practicing this form of meditation. Avoid breathing from your chest but from your belly. It is easier to control the pace of your breathing when you breathe from your belly. Let your abdomen expand and contract with every breath. If you notice that your shoulder is falling and rising, it shows that you are not yet breathing from your belly. Put the focus on breathing from your belly. When you are doing it correctly, your belly will move as though it is a balloon inflating and deflating rhythmically.

There are breathing exercises that can help you practice body scan meditation effectively. For example, you can go for "mindful diaphragmic breathing". This breathing exercise involves closing your eyes and start noticing your breath while you are in a comfortable position. Notice the pace and depth to see whether it is shallow or deep. This will help you become aware of your breathing pattern and relax more when necessary.

You can also consider counted breathing exercises. This breathing exercise involves placing your tongue on the roof of your mouth behind your teeth while inhaling through your nose. While breathing, slowly count from 1 to 5 before you exhale. This breathing exercise will help you control the pace of your breath and stretch your exhalation.

Bring Awareness to Your Feet

While breathing, slowly bring your attention to your feet. Start to observe the sensations in your feet. In case you observe the pain, notice it and also any emotions or thoughts that come with it. Don't increase the pace of your breathing as a result of this action. Slowly breathe as you observe these sensations, thoughts, and emotions.

Focus and Breath into the Tension

In case you observe any sensations that are not comfortable, don't ignore them. Focus on these sensations and breathe into them to notice the reactions. Imagine the tension leaving your body as you breathe. Visualize the tensions evaporating away into the air. When you feel you are ready for the next phase, move on. Remember that meditation is more about the mind rather than physical experiences.

Hence, it is vital that you can visualize your tensions disappearing as you practice meditation. Once you can handle the state of your mind, you are in the driving seat. This simple but powerful method will alleviate you of stress in a way that will amaze you. Hence, you won't see any physical mist or vapor going away but the mental process of visualization is enough to do the magic.

Entire Body Scan

The last phase of body scan meditation is the entire scanning of your body. You will do the same thing you did with your feet to the remaining parts of your body gradually. In other words, you will gently observe the sensations in the other parts of your body by starting with your feet upwards. You will not stop until you get to the top of your head. Observe how you are feeling and notice where you are holding stress. In case you feel any sensation like pain, tightness, or pressure, breathe into it. You will be able to ease any tension or stress this way and learn about it for future reference.

Other Important Tips

There are other important tips that will enable you to make the best out of body scan meditation. Here they are:Feel free to practice body scan meditation any time you feel stress. However, you don't have to feel stress before you practice body scan meditation. You don't always feel the physical comfort in your due to stress but you can always discover any discomfort through the practice of body scan meditation.

There is an abbreviated version of body scan meditation you can practice in case you don't have much time. It involves sitting and paying attention to any part of your body where you have tension instead of moving from your feet upward. It does not come off easily from the onset. Through regular practice of full body scan meditation, you will be able to pull off the abbreviated version with ease over time. However, don't get used to it because it is not as effective as the full body scan. You should only use it when you have a tight schedule and still want to stay healthy via meditation practice. The abbreviated version is not a shortcut but half bread which is better than none but not as good as full bread. Hence, schedule your time to practice body scan meditation at least 30 to 40 minutes daily. However, during days when you can't do that, all hope is not lost.

Chapter Six: Loving-Kindness Meditation

We all want to be loved especially by people we care about the most. However, most people find it difficult to express love towards others. Loving-Kindness Meditation is a type of meditation that will help you find it easier in your heart to love others. You cannot love others if you have issues with accepting and loving yourself.

The word "Loving-Kindness" in Buddhism is "Maitri" which also means friendliness and benevolence. It is one of the ten paramis (perfections) of the Theravada school of Buddhism. In this chapter, you will learn about what loving-kindness meditation is all about, how to practice it, and the benefits you stand to enjoy by practicing it.

What is Loving-Kindness Meditation?

Loving-Kindness Meditation is a meditation practice that is popular for its ability to promote well-being and reduce stress. It is a self-care technique that enables to you living a healthy and happy life. Beyond physical health, Loving-Kindness Meditation helps you to walk in love and forgiveness towards people who hurt you. It also helps you to accept yourself and connect with others around you with ease.

In Loving-Kindness Meditation, while in a still position, you imagine someone who you respect or love stand by you while you meditate. The person may be someone in the present or someone in your past. As you meditate, you imagine the person standing on your right side sending you wishes for your health and prosperity. You will also do the same for your left side. This process of imagining people you love wishing you well is the foundation for receiving loving-kindness in this type of meditation.

You can also send your love and best wishes to people you love via this meditation. You do this by imagining yourself send the love you felt to the person on your left and right side. This meditation helps you to see how other people around you also need love just like you. Hence, your imagination of sending love to others will help your practice loving-kindness towards people around you more frequently.

Benefits of Practicing Loving-Kindness Meditation

Below are the benefits of practicing loving-kindness meditation:

Generation of Positive Energy

During loving-kindness meditation, you will be able to generate a lot of positive energy from loving yourself and others. People around you will start seeing you as a role model and an epitome of sacrifice when you practice this form of meditation.

Treatment of Borderline Personality

Apart from the feeling of relaxation and calmness you get from this meditation, there is more. A study carried out by Johannes Graser and Ulrich Stangier in 2018 reveals that loving-kindness meditation can be beneficial in the treatment of borderline personality and chronic pain. However, the study concluded that more evidences will be needed to support this claim.

How to Practice Loving-Kindness Meditation

There are various Buddhist traditions with different methods of practicing loving-kindness meditation. However, each of these methods has the same core psychological operation. The core principle of every method of practicing loving-kindness meditation is to generate affection towards some specific people in your life, yourself, as well as others. Below are some useful tips as regards the practice of loving-kindness meditation:

Set out Time to Practice

You cannot be too busy to pay attention to whatever matters to you. Whatever you don't have time for, you don't value. Hence, if it matters to you that you should increase the way you show love to people around you and yourself, you have to take out time to practice this type of meditation. You don't need so much time before you can engage in loving-kindness meditation. Just a few minutes are enough to do it. Once you are ready, find somewhere comfortable to sit. I don't have to repeat what I have said earlier about comfortable outfits. While your eyes are closed, relax your muscles, and take a few deep breaths to get started.

Visualization of Emotional and Physical Wellbeing

The next step is to visualize yourself experiencing total emotional and physical wellbeing and inner peace. Imagine yourself accepting yourself totally and loving yourself in an overwhelming way. Think of yourself as a person of worth and value and be grateful for who you are. Kick out every thought of words of ineptitude about your personality. See yourself as a person worth the love and affection of any reasonable person as you meditate. Feel the inner peace you get as you focus on these thoughts. As you inhale and exhale slowly, see it as you breathing in affection and breathing out tension and negative emotions.

Repeat Positive Phrases about Yourself

Don't just stop at thinking about yourself in a positive light and showering yourself with all the love in the world. You need to also say good things about yourself during meditation. Wish yourself well and pronounce positive words about your present and your future. Declare positive things about your health, finance, family, relationship, and other important areas of your life.

Say things like "I stay healthy", "My family is safe from all danger", "My finance is getting better" etc. You don't have to say these exact words. You can modify them according to your desire. What matters is to speak positive words about your life while in this relaxed and comfortable sitting position. Say these words slowly to avoid increasing the tempo of your breath and unsettling your previous equilibrium. Say these words at least three or four times.

Enjoy the Moment

Enjoy the moment as you bask in this moment of showering yourself with love and warmth. Don't let go of this precious moment quickly. Treasure the moment and enjoy the feeling of warmth and compassion towards yourself. Let these feelings of affection and compassion envelope you. It is possible that you find your attention drifting away to another though which may be neutral or contradictory. Don't fight it; just gently redirect your attention back to these thoughts of loving-kindness. Take your time and let the feeling overwhelm you. Focus on yourself completely in this phase before you move on to the next phase.

Focus on Others

After focusing on the feeling of compassion for yourself, the next phase is to focus on other people in your life. You can start with someone very close and dear to you first like your child or your spouse. Feel your love and appreciation for the person as you meditate. Think about how much the person means to you and let the feeling of compassion and affection for the person overwhelm you for a while. Speak the same or similar positive words you spoke about yourself earlier about the person too. Of course, that will imply that you will change the "Is" to "you". Just speak freely about the health and progress of the person as you shower compassion on the person.

One after the Other

After holding the feeling of compassion for the first person for a while, move on to another person who is important to you. Imagine every one of them living happily in good health and having inner peace. Bring in your friends before moving on to your family members, neighbors, and colleagues. The people you focus on does not necessarily have to be people who are living close to you alone. You can extend this loving-kindness to people across the globe. You can spare a thought for people struggling with terminal diseases, malnutrition, and extreme poverty all over the world. Wish them well and feel your compassion towards them. Connect with them and have empathy towards them.

However, the height of this phase is when you focus on people who have hurt you in the past or recently. Shower your compassion on them too and experience tremendous inner peace. It is easy to love people who care about you but it is difficult to have compassion for people who don't wish you well. If you can push yourself to extend your feeling of compassion towards them and wish them well, the inner peace you will feel is immeasurable.

Internalize the Experience

After you are done with the meditation, open your eyes and relish the wonderful journey. You can think about the inner peace and nice sensation you felt during the meditation all day long. Remember the inner peace you enjoyed to remind you to practice loving-kindness towards yourself and other people in your life. Internalize the feeling so that it will spur you to practice it again some other time. Take a few deep breaths before you finally bring the meditation to an end.

Other Important Tips

Other important tips that will help you get the best out of loving-kindness meditation include:

As a beginner, focus on only yourself when meditating. In other words, perfect your ability to imagine the feeling of compassion and speaking positive words with yourself as the sole subject. You will be able to bring in others later when you are comfortable with practicing with yourself first.

Bring in people you find difficult to forgive last. You may not have enough inner strength to genuinely forgive such people until you have practiced loving-kindness towards yourself and the people you love first. Forgiveness is not complete until you can both imagine the offender doing well and speaking positive phrases about the wellbeing of such a person.

Set an alarm if you want to avoid spending too much time practicing this meditation. However, you don't need an alarm as a beginner. The need for an alarm should arise after you have practiced such that you have reaped the benefits consistently.

The above method is not the only way to practice loving-kindness meditation. This is just a sample which you can modify slightly or drastically to suit your need. However, the principle of relaxation and feeling compassion towards yourself and other people remains constant. You can alter other procedures but not these two.

Chapter Seven: Spiritual Meditation

Spiritual meditation is all about knowing yourself the way you are and not based on inaccurate perceptions you had about yourself. It is important to note that different religions such as Hinduism, Buddhism, Daoism, and Christian faith all practice spiritual meditation. In this chapter, you will be introduced to spiritual meditation, its benefits, and practices.

Meditation in Hinduism, Buddhism, Daoism, and Christian Faith

Meditation in Hinduism is an important practice. Meditation in Hinduism is carried out to achieve oneness between the non-dual almighty (Brahman) and the spirit of the practitioner. This state of oneness is called Moksha. In the Hindu scriptures, there were monks who attained supernatural power through the practice of meditation.

Meditation in Buddhism is similar to Hinduism. Historians believe that the practice of meditation was passed from Hinduism to Buddhism as Buddha; the founder of Buddhism was a Hindu. The difference is that meditation in Hinduism has different purposes and ultimately to connect with God. However, Buddhists don't believe in God but see meditation as an integral part of their religion.

Meditation in Daoism is similar to Buddhism. Some techniques used in Daoism were developed from mindfulness practices in Buddhism. Meditation in the Christian faith involves thinking about the scriptures to obtain revelation from God. Do you need to have a religion you practice before you can practice spiritual meditation? No.

What is Spiritual Meditation?

Spiritual meditation is a type of meditation that connects you with your real self. It involves stripping yourself of your perceptions as you delve into a peaceful and still state of mind. This type of meditation involves sitting in a calm manner while clearing your mind and enjoying the moment. It involves deep breaths, visualizing, uttering a prayer, and even humming. Spiritual meditation is not restrictive and you can always modify it to what suits your needs.

Don't assume that spiritual meditation means that you have to be religious. It is true that different religions practice spiritual meditation but you don't have to be religious to practice it. It is all about connecting to something greater and deeper than you. It involves honest self-reflection to increase your level of spiritual awareness. It requires an attitude of integrity and genuineness while looking at yourself and the world.

As your spiritual confidence and awareness increase, you will be able to live a life that will be beneficial to others. Whether you know it or not, you have been on a spiritual journey since you became conscious as a person. Although the journey to spiritual enlightenment takes time, the benefits are worthwhile. Spiritual meditation is not a quick fix to all your problems but a journey of self-evaluation and reflection. For people who place a premium on their spiritual growth (we all should), spiritual meditation is non-negotiable.

Benefits of Spiritual Meditation

There are emotional, cognitive, mental, and physical benefits that come with the practice of spiritual meditation. Below are the benefits of practicing spiritual meditation:

Reduction of Stress and Anxiety

Just like other forms of meditation, spiritual meditation helps in the reduction of stress and anxiety. Spiritual meditation is a short-term and long-term remedy for mental stress and anxiety. Blacks and his colleagues in 2015 discovered in their research that consistent practice of meditation decreases stress and anxiety.

Happiness and Meaning

This form of meditation is also able to make your experience as a person better. It has proven to make people a happy and meaningful life. According to the EOC Institute, there are seven main neurotransmitters that are involved during spiritual meditation. The hormones responsible for happiness, serotonin and endorphin are released during the practice of spiritual meditation. There is a change of mood that occurs during this meditation that will affect your overall happiness in the short and long run.

Enhanced Memory

The EOC Institute also reckons that spiritual meditation can bring about enhanced memory in the long run.

Immunity

Spiritual meditation also improves your immunity against both common and fatal diseases. According to a study carried out by David Black and George Slavich in 2016, the result showed that meditation can bring about a reduction of proinflammatory processes. The study also revealed that meditation can lead to an increase in enzyme activity and cell-mediated defense parameters.

Reduction of Physical Pain

According to the Cleveland Clinic, the practice of spiritual meditation helps you to reduce physical pain. The practice of spiritual meditation helps you to focus on other things apart from the pain thereby leading to a reduction in the pain you feel.

Control Negative Emotions and Increase Life Span

Spiritual meditation can also help you control negative emotions and increase your life span according to the EOC Institute.

How to Practice Spiritual Meditation

It is simple and straightforward to practice spiritual meditation. Below are the steps to follow:

Get a Calm Place to Sit

The foundation of every form of meditation is to find a peaceful place you can practice it and spiritual meditation is not different. This meditation just like other types of meditation requires concentration and a peaceful place where you can be alone with your thought is very vital. Some people are still able to concentrate even in a place with minimal distraction but it is always better to find a serene environment for maximal concentration. After finding the perfect place for you, sit down and concentrate and shut out every form of distraction.

Close Your Eyes

The level of concentration required in spiritual meditation requires that you close your eyes. It is especially important that you close your eyes all through the duration of the meditation if you are just getting to start this form of meditation. When your eyes are open, it is easy for you to pay attention to a stimulus in the environment that will prevent you from totally submerging into a state of meditation. It is not easy for whatever you are not seeing to distract you. Hence, to submerge yourself into a complete state of meditation, it is better you close your eyes.

Be in Charge of Your Thoughts

After closing your eyes, you need to take charge of your thoughts by keeping it quiet. Your thoughts don't make any audible sound to others but they can be the loudest for you. Hence, you need to avoid being distracted by those lousy and cluttered thoughts. Take your time to clear your mind as you get set to surge into a full meditative state.

You need a relaxed state of mind to get the best out of spiritual meditation. It is in the midst of a quiet mind that you can connect with your through and higher self. Remember that the end of spiritual meditation is to strip off wrong impressions and see yourself in the true light. Hence, you need a clear state of mind to achieve this and not pick the wrong perception.

Let Go of Any Grudges

You cannot submerge into a complete meditative state when you have grudges against people. Sometimes, you hold grudges subconsciously and that is why you should do a little bit of soul-searching. Forgiveness is a critical part of spiritual meditation. It is impossible to get the full experience of spiritual meditation when you still have painful grudges in your heart. Let go of disappointments and betrayals by people around you. Meditation is meant to also help you feel compassion towards people in your life. Hence, you will be starting on a wrong note when you are hurting and don't want to let go.

Be Open-minded

You will learn a lot through the practice of spiritual meditation and that is why it is important you keep an open mind. You will grow and get better as a person through this experience and you must be ready to learn. You have to mentally take yourself outside your comfort zone. This is done by forgiving yourself and also people in your life. Let go of negative emotions and your regular thought pattern. This journey of discovering yourself needs you to keep an open mind to get the best out of it.

Pay Attention to Your Breath

You breathe all day long but you don't pay attention to your pattern of breathing most times. In the practice of spiritual meditation, you need to focus on your breathing. Observe the depth of each breath and the movement of your body as you inhale and exhale. Also, observe how long you hold your breath. This breathing exercise will not only help you breathe properly but calm your chattering mind.

Visualization and Muttering

The last phase of spiritual meditation involves visualizing yourself in a serene environment. You can imagine a bright white light touching your head and cleansing your soul of childhood hurt and other grievances. To feel that inner peace en route to self-discovery, speak words that carry positive energy about you. Speak about your health and other areas of your life. Take note of the phrases you spoke that made you feel better the most. Use those phrases often any time you meditate.

Other Important Tips

If you are new to spiritual meditation, it is not an issue. As long as you keep an open mind and a willingness to learn, you will be fine. Below are important tips that can help your practice spiritual meditation effectively:

Ensure you are comfortable both in your sitting position and your outfit. The importance of comfort when it comes to spiritual meditation cannot be overemphasized. It is the foundation of your journey to connecting with your true self.

Make sure your body is in a relaxed state before and during meditation. If you notice that your body is not relaxed, you can deliberately tense up your muscles and relax them as you breathe slowly.

If you find it difficult to keep a quiet mind during meditation, you can hum a favorite tune. Breathe slowly and feel the ambience of a peaceful mind.

Don't be perturbed about how well you are doing but the experience itself. In other words, don't get anxious about whether you are practicing meditation correctly or not. You should get more knowledge before or after the meditation. However, while practicing, the only thing that should be on your mind is the experience of connecting with your higher self and not how well you are doing it.

Don't restrict yourself to any particular environment. You can experiment with both indoor and outdoor meditation. You cannot know what is best for you until you try different options.

Never stop learning about how to improve your meditation practice. Get books and any other material that will help your experience. If you can get a teacher you can trust to teach you one-on-one, it is also a good option. You can take meditation classes also to get better.

If you stop practicing spiritual meditation, you may lose the previous experience. Hence, just like exercises and sports, you need regular practice. A daily habit of practicing meditation will do you a whole lot of good. It is fun and helpful. So, why not daily?

You can set reminders on your phone every day to remind you to practice every day. You can also get friends and family to practice with you so that you can encourage yourselves to practice daily.

Chapter Eight: Focused Meditation

Every form of meditation requires you to focus on it. Hence, focused meditation cannot be all about maintaining your focus any time you meditate. Focus is one of the most important things you can have in life. What you focus on is where you place your attention. Meanwhile, your attention is what determines the direction of your life. You drive, passion, and commitment is towards whatever is the focal point of your life.

What is Focused Meditation?

Focused meditation is a type of meditation in which you focus on a particular moment before moving on to another moment while meditating. It is a popular Buddhist practice where you learn to sustain your attention on selective moments to experience inner peace and release tension. What to focus on during this meditation can be something external. This form of meditation is not rigid. It allows you to bring in external influences to help focus your attention. You can focus on the sound of a gong or just staring at a candle flame. You can also use mala beads and just concentrate on counting them.

Any of your five senses can be used to concentrate during this meditation. This form of meditation helps you to measure the quality of your ability to pay attention to something. As you try to focus on your breath or any other thing of choice, you can find your mind moving to the pain you are feeling in a part of your leg. You may also find your attention drifting to something unpleasant that took place at your workplace or between you and your spouse.

You let go of the distraction and return your mind to the chosen focal point. Basically, you are training your mind to focus more on a selective thing and not wander about during this meditation. The particular thing you are focusing on is your anchor and you will know when you have moved away from it. You will learn from this drifting and bring your mind back to where it ought to be.

Benefits of Practicing Focused Meditation

The practice of focused meditation is fun but also beneficial. Below are some benefits of practicing meditation:

Recognition of Distractions

When you practice focused meditation, you will be able to develop a monitoring awareness that enables you to detect distractions. You cannot know what distracts you unless you have a specific focus. Hence, whatever drifts your attention away from your initial focal point will be labeled as a distraction. This will enable you to detect distractions in your life in your daily life. You will learn to set clearly defined goals and notice when something else is taking away your attention from your goal.

Ability to Disengage from Distractions

During focused meditation, you will learn to disengage from distractions while meditating. Therefore, you will not only learn to recognize distractions but also disengage from them when you practice focused meditation. This will result in you being able to disengage yourself from distractions in your daily activity.

Ability to Refocus

It is not just good enough to recognize and disengage from distractions; you must be able to refocus your attention again on the selected focal point. The practice of focused meditation trains your mind to bring your attention back to where it was before it drifted away. It is actually fun to practice this form of meditation. It feels like playing a racing game where you are racing against the tides. You are holding on to the "steering wheel" of your mind and bringing it back to where the tides have moved it away.

More Productivity

Your performance and productivity are impaired when you are distracted. Once you learn to recognize and disengage from distractions via this meditation, your performance in your daily activities will definitely get better. You will know when something else is taking your attention away from your job, family, or loved ones. You will disengage on time and be better in your career and the way you handle your relationships with others.

How to Practice Focused Meditation

You can become a pro in the practice of focused meditation in no time. Here are some tips that can help you:

Set out Time for Practice

It is always important you decide how long you want to practice to maintain consistency. You can go for 15 minutes daily or 4 times a day. You can do more but just be consistent. As long as you are consistent, you are good to go.

Find a comfortable Place to Practice

If I have to say this a thousand times, it is worth it. Every form of meditation demands that you practice in the correct environment. You cannot focus when you have sounds blaring and people distracting you. Hence, it is vital that you find somewhere with little or no distraction. You don't have to find a place where there is perfect silence as that will make a graveyard the only perfect place to practice.

Decide Your Focus

After finding a place to practice, the next step is to decide what will be your focal point. It is totally your choice to decide what you will use as an anchor for your thought. It can be the sound of a metronome or a nice picture. As long as the stimulus is good enough to stimulate you, you are good to go. You don't have to use what other people use. Focused meditation allows you to be creative with your choice of an anchor.

Get into a Comfortable Position

What you need next is to get into a meditation position that suits you. Relax your body and loosen your shoulder. Breathe slowly from your belly as against your chest to control the pace of your breath. Most people who practice focused meditation cross their legs but you don't have to do that. If you are comfortable with crossing your legs, it is good. However, if you find another position that is more comfortable for you, go for it. Your meditation position should not be such that it makes you sleep. Be active but relaxed when meditating.

Focus on the Chosen Target

Once you are in a comfortable position, focus on the target you have previously selected. Just like a hitman, set your radar on that sound, smell, or image you have made your focal point. Savor every detail and analyze it. The idea of focusing on a target is not to just pay attention to it but to experience it. If it is a sound, notice the tempo, think about how different it could have been. If it is a picture, observe every line and color combination. Let every detail come alive to you. Be fully present and enjoy the moment.

Calm Your Inner Voice

Your chattering mind will try to prevent you from enjoying the moment. The same way you find yourself drifting from a particular thing in your daily life is what also takes place during the meditation. Learn to master the art of bringing calm to your monkey mind during this meditation and translate it to your day-to-day activity. Your inner voice will remind you about something else but you have to gently return your attention to the focal point. It is during this process that you learn to recognize distractions, disengage from them, and refocus again. Learn from the drifting pattern and use it as a template in practical daily activities.

Don't be concerned about Failing

The common pitfall people who practice various forms of meditation including focused meditation fall into is evaluating their success while meditating. Thinking about whether you are doing it right or wrong in itself is a distraction. You have succeeded in taking your mind away from the chosen target to another thought. Therefore, always evaluate yourself after meditation and not while meditating. There is always room for improvement and you should seek to get better. However, you are not doing yourself any good when you allow the thought of doing it correctly or not distract you from focusing on the chosen target.

Other Important Tips

There are other things you need to know that can help you practice focused meditation more effectively. The steps above are to guide you and serve as a template but there is room for modification. You may struggle initially with each step. Below are important tips that can make your practice easier:

Don't be in a hurry to be perfect. It takes practice to practice focused meditation perfectly. It is not difficult but you need to give it time. Giving it time does not mean that you should not practice; it means that you should practice patiently. Celebrate every progress; don't be too critical of yourself. Enjoy the journey and the learning process.

You don't have to start with fifteen minutes. You can start with shorter sessions like 5 minutes as a starter. Patiently increase the time you spend as you get better. There is no in point spending time when you are not effective. Ease yourself into the practice and build your effectiveness over time.

If you are finding it difficult to handle focused meditation, you don't have to quit meditating altogether. You can try other forms of meditating first and try focused meditation later. Every form of meditation has the same basics. Hence, if you are able to "crack the code" with another form of meditation, you can find it easier with focused meditation.

Don't follow stereotypes. For some people, the best time for them to meditate is early in the morning while some people find joy meditating in the cool of the evening. Some people are even comfortable with both. Find the best time for you to practice. Don't just copy what other people do because the fact that it worked for them does not mean it will work for you.

Chapter Nine: Zen Meditation

Zen is a Japanese term that has the same meaning as the Chinese word "Ch'an" and Indian word "dhyana" all meaning meditation or concentration. Zen meditation is also called "zazen" and it is a type of meditation built upon Buddhist psychology and traditions. It is an interesting form of meditation with myriads of benefits. In this chapter, you will learn what Zen meditation is all about and how you can practice it.

What is Zen Meditation?

Zen meditation is often described as a meditation that helps you to "think about not thinking". This description is not far from the truth about Zen meditation. This form of meditation involves looking within and gaining awareness and focus. Unlike focused meditation, it does not involve focusing on any particular target. However, just like focused meditation, Zen meditation enables you to train your monitoring skills.

This monitoring without a specific target is the reason Zen meditation is often described as an "open-monitoring meditation". It does not involve the recitation of any mantra or cultivation of compassion like loving-kindness meditation but there is still a lot of focus on self-awareness. Unlike any other form of meditation, the eyes are kept semi-open in Zen meditation. The target of your attention during the practice of Zen meditation is nothing!

In other words, during Zen meditation, you are not thinking about anything in particular and that is why it is described as a meditation where you think about not thinking. All you do is to fight off any thought that tries to pop into your mind while you are in a calm and relaxed state. The idea of this meditation is to help you tap into your subconscious mind. You will be able to detect preconceived notions and discover your thought pattern and insight into yourself.

Benefits of Practicing Zen Meditation

Just like other forms of meditation, Zen meditation has many benefits. It offers calmness and helps you to release tension just like other types of meditation but much more. There are psychological, physical, cognitive, and spiritual benefits you can derive from this form of meditation. You can enjoy the following when you practice Zen meditation regularly:

Insight into the Nature of your Body and Mind

The regular practice of Zen meditation will help you gain insight into how your mind works. You will also be able to learn about some of your reflex actions. You will be able to shutout mainstream thoughts and learn about your thought pattern.

Enhanced Focus

The interest of scientists to understand how meditation affects the body and mind has led to some researches with interesting results. In 2008, Giuseppe Pagnoni, Milos Cekic, and Ying Guo carried out research on the correlates of conceptual processing during Zen Meditation. Ten Zen practitioners who all have more than three years of daily practice were used in this study.

The result of the study showed that there are activities in the brain "default network" regions. These regions of the brain are linked to wandering minds. This result shows that the regular practice of Zen meditation can enhance your focus and ability to pay attention to specific things.

Limitation of Distraction

The enhanced focus will translate to the ability to keep out distractions. Focus and keeping out distractions are difficult to achieve in the digital world we have today. So much time is spent on gadgets, mobile phones, and computers in the modern world. Therefore, the ability to maintain your focus and avoid distraction is very vital.

Access to the Unconscious Mind

Zen meditation makes it possible for you to access your unconscious mind. This claim has raised some dust but it is true and supported by scientific evidence. Does it really matter that you gain access to your unconscious mind? Yes! Why? Your conscious mind can only focus on one thing at a time but your unconscious mind can do more than that. Therefore access to your unconscious mind can unlock a higher level of creativity and performance.

In 2012, a study was carried out to examine the possibility of gaining access to your unconscious mind via the practice of Zen meditation. The participants were all seasoned Zen practitioners. A group was asked to read magazines while the other group was asked to meditate for 20 minutes. The two groups were then asked to solve a puzzle on the computer screen. The people who meditated were able to solve the puzzle faster than those who read magazines. The result of this study shows that Zen meditation enables you to access your unconscious mind.

Treatment of Drug Abuse

Most forms of meditation lead to a connection between the mind and the body. However, Zen meditation takes it a notch higher as it causes an interaction between the heart and the brain! A study in 2018 carried out by Lo Pei-Chen and other scientists was able to establish this interaction. According to this study, Zen meditation makes it possible to connect with the spiritual heart which is located in the organ heart.

The authors of this study reckoned that years of Zen meditation practice helps the practitioners to have their brain in such a way that it is dominated by the spiritual heart. It is this heart and brain interaction that makes it possible to treat drug addiction with regular Zen meditation. Zen meditation serves as the foundation of drug abuse treatment programs in Taiwan. This type of meditation affects the autonomous nervous system which is the system that is responsible for bodily functions such as breathing, digestive processes, and heartbeat.

People suffering from drug abuse often have issues with their autonomous system during their recovery. Zen meditation improves mood and people recovering from drug addiction needs an improved mood to prevent them from abusing drugs again.

How to Practice Zen Meditation

You don't have to find a monk before you can practice Zen meditation. Below are steps you can follow to practice this form of meditation:

Sit in a Relaxing Place

You need a place devoid of distractions to practice Zen meditation. It may be indoors or outdoors as long as you can meditate there without distractions, it is fine. You can create a special atmosphere if you are meditating indoors by creating an altar. You can make the altar with items like flowers, seashells, and stones. Lighting a candle can also help you create a serene and spiritual atmosphere to meditate.

Get into a Stable Position

The way you seat is crucial in Zen meditation. Hence, ensure you are sitting comfortably such that you keep your back straight. You can cross your legs or support yourself with a pillow to ensure that you are comfortable and ready for meditation.

Position Your Head Correctly

The way you position your head is also important in this form of meditation. Let your head be in a position that is natural such that you don't strain your body. Let your spine align with your neck as though a straight line is running up your spine to your neck.

Relax the Muscles of Your Jaw and Face

It is important that you don't strain your body when meditating. Hence, ensure you relax your jaw and facial muscles. Before you start meditating, notice if there is any tension in the jaw or facial muscles and release them.

Breathe Through Your Nose

There is a lot of focus on breathing in the practice of Zen meditation. You need to breathe through your nose and feel the cooling and warmth sensation produced via your inhalation and exhalation. Nasal breathes will enable you to monitor the rhythm of your breath all through the meditation.

Pay Attention to your Breath

You have to focus on your breath when you start meditating as much as you can. Focus on the rhythm and sound of your breath as you inhale and exhale. Feel the warmth and cooling sensations as air passes in and out of your lungs. You will pay attention to your breath not just at the beginning of the meditation but all through the meditation.

Decide on what to do with your Eyes

Many people keep their eyes closed when practicing Zen meditation. However, there is no harm in keeping them open or semi-open. However, if you are keeping your eyes open, you need to focus on a particular point in the room. What matters is that you feel natural, comfortable, and not distracted.

Be in Charge of your Mind

Your mind will wander because you are sitting in silence but you have to be in charge. Your mind can go to other things you need to do later in the day or the mistakes you made in the past. There is no limit to what your mind can ponder about. However, you have to gently redirect it back to your breath all through the meditation. Your mind may even drift to thinking about whether you are carrying out the meditation correctly. However, you have to be in charge of your mind and not let it wander.

Other Important Tips

Apart from the basics, the following information should be beneficial to you:

If you are struggling with the alignment of your neck and spine, tuck in your chin.

Use your fingers to massage your jaws slightly if you notice that your jaw feels tense to loosen up the muscles of your face.

Struggle with keeping your mind quiet in the early stage of practice is not an anomaly. Don't be discouraged because you will get better with regular practice over time.

Avoid meditating for long as a starter. You may struggle to focus on your breath if you meditate for long as a beginner.

Hence, start by meditating for two minutes and improve on it with practice.

You can buy a small or zafu pillow to make your practice more effective. A zafu pillow is designed specifically for Zen meditation and you will do well to get one.

Just like other forms of meditation, don't be perturbed about perfection from the onset. Be excited and contented about the fact that you were able to start. Enjoy the experience and learn from your mistakes as you seek to get better.

Chapter Ten: Mantra Meditation

The words you speak reflect the state of your mind. You cannot know a person who is pessimistic by just looking at the face of the person. You will know a pessimist by the words spoken by the person. In the same way, you can only know an optimist when the person speaks. In the same way, you can change the state of your mind by speaking the right words. Mantra meditation is a form of meditation that takes advantage of speaking positive words. This chapter is a compendium of important things you need to know about this type of meditation, its practice, and its benefits.

What is Mantra Meditation?

Mantra meditation, just like most forms of meditation has Hindu and Buddhist roots. However, recitation of sacred words is also a tradition found in Judeo-Christianity as well. However, in recent times, the practice of mantra meditation is becoming more popular in non-religious mindfulness practice. A mantra refers to a word, syllable, or phrase that is spoken repeatedly during meditation. You don't have to speak audibly before it can be called a mantra. You may whisper it, chant it, or just repeat it in your mind.

It is important to note that it is not any word or syllable you chant that is a mantra. It is the energy associated with the muttering or chanting that produces the powerful effect that makes it a mantra. During meditation, mantra serves as an anchor point for a wandering mind. In other words, mantra meditation involves chanting or thinking about a set of words or syllables to train your mind to focus and experience the moment. You should know the meaning of the mantra to make the practice more effective. A mantra can be something like "I have much to celebrate" or "I am kind to myself".

There are various reasons people practice mantra meditation. For some people, they practice it to protect themselves against negative emotions. For other people, it is what they do to improve their sleep. However, in both Christian and Hindu tradition, mantra meditation recitation has a spiritual purpose. It is practiced to gain connection and intimacy with the divine. However, it is different in Buddhism because of the lack of belief in God. In Buddhism, mantra meditation aids focus and enjoyment of the present moment.

Benefits of Practicing Mantra Meditation

Mantra meditation is not without benefits and that is why a lot of people practice it regularly. According to the Eco Institute, below are benefits of practicing mantra meditation regularly:

Improvement of the Brain Functions

The regular practice of mantra meditation improves 9 key regions in the brain. The result of this improvement is that your stress level will reduce and you will also find it easier to sleep. Other benefits of this improvement include enhanced memory, ease of learning, higher EQ & IQ as well as more happiness.

Increased Life Span

Regular mantra meditation makes people who practice it look younger and live longer. According to the Eco Institute, mantra meditation boosts glutathione (GSH) which is an antioxidant. Glutathione is the most important antioxidant in the body. People who have terminal diseases like cancer or AIDS usually have their level of glutathione depleted. Glutathione is important for the maintenance of intracellular health. Hence, don't be surprised to know that regular mantra meditation can make you look way younger than your age and increase your life expectancy.

Prevention of Weight Loss

Stress can lead to an increase in heart rate and the tension can become unbearable when it is intense. One of the results of intense stress levels is the loss of weight. When you practice mantra meditation regularly, you will be able to keep your mind quiet and reduce your stress level. Indirectly, you are preventing yourself from suffering the loss of weight.

Access to your Subconscious and Unconscious Mind

Your subconscious and unconscious minds contain the requisite creative solution you need to take your life a notch higher. You will have a little taste of what lies within when you are half-awake early in the morning. You find great ideas come into your mind and you begin to wonder why you have never thought about them before. Where did these wonderful ideas come from? Your subconscious and unconscious mind! Imagine how much you will be able to do when you can expressly access your subconscious and unconscious mind! Thankfully, consistent practice of mantra meditation is the key that gives you access to your subconscious and unconscious mind.

Boost of Brain Chemicals

Key brain chemicals such as Endorphins, GABA, and Serotonin are boosted through the practice of mantra meditation. Cortisol is the hormone in the body linked to stress. In 2013, Turakitwanakan and his colleagues studied the effects of mindfulness meditation on serum Cortisol of medical students. The result of the research revealed that mindfulness meditation decreases the Cortisol levels in the blood thereby reducing stress and preventing psychiatric disorder.

Improved Immune System

The practice of this form of meditation boosts your immune system. Consistent mantra meditation is more like training your body to act like a fully loaded Mack truck to crush germs that comes against it. Your body has "soldiers" that protect it against germs and these soldiers are "T cells" and "antibodies". When you practice mantra meditation regularly, these warriors are boosted and help your body to fight against diseases without you even knowing about it.

Fight against Addiction

The brain "happiness center", the prefrontal cortex, is activated when you practice mantra meditation regularly. The implication of this activation is that you will have a "natural high" which ensures that you don't need to depend on any drug. Therefore, you will never have any reason to deal with addiction.

Development of Willpower

Willpower is important for success in the future. It takes willpower to have confidence in your ability to work hard and achieve your goals in life. Willpower is never automatic; it is developed by training and practice. The kind of training of the mind you get through mantra meditation develops your willpower and set you up for success in the future. Top executives are beginning to understand this benefit and they are practicing meditation more than ever in recent times.

How to Practice Mantra Meditation

By now, you already know that you need to get a serene environment to practice no matter the form of meditation you prefer. Regardless of your purpose for practicing mantra meditation; the following steps will help you:

Decide the Purpose of the Meditation

The reason for your practice of mantra meditation is what will determine the mantra you will use. Hence, you need to settle on whether you want to practice this form of meditation for the health benefit it offers or to achieve spiritual connection. Once you decide the purpose of the meditation, you are ready for the next step.

Get an appropriate Mantra for your Purpose of Meditation

Don't let this step bother you because there are already universal mantras you can use that supports your intention. The right mantra creates vibrations that resonate with your purpose. Every mantra has its own energy and you need to find the mantra whose vibration corresponds with your purpose for meditation. Regardless of your purpose, you can chant the universal mantra, "aum" repeatedly. It creates such a powerful vibration in your lower abdomen that makes you want to do it again. For peace of mind, you can chant "Hare Krishna, Hare Krishna, Krishna Krishna, Hare Hare, Hare Rama, Hare Rama, Rama Rama, Hare, Hare".

Sit Appropriately

The ideal sitting position for this form of meditation is sitting comfortably such that you cross your legs and your hips are elevated. This sitting position will help you align your spine with your neck in a straight way. In this sitting position, close your eyes for maximum concentration.

Focus on your Breathe

Focus on your breath but avoid the temptation to try to control it. Focus on the feeling of warmth and cooling sensation while exhaling and inhaling. The essence of this breathing exercise is to keep you relaxed in a meditative state.

Chant your Chosen Mantra

Having gain mastery over your breath, you are ready to chant your chosen mantra. There is no particular way to chant your chosen mantra. Chanting mantra is so powerful that you will get a lot of benefits from a small amount of chanting. You should also decide whether you want to continue to chant silently in your mind or audibly. It is not good to drift from audible chanting to mindfulness. You need focus and stability and that is why you should make up your mind on time. Stick with one because anyone you choose will be beneficial to you.

Meditate until you are Satisfied

There is no limitation to the time you can meditate. However, the longer you meditate the better for you. Just like sports, an athlete who practices longer and consistently will be fit and record better performance than a sloppy athlete. In the same way, the more you practice meditation, the more you will reap the benefits. It is only by practice, dedication, and commitment that you can move from being a naïve practitioner to an expert who can train others.

Other Important Tips

Other helpful tips you need to enjoy the practice of mantra meditation include:

Controlling your breath is not that easy and you should not be discouraged if you struggle initially. You will get better with time as you continue to practice.

If you find it difficult to meditate while sitting, you can use a chair and you can even do it while lying down.

If you don't want to use "aum" or any other mantra because you are not familiar with them, you can chant words that you know. As long as the words resonate with your purpose, you are doing well.

The best time to practice mantra meditation is early in the morning before your mind is encumbered by other thoughts. However, if you are not able to do it in the morning, do it at other periods of the day. The most important thing is regular practice because consistency is key in mantra meditation.

Chapter Eleven: Transcendental Meditation

Transcendental meditation is growing in influence and popularity as it is being incorporated into the programs of prisons, schools, and colleges in Europe, the US, Latin America, and India. What is so special about this form of meditation that is making various people practice it? You will find out in this chapter as we delve into what this meditation is all about, its benefit, and the way to practice it.

What is Transcendental Meditation?

This type of meditation was developed by Maharishi Mahesh Yogi. It is a silent meditation where you meditate to avoid distractions and attain a state of calmness and awareness. It is a meditation that can be practiced whether you are religious or not. It is a religious practice in Hinduism but you can practice it for the purpose of self-development if you are not religious. Transcendental meditation has been around for more than 50 years and it is endorsed by celebrities and various media outlets.

One of such celebrities that endorse transcendental meditation is Jonathan Rowson, the Scottish chess grandmaster. According to him, transcendental meditation offers you a feeling of balance, serenity, and energy. Other celebrities who practice this form of meditation regularly include Sam Allardyce, a football manager; Jennifer Aniston, an actress; Russell Brand, a stand-up comedian; and Ray Dalio, an investment banker. Therefore, if you choose to practice transcendental meditation, you are in good company.

Maharishi reckons that your thoughts are like bubbles that keep pouring in relentlessly like a stream. Hence, you need to be calm and aware to be able to have a proper thought. A proper thought is that thought that is devoid of sentiment and emotions. During the practice of transcendental meditation, you silently repeat mantras while seating comfortably. There is no specific posture or sitting position that you must assume before you can practice this type of meditation.

The mantra serves as a vehicle with which you evade noises in your mind and attain a quiet and calm state. The ordinary thinking process becomes transcended and replaced by a state of unadulterated consciousness. Every mental boundary is depleted and you will be able to attain a state of tranquility and orderliness.

Benefits of Practicing Transcendental Meditation

According to Dr. Norman E. Rosenthal, an award-winning psychiatrist from Georgetown University, if transcendental meditation can be put into a capsule and sold like a pharmaceutical product, it would have been a billion-dollar blockbuster! A remarkable statement, isn't it? Why will these celebrities and much more practice transcendental meditation if it is pointless? Definitely, there are benefits attached to the practice of this type of meditation. Do you care to know? Here they are:

Peak Performance

Many people have wondered what exactly makes transcendental meditation unique. One of the uniqueness of this form of meditation is that it aids the performance level of the practitioners. How? When you practice this meditation, the whole of your brain is turned on to function properly as a unit. A study in 2005 by Chandler and his colleagues on the effect of transcendental meditation technique on cognitive stage development revealed that regular practice of transcendental meditation enhances brain function. Therefore, don't be surprised that athletes with top performances and top businessmen and women are practicing transcendental meditation.

Reduction of Stress and Anxiety

The regular practice of transcendental meditation brings about a reduction in stress and anxiety. A study in the Harvard Medical School on the effect of transcendental meditation on cardiovascular function by Vernon Barnes and his colleagues in 2001 confirms that transcendental meditation reduces stress and anxiety.

Enhancement of Cardiovascular Health

In 2007, Anderson and his colleagues carried out a study to investigate the effect of transcendental meditation on blood pressure. The result of the study showed that transcendental meditation practices boost cardiovascular health.

Prevention and reduction of Depression

Depression is a major issue in the world today. The pressure to perform is on the rise and many people find it difficult to get to grips with the loss of their jobs and confidence in modern times. Transcendental meditation has proven to be a remedy and preventive measure against depression. A study on the treatment of Post Traumatic Stress Disorder (PTSD) by Boyd and his colleagues in 2013 has confirmed that the practice of transcendental meditation can remedy depression.

Prevention and Treatment of Addiction

Drug abuse is a malaise the government of different countries are doing all they can to fight against. However, people who practice transcendental meditation consistently does not have to worry about being infected by this "virus". Your general mood improves when you practice this form of meditation and you won't need any chemical substance to make you happy.

Treatment of Sleeplessness

You will not be able to perform up to the maximum level when your sleep is not regular. However, you don't have to worry about issues with sleepless when you are a consistent practitioner of transcendental meditation. The effect of transcendental meditation on sleeplessness is not a farce but a fact backed up with scientific evidence. One of the numerous studies that confirm the effect of transcendental meditation on sleeplessness was carried out in 2014 by Charles Elder and his colleagues. This study revealed that consistent transcendental meditation practice is effective against insomnia.

How to Practice Transcendental Meditation

For the best transcendental meditation, you will need a qualified and experienced transcendental meditation teacher. Such a teacher must be certified by the Maharishi Foundation, a non- profit organization recognized by the government of the United States of America. However, you can still practice on your own if you want to. To practice transcendental meditation, below are some useful tips:

Set out Time to Meditate

The best transcendental meditation practice requires you to practice at least twice a day. An average of twenty minutes each is good enough to practice. You have to ensure you are consistent to enjoy the full benefits of practicing this type of meditation.

Sit Comfortably in a Serene Environment

"Serenity" is relative when it comes to the practice of transcendental meditation. What matters is that you are in an environment that is comfortable for you to practice. Avoid practicing in a place where you will have to fight the thoughts going through your mind and external stimuli. Practice in a place where there is a level of noise that is acceptable for you so that you can focus. It is hard enough to focus during meditation. You don't need to make it further difficult for yourself. You can either sit on the ground or on a chair. What matters is for you to sit comfortably such that you don't strain your body or too relaxed such that you feel like sleeping.

Take a Few Deep Breaths

Take a few deep breaths while closing your eyes to keep you calm and release tension. Ensure you don't strain your body. Observe if there is tension in a part of your body especially the muscles of your face. Let go and relax to delve into a full meditative state.

Open your Eyes and Close Them Back Again

You will have to close your eyes all through the time of the practice. Hence, before you start muttering a mantra, you can close your eyes for the last time before you finally close them again to concentrate all through the period of the meditation.

Mutter a Mantra Repeatedly

A mantra is the anchor point on which you will focus all through the period of the practice. To enjoy a full experience of transcendental meditation, you should use a Sanskrit sound given to you by a certified transcendental meditation teacher.

The mantra for meditation in this form of meditation is not just a random positive mantra; it has to be a mantra whose energy and vibrations are endorsed by experts. This specific use of specially designed mantras is what makes the practice of transcendent meditation different from other forms of meditation.

Focus on the Mantra

Pay attention to the mantra all through the period of the practice. Your mind will wander off into a series of thoughts but you have to gently bring it back to the mantra. Your mind is prone to distraction and that impairs your performance in your daily activities. The practice if transcendental meditation enables you to train your mind to focus on what you want it to focus on. Don't fight it or feel bad about your mind drifting away, just calmly bring it back to the anchor point.

Ease yourself back to the World

Once you are done with the meditation, ease yourself back to the world by slowly moving your fingers and toes. Then open your eyes as you complete the meditation and enjoy the inner peace you have because of the meditation.

Other Important Tips

I believe you should also find the following tips useful to help you to practice transcendental meditation effectively:

Set an alarm to know when to stop meditating. You cannot afford any form of distraction while meditating. Hence, it is not ideal to check time to find out if you have meditated long enough. You may also assume that you have meditated for 20 minutes when you have only meditated for 5 minutes. You don't need that feeling of disappointment, just set an alarm to know when your time is up.

Don't forget that you should not access your performance while meditating but after meditating. There should not be any other thought occupying your mind all through the period of the practice apart from the mantra you are muttering. Strive for perfection as much as you can but ensure you do that before or after the meditation.

You can still practice transcendental meditation without getting a particular mantra from a transcendental meditation teacher. You can simply use "Homm" because it is a universal mantra used by monks for the practice of meditation. You can also use "Kirim" or "Shirim". Mutter them slowly to intentionally drag the pronunciation. I mean something like "Kiiiiiiriiiiiiiiim" or "Shiiiiiiiiiriiiiiiiiiiiiiiiiiiiim".

The most important thing about the practice of transcendental meditation is not the muttering of the mantra but to achieve inner peace and ease off stress. The idea is to transcend your mind by focusing on a meaningless word. Hence, if you notice that the mantra you are using sounds like a world you are familiar with, change it because it can distract you in the long run.

Chapter Twelve: Guided Meditation

We all need guidance in life. If you don't want to practice meditation by yourself because you want to be absolutely sure that you are doing it correctly, guided meditation is for you. Guided meditation? You don't need to be worked up about what it is all about and how you can practice it or what you stand to gain by practicing this type of meditation. You will get every answer you need in this chapter. You are about to be guided to meditate!

What is Guided Meditation?

This is a form of meditation in which you are guided by an experienced and qualified meditation teacher. Guided meditation takes away the burden of learning how to go about meditation. Your teacher will guide you through to know the best meditation posture and breathing exercise that will enable to practice effectively. You will not also need to worry about the mantra you can use during meditation because your teacher has got your back.

Your teacher does not necessarily have to be physically present with you during the meditation. The advancement in technology has broken the barrier of distance in learning. You can learn anything from a teacher at the comfort of your home including meditation. Hence, your learning may be through a video or podcast. Whether it is physically or via a video, you will be provided with each step you need and techniques as well as tips for meditation.

All you have to be concerned about is paying attention and practicing what you are taught. Guided meditation is recommended for beginners to enable you to explore and enjoy the full experience of meditation. You may be frustrated if you are trying so hard and you can see the benefit you expected to enjoy from the practice of meditation. Instead of reducing your stress level, you will end up increasing it. When you are not getting it right, meditation can often feel like buying a machine without a manual. You can practice on your own later after receiving guidance as you take your first steps on your journey of meditation.

Benefits of Practicing Guided Meditation

Unguided meditations are beneficial and guided meditations are not different. Below are the benefits of guided meditation:

Perfect for Meditation Beginners

Guided meditation is perfect for you if you are just trying to get to grips with meditation practices generally. Your first steps are important because they go a long way in determining your perception of meditation. If you don't have the right guidance when you are just starting to learn to meditate, you may assume that meditation is a worthless practice not worth your time. Hence, guided meditation ensures that you learn without experimentation.

Assurance and Confidence of Being on the Right Path

One of the greatest battle people who practice meditation by themselves have is the evaluation of how well they are practicing. Some people get distracted by the thought of whether they are practicing correctly or not while meditating. Guided meditation eliminates any worry about meditating correctly. You are learning from experts and you can rest assured in their rich experience and expertise.

Enhanced Calmness

Any form of meditation will make you comfortable and calm. However, it is better when you are meditating with the aid of a guide. You are sure that you are practicing correctly because of the credibility of your guide. Hence, you will be able to find it easier to delve into a full meditative state. Your mind and body is at peace with one another and you can focus on your breath or mantra easily. Every form of meditation makes you calm by taking your mind off your monkey mind and making it focus either on a mantra, your breath, or absolutely nothing. Guided takes this ability to focus a notch higher due to the fact that you have a definite and trusted guide.

Focus

Just like other forms of meditation, guided meditation enables you to retain your focus. The importance of focus cannot be overemphasized in your daily activities. The U.S. Marines have embraced mindfulness because they realized that it helps them to focus better on the job. If a credible organization like the U.S. Marine sees meditation as a helpful practice for enhanced focus, then, you are in good company when you choose to meditate consistently.

Prevention and Cure of Depression and Chronic Pain

You will not have reasons to bother about depression when you practice guided meditation. If you are already suffering from depression, it is not too late because guided meditation is also a remedy to depression. Psychologists from the University of Exeter recommend meditation as a cure for depression. They reckon that mindfulness is a better cure than drugs. According to their study, patients who practiced meditation for four months were better enough such that they did not need antidepressants again.

Prevention and Cure of Chronic Pain

According to a study conducted in the Wake University in 2011 by Fadel Zeidan and his colleagues, meditation was found to offer both preventive and curative effects to pain. In the study, the brain of the participants who practiced meditation was scanned with MRI. The scans revealed that there was a 40 percent reduction in pain! Therefore, instead of spending money on treating chronic pain like many people today, your lot can be far better with the consistent practice of meditation.

How to Find a Guide

In guided meditation, your guide will help you understand how your mind works as well as meditation techniques. You will know what to expect and how to go about it exactly. I don't need to give you steps on how to go about practicing guided meditation. What you need is a guide and you will get every step you need and more. How can you get someone to guide you? You can find a guide through the following ways:

Find a Local Meditation Class

By searching online with the aid of Google, you can find local meditation classes around you. There are many people like you around you who know the importance of meditation and are committed to practicing it. These people meet regularly and you can also join them. These groups are led by an expert who gives the requisite instructions and guidance for effective meditation. The style of meditation that will be practiced in a particular group depends on the teacher. Hence, you can find another group if you find it difficult to cope with the approach of the teacher of a particular group.

Download an Instructional App

If you are not comfortable with meditating in a group or for the sake of comfort, you can get an instructional app that will guide you. Search online for a tested and trusted digital app you can use. Ensure you read the reviews of previous users of the app before you download it. There are many people out there waiting to pounce on the ignorance of naïve people. So, you need to be careful. Instructional apps contain audios and videos of experts who will guide you on how to go about meditating. They provide you with techniques and other details you need to help you meditate effectively.

Online Music Services

Streaming music services like Spotify or Apple Music comes in handy when it comes to access to guided meditation sessions. All you need to do is to subscribe and you will gain access to guided meditation sessions of various lengths and practice styles.

Podcasts

Podcasts also provide you with guided meditation sessions that can be beneficial to you in various ways. Some podcasts provide you with information about meditation and its benefits while some will give you steps on how to practice it. Hence, regardless of your purpose of meditation, you will find podcasts beneficial. Without leaving your room or any other designated place where you can practice without distractions, you can practice with ease.

Websites

There are several mindfulness websites that offer you free guided meditations. Just search for such websites online and you will find a couple of credible ones. You will find guided meditations in both visual and audio formats in these sites.

YouTube

You can also get qualitative and quantitative guided meditations on YouTube and other video websites. These kinds of sites are the best for you if your preference is visual guided meditation sessions.

Other Important Tips

On the flip side, your decision to go for a teacher may be a result of low self-esteem which will not be good. If you just don't want to bother about the complexities or complications around meditation, guided meditation is a good choice. However, you can try to meditate by yourself first and then get a guide later. Compare the benefits of both before you finally make a decision. There is no scientific evidence that proves that you are better off with guided meditation.

Consider shorter sessions when you are just starting especially if you are not practicing with a physically available teacher. In other words, if you practicing with the aid of podcasts or YouTube videos, start with shorter sessions so that you can build your confidence and expertise steadily. You will do yourself a lot of good by switching off your phone or putting in on airplane mode when you want to meditate. You don't need any form of distraction in order to get the best out of guided meditation.

Don't procrastinate because you will never be consistent and enjoy the full dividends of meditation when you procrastinate. Set out time that is convenient for you and once that time comes, don't postpone it until some other time. The best time to meditate is now! Yes! Now!

Since meditation helps you to focus and get better sleep, it is better to practice it early in the morning to start the day on the right note or in the evening to make you relaxed to sleep well.

Avoid overconfidence because you are practicing guided meditation. Ensure you thoroughly scrutinize the credibility of your guide. All that glitters is not gold. Before you commit to a guide, ensure it is the right one.

Every form of meditation requires practice. Hence, don't think that guided meditation is some kind of shortcut. You will have to practice consistently to get the best out of any form of meditation you choose.

Chapter Thirteen: Dynamic Flow/Meditation in Motion

One indisputable fact about human beings is that we are not the same. The uniqueness of humans can be seen in our choice of food, spouse, dress sense, among other intricacies. Human uniqueness also spills into our choice of meditation type. Most of the type of meditation I have discussed so far involves sitting in a comfortable position. However, some people cannot imagine themselves doing that. They want to meditate but they are too "active" to meditate while sitting still.

You will not be the first person if you think meditation is not for such people. However, such people can also practice meditation. That should be good news for you if you are one of such people. Dynamic flow/meditation in motion is the perfect type of meditation for such people. All you need to know about this form of meditation and its practice are available in this chapter.

What is Dynamic Flow/Meditation in Motion?

This form of meditation emphasizes movement while attaining calmness. It was created by Osho (Bhagwan Shree Rajneesh), an Indian mystic sage. Osho believes that the modern world will benefit more from a meditation style that involves physical activities. He proposes over 100 meditation techniques that can be employed in the practice of this form of meditation. Dynamic flow meditation has stages but the end is to give you calmness and awareness.

Meditation in motion is not rigid as it does not have any particular method of practice. The flexibility of this type of meditation is one of the reasons it is gaining grounds in recent times. This method of meditation totally changes the perception of meditation as a practice meant for only monks who sit is a calm state in silence. Dynamic meditation brings a sense of "fun" to meditation which makes it attractive and exciting.

There is nothing weird about dynamic flow meditation because it is built on the core principles of meditation generally. Though there are many benefits of various forms of meditation, the three primary benefits are awareness of the present moment, focus, and calmness. The practice of meditation in motion offers you these three benefits and more. Hence, there is nothing to worry about because this form of meditation is not inferior in any way to other forms of meditation.

Tai chi and Kundalini yoga have the ingredients of dynamic flow meditation. Tai chi is a martial art that is based on the mind-body connection. The core principle of Tai chi is to create a balance between the forces of Yin and Yang. These are two opposing forces in the universe that needs to be in balance for you to be healthy. Tai chi involves movement, meditation, and deep breathing which are the core principles of dynamic flow meditation.

Kundalini yoga is a blend of chanting, mindfulness, and expression of power and energy. When you practice Kundalini yoga correctly, you will feel as though you have gone to the gym, gone for therapy, and had fun singing with friends at the same time. You stand to enjoy these same benefits when you practice meditation in motion.

Benefits of Dynamic Flow/Meditation in Motion

It is important you are aware of the things you stand to enjoy when you practice dynamic flow meditation. These benefits will spur you on to practice consistently especially during times when you are stressed out. Below are the benefits of practicing meditation in motion:

Calmness, Awareness, and Focus

Just like other forms of meditation, dynamic meditation offers you calmness and leaves you in a relaxed state. The fact that it involves movement makes it sound impossible but at the end of the practice of this form of meditation, you will enjoy an amazing state of calmness. Your awareness and focus are also heightened when you practice this type of meditation.

Reduction of Stress Level, Tension

The physical activity involved in dynamic flow meditation ensures that your blood circulation is enhanced. There will be more oxygen in your bloodstream and the front of your heart and spine will open up. The resultant effect of the enhanced blood circulation is that your stress level will reduce and you will be able to release tension.

Loads of Fun

Meditation in motion is fun and that ensures that you will not have issues with depression. This form of meditation heals your body and mind. You will be energized and feel alive and aware of your world. Dynamic flow meditation is a complete package of health benefits and fun.

How to Practice Dynamic Flow/Meditation in Motion

Practicing meditation in motion is not difficult. Like I have said earlier, there is no particular method you have to follow to practice this form of meditation. However, just like every other form of meditation, you need to schedule the meditation and find somewhere conducive enough for you to practice. Apart from these, below are the steps you can follow to practice meditation in motion:

Get Enough Space

It is not just good enough to find a place that is comfortable in the sense of serenity, it is more important you get enough space. Remember that you need space to move around while meditating; hence, ensure you choose a place where you can move without inhibition. Once you are restricted during meditation in motion, you cannot get the best out of this type of meditation because it is not a sitting meditation.

Begin by Breathing Slowly through Your nose

The practice of dynamic flow meditation begins by breathing slowly through your nose. Inhale and exhale slowly as air fill your lungs and leave them. You need to master these slow deep breaths because it is the foundation upon which this form of meditation is built. All through the period of meditation, you will have to take deep breaths.

Slightly increase the Pace of your Breaths for Ten Minutes

After the initial phases when you take breathe slowly, you will increase the pace and breathe faster for ten minutes. Focus on thorough exhalation and inhalation. You will continue to breathe faster but you must ensure that you continue to take deep breaths. Breathe deeply into your lungs and exhale completely before the next breath without reducing the pace. It may not be easy initially but you will master it by practice. The essence of this breathing pattern is to make you lose track of the sensations in your body while breathing.

Move in an Uncoordinated Manner

If you think the earlier steps have been boring, things are about to get more interesting now. The next phase involves moving chaotically. You can be creative about the way you go about this stage. You can choose to jump, dance, laugh out loud, or scream. The essence of these uncoordinated movements is so that you will further lose track of your body by creating a catharsis for your body. Don't forget to continue with the deep breaths while moving around without paying attention to the pattern of movement.

Raise your Arms above your Head

You are going to settle for a pattern now after the uncoordinated movement phase. You will start by raising your arms above your head.

Jump Up and Down as you Shout "Hoo!"

With your arms still raised above your head, jump up and down and shout "hoo!" each time. Each time you land on your feet, you will feel your feet sending a vibration through the center of your body. Savor this sensation without stopping the jump. Continue like this for ten minutes before you move to the next stage.

Stop Moving and Stay in a Position for 15 minutes

Freeze in a position and pay attention to what is happening to your body. You have created positive energy in your body through the earlier activities and you should feel it. The essence of this is to train your mind to be aware of the moment and enjoy it. Continue taking deep breaths while doing this. The recommendation of Osho meditation is that you should not move at all during this phase. You are completely in charge and you are savoring every sensation going on in your body during this stage.

Celebrate for 15 Minutes

The climax of dynamic flow meditation is the last phase when you celebrate your progress. Meditation in motion is such that you don't have to celebrate your progress later but within the meditation. Do whatever you do when you are in a happy mood at the end of the meditation. You can laugh, dance, run around, or sing. The essence of this meditation is not just to celebrate your progress but to let go of your body in an excited state.

Other Important Tips

I am convinced that the steps to follow to practice meditation in motion as highlighted above are straightforward. Below are other tips that can aid effective practice:

There is no method of meditation that is superior or inferior. It is all about what you feel is best for you. Hence, if you practice meditation in motion and it suits you, why not? However, if you prefer a meditation style where you sit still, stick with it. Never practice a method of meditation just because people around it practice it.

As a beginner, you can reduce the recommended minutes to half and increase it with time. You are permitted to have your own abbreviated version initially but you must ensure you get better over time.

Don't allow anyone to discourage you. What you are doing may not make sense to people who have not experienced the power of meditation before. Focus on what you need to do and critics will end up asking you to teach them later when they see your progress as a result of regular practice.

Meditation in motion is a physical exercise. Hence, don't forget to wear flexible clothing and shoes with soft soles that can support you when you jump. A towel and water around you is a good idea so that you can look after your body immediately after the meditation.

Chapter Fourteen: Prayer, Even if You are Not Religious

When you hear "prayer", it is likely that what comes to your mind that it is a sacred activity that people who are involved in one religion or the other carry out. However, you don't have to be religious before you can pray. Are you surprised? I am glad if I am the first person to tell you. What do you have to pay me for that? A lot of attention in this chapter! You will learn how to pray in this chapter even if you are not a religious person.

Changing your World with your Thoughts

You are not the only one if what prayer meant to you is clasping your hands and asking a deity to grant you your heart desire. Some people stopped believing in religion when they realize that people who are not religious are enjoying the same things they ask a deity to grant them. The right mindset is more important than cowering before a deity to grant your desires. I am not in any way saying that religion is obsolete.

However, you need to know that there is so much you can do with your mind without any religious affiliation. In other words, the only time you pray is not when you are reciting "Our Father" (Christianity) or "Mrityunjaya Mantra (Hinduism). In other words, you can be spiritual without any religious affiliation.

According to Dr. Brian Weiss:

"One way to raise your vibration is to fill your heart and mind with loving-kindness, with tranquility, and with peace. When you can create and manifest such an energy field, your burdens will be eased, even in the toughest of times."

You can connect with your "Higher Power" through prayer without beseeching a deity. You need to change your perception about prayer if you have always only seen it in a religious way. It is high time you saw prayer as an activity that enables you to align your thoughts and strengthen your energy. The result of prayer is that it enables you to have the right thoughts and make the right decisions. You get guidance to go in a particular direction or talk to someone or say something that will make a positive difference in your life.

Affirmative Prayer

Affirmative prayer involves setting your heart to the possibility of something positive happening and affirming it with your words. Your thoughts create vibrations that go out into the world. Your thoughts have the capacity to create situations. You are a powerful creator and there is no limitation to what you can do when you align your thoughts with your dreams. Hence, you have to avoid filling your mind with negative thoughts.

You can experience the energy of people be it positive or negative when you are around them. You can know someone who is in a bad mood even before the person speaks to you because the state of the person's mind radiates energy. In the same way, you can tell when a person is in a good mood because of the kind of vibration the state of their mind produces. Hence, you radiate energy with your thoughts and this energy may be creative or destructive. The energy you radiate can work against you or work for you.

You can take advantage of prayer to ease your burdens and calm yourself down without necessarily believing in a deity. When you think about something and affirm it with your words in prayer. You will be surprised that circumstances arrange themselves and your request is somehow granted. You will ride on the ripple effect of the energy you created by praying and meet people who can help you achieve or find what you want.

Tips on Praying Without Being Religious

To create your own spiritual pathway with prayer, below are some helpful tips to pray without a religious affiliation:

Meditate

Meditation provides you serenity and calmness of mind. You can have your own sacred place where you meditate and connect to your higher self. You can choose any form of meditation and practice it regularly to regulate the thoughts of your mind and be at peace with yourself. You can create somewhere in your house and make it sacred to you. A place you go to unburden your stress and lose yourself in a meditative state and create positive energy.

Be Grateful

Nothing creates more negative energy than a hurting or bitter heart. It will prevent you from seeing the positive things happening around you and kill every sense of optimism. However, if you think deeply enough, you will realize that you have many reasons to be grateful in spite of the challenges and difficulties you are going through. When you practice meditation, you will be able to have a better perception of your life. You may not have money but you have people around you who love you. Be grateful for the relationship you have and the gift of life. Make it a daily practice to take out like fifteen minutes to deliberately find reasons to be grateful in your life. Reflection and gratitude will enable you to connect with your spiritual self and find comfort money cannot buy.

Enjoy the Moment

There are many things around you that are wonderful and lovely but you will never pay attention to them when you are not aware of the moment. Walk in the woods when you are not busy in the evening and just admire the beauty of nature. Enjoy the ambience of the moment and appreciate the beauty of something greater than you. Look at how vast the earth is and how it supports life. Secular spirituality is all about enjoying the moment and refusing to get lost in negative thoughts. Become alive and aware as you create positive energy around you with your thoughts. Prayer goes beyond just making requests. Create positive vibes with pure positive thoughts and words and create a comfortable atmosphere to attract the right people and the right circumstances to yourself. Don't allow whatever you change about your life cannot overwhelm you. Let the thoughts of possibilities about the things you can change in your life consume your thoughts.

Look Within

You can easily drift such that you value yourself on the basis of the things happening around you. However, your true worth lies with you. Only you can know what you are worth. There is no great person today who has not been misjudged and deemed useless by people at one point of their lives. Hence, it is your choice to either see yourself as a worthless person or a person of worth. People will learn to see the true you and appreciate your qualities over time. However, your voice will never be heard when you drown in the thoughts of the negative things people have said about you. Focus on your strength and work on improving areas where you are not strong.

Keep a Journal

You can take things a notch higher by writing down your thoughts in your personal journal. Don't just write down random thoughts that come to your mind. Filter your thoughts and write down the positive things you think about yourself. There is no amount of appreciation or acceptance you can get from people that can rival your appreciation and acceptance of yourself. Ensure you keep your evaluation of yourself honest. Begin by writing about the qualities you have and smile all the way as you write. Then, move on to writing down areas where you need to improve. Don't stop there; write out practical ways with which you can improve on your deficiencies. The best time to do this is after meditation when you mind is calm and your thoughts are fully under your control.

Listen to Music

Listening to songs that resonate with you helps you to create positive vibes around you. Meditate on the lyrics and appreciate the creativity that has produced the song. Enjoy the tune and notice the tempo as well as the musical instruments used to create the work. Appreciate the symphony and the beautiful synchronization of the singing and the musical instruments. Music has the ability to move people to tears or create a state of elation. It is a vehicle that can connect you to your higher self with ease.

Practice Empathy

Having an awareness of the struggles and pains of people around you connects you spiritually to them. Practicing loving-kindness meditation gives you a head start in connecting with people around you. Don't just think about what they are going through; seek how to alleviate them of their pain. You will be able to attain inner peace every time you make the choice to lift up others. We all need ourselves and the height of spirituality is to live for the common good. Religion without love stinks and it is hypocritical. We are not designed for isolation but a community where love is the watchword.

Create Rituals

You need a routine if you are serious about your spiritual life. You must create time for your personal growth. You can do the dish while keeping an eye on the birds having a jolly ride in the sky outside your window. Be creative about your ritual. The most important thing is to do something that takes your mind away from your worry about debt or work or other things that makes you stressed. Just live every moment and be fully aware of what is going on around you.

Celebrate Life

Activities such as running in nature can give you a spiritual connection with the universe. Running in nature is a physical exercise that has both physical and spiritual benefits. Celebrating in a healthy body ease you of tension and makes you feel alive. During holiday celebrations, say words that show you are grateful for your life and the beauty in it. Be the best version of yourself every day by creating positive energy with spiritual activities. You don't have to go to parties and get drunk or have sex before you can feel elated and alive. It is the absence of a culture of practicing spirituality that makes people seek such unprofitable alternatives.

Chapter Fifteen: How to Establish a Consistent Meditation Practice

When you see people who practice meditation regularly, you will admire them. They look younger than their age, full of life, and have no worries. They are on top of their game in their daily activities with an incredible level of awareness and focus. They live life to the fullest with a moment-by-moment approach that makes them buzz with positive energy.

Such people are not freaks but regular people who have made the choice to commit and dedicate their time to practice meditation come day come shine. They are good role models and you can also follow in their footsteps. I know one or two things that help people to maintain a consistent meditation practice. Here are a few things I believe can also help you on your journey to practice meditation consistently:

Find People of Like Minds

You need the right company to achieve anything in life. Whether you believe it or not, you are a product of the influence of people. These people may be close to you or far away from you but you definitely have people whose actions or inactions influence your decision. You may not be able to realize quickly until you think and trace where the influence came from. In fact, your decision to read this book on meditation is a product of the influence of someone or some people on you. There is nothing wrong with having people who inspire you or influence you as long as they are leading you in the right direction.

The journey is smoother when you have someone you can discuss your success and failure with. Hence, if you want to be consistent in your practice of meditation, you need people of like minds. You need people who believe in the power of meditation and are also willing to or are already practicing consistently. When you have someone you are accountable to, things become easier. It is easier especially when you and the person meditate at the same time and at the same place. You know that the person will ask why you did not come around and that alone will keep you on your toes to be consistent.

Never forget that the Benefits of Meditation is only for the Consistent

I have mentioned many benefits of meditation so far in this book. I am convinced that you will like to enjoy these benefits too. However, meditation is not something you can just do and stop whenever you feel like. You have to be committed to it to enjoy the benefits. Since you want to enjoy these benefits; you should also maintain a committed attitude towards practicing it. If you keep reminding yourself that it is only with consistent practice that you can reap the benefits of meditation, you will have enough motivation to practice consistently.

It is just like trying to lose weight and not willing to be committed to your regiment. Such a person will not be able to achieve any reasonable result. Meditation can even help you lose weight as backed up by scientific evidence which I have explained earlier. If you have the right tool in your hands, then, you should not let anything stop you from using it consistently for your own benefit.

Practice Every Morning

As much as you can actually practice meditation at any time of the day, it is better you practice it early in the morning for the sake of consistency. In the morning, you are still fresh especially if you have had a good night's rest. You still have enough energy to practice and enjoy the meditation. Besides, you will have enough calmness and focus that will help you record peak performance for the rest of the day. By the time you go into the day and you are encumbered by the stress of the day, you may find it difficult to practice again. Hence, unless it is absolutely impossible, ensure you practice meditation early in the morning so that you can be more consistent. That does not mean that you will not enjoy the benefits of consistent meditation at other times of the day. However, you will open your path to consistent practice with an early morning meditation.

Connect it with an Activity you do daily

I doubt there is any day you don't brush your teeth. You don't want to even imagine how your breath will be when you don't brush your teeth for just a day. I am sure you are even uncomfortable with the fact that I called it "just a day". Most people will lose their confidence and will keep a distance from other people when they speak if they have not brushed their teeth that day. Mind you, when you meditate, you are not only taking care of your body but primarily your mind. See meditation daily as "washing your mind daily". It may sound funny but that is exactly what you are doing.

You are taking charge of your mind and "washing" away negative thoughts and sensations. Hence, don't just feel uncomfortable when you have not brushed your teeth in a day, you should also feel uncomfortable when you have not meditated away. Remember that one meditation per day keeps the medical doctor, psychologists, and psychiatrist far away from you. Consistent meditation indirectly reduces your bills because you will have fewer reasons to pay physical and psychological health practitioners.

Use the Same Time and Place

It is good to experiment with different times and places when you are a beginner so that you can know what works best for you. However, you have to find the best time and place for you quickly so that you can settle and practice consistently. Chopping and changing your meditation time and location consistently will not make you consistent. Your practice of meditation has to be a routine – a ritual. Your mind and body must get used to that time and location such that it almost becomes a reflex action. Meditation must move from one of your activities and become a permanent habit. You need to be consistent with the timing and place where you meditate to make this possible. Once it becomes your habit, you will become "addicted" to it. Meditation is a positive addiction that kicks out negative addictions.

Don't Let Guilt Stop you

It is good that you make yourself feel uncomfortable with missing your meditation every morning. You should be your own best critic and should not allow yourself to lose your discipline. However, if it happened that you missed it one morning; ensure that you make up for it in the evening. Don't fall into the trap of feeling so bad because you missed your meditation in the morning such that you skip it altogether.

In the same way, if things got so bad that you missed your meditation all day long (it should never happen!), don't decide to quit altogether because of guilt. You may miss your meditation a day or two when you are just starting because your body is trying to get used to it. Make you encourage yourself to continue. You stand so much to gain from consistent meditation practice. Hence, don't allow anything to stop you; not even guilt!

Don't Be Too Hard on Yourself

Self-evaluation is good because it enables you to measure your progress. However, you need to avoid being too critical of yourself as regards whether you are good or bad in meditation. Judge your progress on the basis of your consistency. In other words, you should feel bad when you are not practicing consistently and double up on time. However, when it comes to the actual practice of meditation, you need to avoid being judgmental. Remember that various forms of meditation exist and most are flexible. Hence, if you are practicing consistently, you will reap the benefits. I don't mean that you should not seek new and better ways to improve your effectiveness in meditation. However, let your primary basis of evaluation be your consistency.

Be Realistic About your Expectation

I need to say it loud and clear that meditation is not a magic wand that will take away all your problems. In the long run, you can attain financial independence through consistent meditation practice. How? If your parents don't own the oil wells in Saudi Arabia or a business empire, you know you have to work hard to attain financial independence. The decisions you make every day, as well as your focus on your goal, will determine whether you will succeed or not. Consistent meditation practice enables you to have a still mind such that you can make consistent quality decisions. Quality decision making can, in the long run, enable you to achieve your dream.

However, you should not practice meditation consistently as a means to earn wealth. It does not directly make you prosperous. There are various factors including unforeseen circumstances that contribute to your success or failure. Hence, practice meditation for the immediate rewards of a calm mind, awareness, and focus. Other indirect benefits can come in later but you have to be realistic. If you have an undue expectation of what you stand to enjoy from the practice of meditation, you will be disappointed in the short run and may even quit. Hence, if you want to be consistent in your practice of meditation, your focus must be on the short-term gain first. Just enjoy meditating daily and enjoy each day as it comes.

Keep an Excuse Book

An excuse book is a book where you write down the reason you did not do what you have planned to do. In this case, keep an excuse book where you write down why you did not meditate in case you missed out on any day. You will not want to keep writing excuses that remind you of your ineptitude. Hence, it will spur you on to practice consistently.

Chapter Sixteen: Stages of the Path

Meditation is a journey; a path that leads to may promising destinations. It is a path that leads you to find your spirituality and a path to self-discovery. It is a journey that will help you develop various aspects of your life. In this last chapter, I will help you with practical tips on how you can develop your emotions, senses, relationships, career, and your personal life as well as dharma via consistent meditation practice.

Emotions

According to the Eco Institute, consistent practice of meditation boosts your emotional quotient (EQ). In other words, when you practice meditation consistently, you will be able to manage your emotions effectively. Emotional intelligence is a big deal. Emotional intelligence refers to the ability to manage your emotions and the emotions of people around you effectively. It is not only negative emotions that you have to manage effectively but also positive emotions too! In fact, you need to be more careful about managing positive emotions because you normally want them to run wide.

Negative emotions are easy to spot and they don't make you comfortable with yourself and you will want to snap out of them as soon as possible. However, you want to let yourself loose when you are elated because something pleasant happened to you. You can feel on top of the world such that you begin to feel you don't need anybody in your life. Hence, you need meditation for both positive and negative emotions.

Emotions exist in eight main forms which include love, sadness, anger, shame, disgust, jealousy, happiness, and fear. Other forms of emotions like defeat and bitterness are derivatives of these eight emotions. The most important factor when it comes to the development of your emotional intelligence is for you to be able to recognize the source of the emotion. Sometimes you feel so sad and you really don't know why you are feeling that way. There are also days when you feel extremely happy and glowing inside of you but you can't get hold of the source.

When you practice meditation, you will be able to have a clear and calm mind that helps you monitor your thinking pattern adequately. Consequently, you will be able to find out the source of your emotions. Once you locate the source of your emotions, you can easily diffuse it if it is a negative emotion or keep it at bay if it is a positive emotion.

Senses

It may sound ridiculous but you can also develop the use of your senses with consistent practice of meditation. What I mean by the good use of your senses is not as though you want to make them function properly but to use them to stay aware of your environment. You may be staring but seeing nothing without being blind. You can be smelling something but not perceiving any sensation. There is a way stress and anxiety can make you dumb. Your senses are working perfectly but you are not aware of what is happening around you.

You can be eating the most delicious meal in the world but not enjoy it. Meanwhile, someone else will be eating a meal that is not as palatable and nutritious as your meal and the person will be having a good time. Your emotions can mess up with the function of your senses. If you are troubled in your mind, you will be looking at things happening around you but nothing will be colorful. You will not be able to experience the beauty of life even when it is all around you.

Hence, you need to take charge of your mind so that you will be able to stay aware and conscious about your environment. When you practice meditation consistently, you will be able to have good use of your senses. You will not just stare at things but see the beauty of life and creativity around you. You will live in the moment and savor every aroma and taste gleefully. You will not just touch, you will feel. It all begins with your mind before your body can experience life to its fullest.

Relationships

Your relationship with the people around you is the most important treasure you have. What about money? You cannot have money without people and money is worthless without people. If you are a business owner, your relationship with your customers goes a long way in determining whether you will succeed in business or not. If you have happy customers, you will be happy because you will also smile to the bank. However, if your customers are not happy with you, you are going to lose your investment.

Apart from business, you must be able to have healthy relationships with various people in your life. You cannot live a happy and peaceful life if you are always at loggerheads with people around you. It is not possible to be in the good books of everyone but it is a serious problem when nobody wants to be around you. The way you manage and handle your emotions and the emotions of people around you is the foundation of healthy relationships. If you are easily irritable and intolerant, people will avoid you.

All hope is not lost if you have struggled with keeping friends because of your struggles with your emotions. The practice of a form of meditation like loving-kindness meditation can help you live in peace and harmony with yourself and the people around you. Meditation helps you to handle your emotions so that you can handle the emotions of people around you properly. When you are able to handle the emotions of people around you effectively, you will be able to maintain stable and healthy relationships consistently.

Work

I will only be wasting my time if I am trying to convince you about the importance of your work. For some people, their job is the most important part of their lives. The truth is that there is hardly anyone who will readily admit that their job is the most important part of their lives. However, you can know if your job is the most important thing for you when you find it easy to sacrifice your personal happiness and the family of your friends and family for your job.

You should be committed and dedicated to your job and give it your best. However, it should not be at the cost of your personal happiness and the happiness of people who matter or should matter to you the most. You should do all within your means to reach the peak of your career. If you are going to reach the peak of your career, you need these three important qualities: awareness, focus, and calmness.

You need to focus to achieve your dream and carry your team along as a leader. You need to be calm to remain productive and emotionally intelligent when you are under pressure. Calmness enables you to make quality decisions, especially during tough situations seamlessly. Awareness guarantees that you are in control and conscious of your environment and the people around you. It takes awareness to be empathetic towards others. Regular practice meditation offers you awareness, calmness, and focus which are three important qualities you need to succeed in your career.

Life

It will not be complete and proper if I talk about every other aspect of your life and fail to mention your personal life. Some people get it wrong by mixing their relationships and work with their personal life. It is true that you are designed to be a functional part of a community but you must never at any point lose your personal identity. You are a unique individual who needs to find expression. It is when you are personally healthy that you can contribute as an integral part of a team or a community.

Despite the fact that you will share a lot of things in common with your spouse, your personal identity and difference cannot diminish. Some people find marriage suffocating and end up pulling out because they lose themselves in the union. They feel lost, jaded, and out of sort. You must have activities you do regularly to keep your body and mind functioning properly. Meditation is an activity that is beneficial to you as a person. Your personal life needs positive generated with consistent practice.

Dharma

The teaching of Buddha is the "dharma" which is a pragmatic approach to life issues based on the development of the mind. It is a teaching that promotes the cultivation of a liberated and peaceful mind. This teaching encourages you to discover your personal truth which is practicable for you rather than pursuing speculative views in the name of faith. Dharma has to do with being free from cravings, complexities and any other form of complexities.

In the words of the Buddha:

"The Dharma is well proclaimed by the Blessed One; it is visible here and now, immediate, inviting to be seen for oneself, onward leading, and to be personally realized."

You are on a journey to self-discovery and further self-discovery which is a life-long journey. Your journey has a direction with a consistent practice of meditation.

Conclusion

We have finally come to the end of this incredible journey. I believe you thoroughly enjoyed the ride. Life is easier and enjoyable when you know what to do, how to do, and when to do it. If you were a complete novice before you started reading this book, I believe you have a clear idea about what meditation is all about now. You have a good grasp of what you stand to enjoy when you practice regularly and how you can practice.

I guess you must have been intrigued by the fact that there are numerous forms of meditation. However, you can actually summarize them into two distinct categories based on guidance: guided meditation and unguided meditation. Unguided meditations are all the forms of meditation I mentioned in this book apart from guided meditation. The variety of meditations available for you to practice shows that you don't have an excuse not to meditate.

If you prefer a form of meditation where you can have a semblance of monks, you can have your way. On the flip side, if you prefer a meditation that is kind of funky where you can move and groove, meditation in motion is available for you. Therefore, no matter your purpose for meditation or preference, there is always a form of meditation that suits you. Having taken your time to read through the different types of meditation and techniques, I believe you must have found one that suits you by now.

I believe you must have been impressed by the fact that meditation is not as rigid as most people think. You can always modify your meditation to suit your need for consistent practice. I have also deliberately gone for an evidence-based approach as regards the benefits of practicing meditation regularly. I notice that a couple of books about meditation out there stated the benefits without providing scientific evidence that supports their claims. It is okay to have your doubts because credibility is a serious issue in the modern world where a lot of people claim to be what they are not.

Some people wish that the benefits they expect to find through the practice of meditation are real. You don't need to bother about that because they are real. You are not the only one who is interested in the credibility of the claims that meditation offers consistent practitioners long life, stress reduction, calmness, awareness, and other benefits.

It will be a huge shame and a total waste of time if you took your time to read this book and you did not make a commitment to practice meditation consistently afterward. The essence of every chapter of this book until the last is to give you reasons why you should practice meditation every day. I have failed if I am not able to give you enough reasons to commit yourself to regular meditation practice. This is not one of the books you should read and forget about the information you have received.

I did not write this book to uncover anything mystical because there is nothing mystical about meditation. I have taken my time to research thoroughly to compile this material because I am convinced that your life will be better when you choose to commit to regular meditation. You know what meditation is all about now and you have also seen the benefits of practicing it which is based on empirical evidence. You have been exposed to the techniques involved and what you need to do to practice either guided or unguided meditation.

The ball is now left in your court to take advantage of this quality information and turn your life around. You have been equipped with the knowledge you need to live a happy and meaningful life through the practice of meditation consistently. You have a world to explore, opportunities to utilize, and people who need your contribution. I know you will make the right choice which is to begin or continue a regular practice of meditation. See you at the top of your game on top of your world.

Thank you and congratulations you for reading this book. I know you could have picked any number of books to read, but you picked this book and for that I am extremely grateful.

If you enjoyed this book and found some benefit in reading this, I'd like to hear from you and hope that you could take some time to post a review. Your feedback and support will help this author to greatly improve his writing craft for future projects and make this book even better.

I want you, the reader, to know that your review is very important and so, if you'd like to leave a review, all you have to do is post a review where you purchased this book. I wish you all the best in your future success!

Harini Anand

References

Anderson, N., Lau, M., Segal, Z., & Bishop, S. (2007). Mindfulness-based stress reduction and attentional control. *Clinical Psychology & Psychotherapy.* 14. 449 - 463. 10.1002/cpp.544.

Barnes, V., & Treiber, F., & Davis, H. (2001). Impact of Transcendental Meditation(R) on cardiovascular function at rest and during acute stress in adolescents with high normal blood pressure. Journal of psychosomatic research. 51. 597-605.

    10.1016/S0022-3999(01)00261-6.

Blacks, D., & Slavich, G. (2016). Mindfulness meditation and the immune system: a systematic review of randomized controlled trials. *The New York Academy of Science.* Doi: 10.1111/nyas.12998.

Blacks, D.S., O'Reilly, G.A., Olmstead R., Breen E.C., & Irvin M.R. (2015).

Mindfulness Meditation and Improvement in Sleep Quality and Daytime

Impairment Among Older Adults with Sleep Disturbances: A Randomized

Clinical Trial. *JAMA Intern Med* 175(4):494-501. Doi: 10.1001/jamainternmed.20148081.

Boyd, J. E., Lanius, R. A., & McKinnon, M. C. (2018). Mindfulness-based treatments for posttraumatic stress disorder: A review of the treatment literature and neurobiological evidence. *Journal of Psychiatry & Neuroscience, 43*(1), 7–

25. https://doi.org/10.1503/jpn.170021

Chandler, H.M., Alexander, C.N., & Heaton, D. (2005). The transcendental meditation program and postconventional self-development: A 10-year longitudinal study.

Journal of Social Behavior and Personality. 17. 93-121. Elder, C., Nidich, S., Moriarty, F., & Nidich. (2014). Effect of Transcendental Meditation on Employee Stress, Depression, and Burnout: A Randomized Controlled Study.

The Permanente journal. 18. 19-23. 10.7812/TPP/13-102. Gaiswinkler, L., Unterrainer, H.F. (2016). The relationship between yoga involvement,

mindfulness and psychological well-being. *Complementary Therapies in Medicine,*

26(1), 123-127. doi:10.1016/j.ctim.2016.03.011 Graser, L. & Stangier, U. (2018). Compassion and Loving-Kindness Meditation: An

Overview and Prospects for the Application in Clinical Samples. Harvard Review of Psychiatry. 26. 201-215. 10.1097/HRP.0000000000000192.

Hacker, P., Davis, Jr., D.R. (2006). Dharma in Hinduism. *Journal of Indian Philosophy, 34(5)*, 479-496. doi:10.1007/s10781-006-9002-4

Hatcher, B.A. (2007). Bourgeois Vedanta: The colonial roots of middle-class Hinduism. *Journal of the American Academy of Religion, 75(2)*, 298-323. doi:10.1093/jaarel/lfm005

Lo P., & Tsai P., Kang H., & Tian W. (2018). Cardiorespiratory and autonomic-nervous-system functioning of drug abusers treated by Zen meditation. Journal of

Traditional and Complementary Medicine. 9. 10.1016/j.jtcme.2018.01.005.

Lu, F., Xu, Y., Yu, Y., Wu, T., Liu, B., Xu, S., ... Li, M. (2019). Moderating Effect of

Mindfulness on the Relationships Between Perceived Stress and Mental Health

Outcomes Among Chinese Intensive Care Nurses. *Frontiers in Psychiatry*, 1664-0640. Doi:10.3389/fpsyt.2019.00260.

Pagnoni G., Cekic M., & Guo Y. (2008). "Thinking about Not-Thinking": Neural

Correlates of Conceptual Processing during Zen Meditation. PloS one. 3. e3083.

10.1371/journal.pone.0003083.

Trousselard, M., Steiler, D., Claverie, D., & Canini, F. (2014). The history of Mindfulness put to the test of current scientific data: Unresolved questions. *Encephale-Revue de Psychiatrie Clinique Biologique et Therapeutique, 40(6),* 474-480. doi:10.1016/j.encep.2014.08.006

Turakitwanakan, W., Mekseepralard, C., & Busarakumtragul, P. (2013). Effects of

mindfulness meditation on serum cortisol of medical students. *J Med Assoc Thai.*

96 Suppl 1. S90-5.

Woods-Giscombé, C. L., & Gaylord, S. A. (2014). The Cultural Relevance of Mindfulness Meditation as a Health Intervention for African Americans: Implications for Reducing Stress-Related Health Disparities. *Journal of holistic nursing : official journal of the American Holistic Nurses' Association*, *32*(3), 147–160. doi:10.1177/0898010113519010

World Health Organization: WHO. (2018). Depression. Retrieved November 23, 2019, from https://www.who.int/news-room/factsheets/detail/depression

Zeidan, F., Martucci, K., Kraft, R., Gordon, N., McHaffie, J., & Coghill, R. (2011). Brain Mechanisms Supporting the Modulation of Pain by Mindfulness Meditation. Journal of Neuroscience. 32. 5540.

[FIND OUT MORE](#)

www.ingramcontent.com/pod-product-compliance
Lightning Source LLC
Chambersburg PA
CBHW071214080526
44587CB00013BA/1368